CHRISTIAN RECONSTRUCTION IN THE SOUTH

CHRISTIAN RECONSTRUCTION IN THE SOUTH

BY

H. PAUL DOUGLASS

BOSTON
THE PILGRIM PRESS
NEW YORK   CHICAGO

Copyright, 1909
BY H. P. DOUGLASS

THE UNIVERSITY PRESS, CAMBRIDGE, U.S.A.

To

THE MEMORY OF HENRY LEE
one of " the unfit "
of whom the world was not worthy

PREFACE

THE writing of this book was undertaken at the request of the Executive Committee of the American Missionary Association and primarily with its constituency in mind. From the work of that organization, therefore, with which the author is personally familiar, the illustrative matter has largely been drawn, especially in those chapters which describe missionary operations concretely. I have tried to interpret that work in its representative character and in relation to that of the whole group of agencies making for the complete Americanization of the South. Further and particularly the attempt has been to provide a sociological perspective and background for the problems presented by the undeveloped peoples of the South. The approach has been through a particular group of interests, the purpose to throw light on the larger issue involved.

The author misses in his book that deliberately laudatory mood which, by the recent usage of high authority, seems to be the proper way for the Northerner to discuss the South. Beginning with the Ogden parties, a succession of distinguished Yankees have journeyed thither on all manner of speech-making occasions. There is so much compelling praise in that marvelously awakening section that these gentlemen have had little difficulty in filling the time allotted by program maker and interviewer with merited congratulations. The echoes of their speeches as reported back home have largely given tone to latter-day Northern thought on Southern problems. But one cannot easily be at the same time both guest and philosopher.

PREFACE

Socrates, in Plato's "Banquet," when his turn comes to speak, assumes ironically the vein of his companions. When they protest that he is manifestly insincere he rejoins that the occasion demands politeness rather than truth. The Northern orators who have had popular hearing have spoken as guests and have played up to the occasion. Consequently nearly all the plain and hard-hitting telling of truth about the South is coming from Southerners.

There is a striking contrast between some of their utterances and those which the North has been hearing from its own authorities. The professor of English, for example, in a Southern university made an original and highly successful attempt to get interest into his students' literary themes: he assigned the race problem as a topic. The resulting product did not lack in interest. Under the caption "The Young Southerner and the Negro"[1] the professor summarizes his experiment as follows: —

> These, then, are the views of forty-eight young men from seven states of the South. They unanimously opposed any idea of social equality; thirty-nine were opposed to higher education of the African; twenty-five favored only reading, writing, and a trade; thirty believed that he should possess no political rights; nine were without faith in his religion; eleven believed him to have been a better man in slavery days; thirty-one declared that he must always be a common servant to the white man; twenty-five thought that he possessed no ability in self-government; seventeen were in favor of retaining him in the South; seven favored giving him a separate territory; three favored "black cities"; nine believed that his dissipa-

[1] South Atlantic Quarterly, vol. viii, pp. 117 ff.

tion and uncleanliness would solve the problem by exterminating him; twelve were content to leave the whole question to Providence; seventeen declared that fornication and the resulting amalgamation of the races were endangering the white blood of the South; ten were opposed to lynching; and fourteen considered a race war highly probable. Remember, once more, that these writers are not a crowd of ruffians from the lower strata of Southern life, but representatives of refined families, and of a student body, ninety-six per cent of whom are confessing Christians and forty per cent candidates for the ministry.

Is such a study of existing tendencies just ground for optimism? . . . Are not the indications plain that the black man is to be restrained, hampered, browbeaten, discouraged within the next quarter of a century as never before in all the bitter years of his existence on this continent?

In a similar vein of courageous candor the Rev. Quincy Ewing, a Southerner of Southerners, has recently diagnosed the spirit of his section.[1] The race problem, he says, is not the negro as an objective burden to civilization. It is not his economic inefficiency, for the South wants him as a laborer; nor his excessive criminality, for he is not more criminal than whites of corresponding social status; nor his ignorance, for according to Governor Vardaman, at least, it is the difficult, educated negro, not the docile, ignorant one who is the burden. Neither has the Southerner any personal aversion to the negro race. On the other hand, Mr. Ewing asserts, the race problem is distinctly subjective. It originates in the white man's mind, in his convictions that the negro is "not human in the sense that he is human, not entitled to the exercise of human

[1] Atlantic Monthly, "The Heart of the Race Problem," vol. ciii, pp. 389 ff.

PREFACE

rights in the sense that he is entitled to the exercise of them." It is not what the negro now is or is not, but " how to keep him what he is in relation to the white man, how to prevent his achieving or becoming what would justify the belief on his part or on the part of other people that he and the white man stand on common human ground." In Southern usage, then, " bad nigger " means not the criminal negro, but the one who shows signs of achievement and thus gets out of focus with the traditional view. " The problem arises only when people of one race are minded to adopt and act upon some policy more or less oppressive and repressive in dealing with peoples of another race. It is the existence of such a policy, become traditional and supported by immovable conviction, which constitutes the race problem of the Southern states."

What shall we say to these things? In answering certain comments of Northern papers on the street duel in which Senator Carmack was killed, the Richmond *Times-Dispatch* characterized such affairs as *typical* of the South but not *characteristic*. It further explains the distinction to mean that, while there are undoubtedly a considerable body of Southerners who approve and practise the street duel, it is not a trait of those who are profoundly representative of the life of their section. Now here are the attitudes of the professor's forty-eight young Southerners, and over against them the wholly opposing attitude of the able and courageous *Review* which publishes the study. Using the *Times-Dispatch's* distinction, they are alike typical of the South; but which is characteristic?

One prefers to answer that the issue is still in doubt. The South is not homogeneous, hence cannot have a single sectional character. Since the war it has not reached stable equilibrium. It is in intellectual and moral transi-

PREFACE

tion. Its sifting is under way. The battle is on but the end is not yet. God defend the right! But if forced to generalize on the basis of present facts, one would have to confess that the tendencies represented by the young Southerners have political and social power beyond that of the *South Atlantic Quarterly* and its kind. The forty-eight are with the majority; the Trinity College group are in the minority. The repressive policies which Mr. Ewing expounds are characteristic, his personal attitude is exceptional. In view of these facts the author of this book sorrowfully finds his olive branch less wide-spreading than those of ex-President Eliot and President Taft seem to be.

The book is dedicated to the memory of a negro teacher of manual training who died of tuberculosis at the age of thirty. The individual is typical of his race and his race of humanity. All stocks of men are always being sifted by one or another of the great secular processes. In contemplating the destiny of others, men stand in the shadow of their own and are led to the ultimate question, What significance in the economy of existence have those who go to the rubbish heap of temporal history? Are the verdicts of sociology as to human values necessarily the verdict of the Last Judgment?

No soul which hopes for itself can call that august verdict *good* unless the universe, somehow and somewhere, saves and utilizes much which fails of measurable human fruition. For the " unfit " (speaking as the evolutionist does) are infinitely outnumbered and outweighed by our multitudes of bankrupt aspirations, those subtle waifs of the inner life, dearer to the heart than the acknowledged sons of the home. Their fate — the fate of the " unfit " portions of ordinarily " fit " experience — constitutes a graver philosophical problem than the mere temporal fall-

PREFACE

ing out of nations or races. If existence fails here it fails altogether.

> "What hand and brain went ever paired?
> What heart alike conceived and dared?
> What act proved all its thought had been?
> What will but felt the fleshly screen?"

If existence be good these discrepancies in the most fortunate experience must somehow find healing in a reuniting of the scattered elements of life. Whatever earth or seas hold these dead must give them up.

Such is the salvation of the most fortunate, and it carries with it a possible salvation for the least fortunate. Where the most fortunate find their indispensable completion, the least fortunate may repair a whole life-failure. Death logically is no more unconquerable than unhappiness.

> "All that I hoped to be and was not comforts me."

If so, maybe eternal values are buried in the secularly unfit and, for the idealist at least, the ultimate background of the solemn sifting of humanity is a universe of unfathomed possibility which the Christian confesses as "the life everlasting."

Many of my fellow workers and officers of the Association with other friends have aided me by information and suggestions. I thank them. I am particularly indebted to Rev. William H. Holloway; also, especially for help in the sociological interpretation of the race problem, to my long-time friend, Prof. Carl Kelsey.

NEW YORK, June, 1909.

CONTENTS

I. TEMPERING THE BODY TOGETHER

		PAGE
I.	"Men of Every Tribe and Tongue and People and Nation"	17
II.	The Unassimilated Populations	19
III.	The New Struggle for the Union	25
IV.	The Race Problem	28
V.	The Underlying Struggle for Democracy	32
VI.	Competency of Missionary Judgment on National Problems	35

II. THE SOUTH AS MISSIONARY GROUND

I.	Sectional vs. National Problems	44
II.	The South as Missionary Ground	46
III.	The Division of Labor between Assimilating Forces	56

III. THE SIFTING OF THE SOUTH

I.	The Two Souths and the Two Southerners	66
II.	The Varied South	70
III.	The Crisis of the Sifting	77
IV.	Study of the Well-Sifted Negro Community	86

IV. THE SIFTING OF SOUTHERN SENTIMENT

I.	Sifting the Hearts of Men	99
II.	The Color-Line	116
III.	Clues to Prophecy	119

V. WHAT THE NEGRO HAS DONE FOR HIMSELF

I.	Success with a Minimum of Assistance	127
II.	Within the National Life	132
III.	Within Racial Lines	140

CONTENTS

VI. A BACKGROUND FOR BLACK

		PAGE
I.	Dubious Verdicts from Conflicting Facts	166
II.	Need of a Sociological Background	169
III.	Alleged Racial Traits and their Sociological Explanations	171

VII. TYPICAL MISSIONARY ACTIVITIES

I.	Spirit and Policy	209
II.	Strategic Location	211
III.	Classification of Institutions	212
	A. Ungraded Schools	213
	B. Graded Elementary Schools	216
	C. Secondary Schools in Cities	223
	D. Rural Secondary Schools	229

VIII. TYPICAL MISSIONARY ACTIVITIES (*continued*)

III.	Classification of Institutions (*continued*)	237
	E. Girls' Seminaries	237
	F. Colleges and Universities	240
	G. Specialized Instruction	247
IV.	The Outreach of the Mission Schools	253

IX. PROBLEMS AND PROGRAMS OF NEGRO EDUCATION

I.	Higher vs. Industrial Education	267
II.	The General Educational Parallel	278
III.	Expert Interpretations of the Lessons of Experience	281
IV.	Principles of Democratic Education	295

X. THE OLD MEN OF THE MOUNTAINS

I.	The Problem of the Mountains	304
II.	How the Mountain Man Lives	312
III.	Mountain Life Reflected in the Mountaineer's Traits	317

CONTENTS

XI. THE PASSING OF THE MOUNTAINEER

	PAGE
I. The Exploitation of the Mountains by Industry	335
II. The Exploitation of the Mountains by Leisure	343
III. The Uplift of the Mountains by Education	350

XII. DOES THE PURPOSE OF GOD THWART THE SPIRIT OF CHRIST?

I. The Moral Sifting of the Nation on the Race Issue	367
II. Moral Struggle Complicated by Intellectual Difficulties	369
III. Examination of the Alleged Verdict of Science	373
IV. The Purpose of God and the Race Question	388

ILLUSTRATIONS

	PAGE
Tenants on School Farm, Brick School, Enfield, N. C.	28
Carnegie Building, Fessenden Academy, Fla.	28
Two Congregational Deacons of Rural Churches	36
Agricultural Peasant of the Black Belt	42
City Slum, Tradd Street, Charleston, S. C.	42
A. F. Beard, D.D.	62
Old Memphis	78
New Jackson	78
Home of Negro Landlord, Thomasville, Ga.	88
Negro Artisan and Street of Artisans' Homes, Thomasville, Ga.	88
Negro Business Men's Homes, Thomasville, Ga.	92
Negro Drug Store and Proprietor, Thomasville, Ga.	92
Negro Rural Home, Piedmont Region	134
Negro Business Street, Thomasville, Ga.	134
Representative Negroes	140
Ingram Chapel, J. K. Brick School, N. C.	148
First Congregational Church, Atlanta, Ga.	148
The Yamacraw Section, Savannah, Ga.	152
Negro Tenements, Charleston, S. C.	152
Aged Breadwinners	156
Servants' Quarters in Rear of a Modern Memphis Home	160
The Cotton Levee, New Orleans, with Negro Longshoremen	160
Transportation, Liberty Co., Ga.	220
Homes in the Land of Mud-Daub	220
The Environment of Dorchester Academy	232
Primary Grade, Andersonville, Ga.	236

ILLUSTRATIONS

	PAGE
Graduating Class, Straight University, New Orleans	236
Swayne Hall, Talladega College; Chase Hall, Fisk University	242
Jubilee Hall, Fisk University; DeForest Chapel, Talladega College	242
Strieby Hall and Beard Hall, Tougaloo University	242
Cotton Picking on School Farm	250
Football Team, Burrell Normal Institute, Florence, Ala.	250
College Choir, Fisk University	256
College Y. M. C. A., Fisk University	256
Domestic Science Laboratory, Talladega College	280
Blacksmith Shop, Tougaloo University	280
Theological Graduates, Talladega College	298
Trained Nurses, Talladega College	298
Primitive Industry of the Mountains	310
Modern Industry of the New South	310
Domestic Grinding-Mill	318
Old Water-Mill	318
The Mountain Weaver	332
The Cotton-Mill	332
Black Mountain Academy, Evarts, Ky.	350
Elementary Grades, Black Mountain Academy	350
Professors and Students, Atlanta Theological Seminary	360
Girls' Dormitory, Piedmont College	360
Typical Makers of Evidence on the Race Problem	388

CHRISTIAN RECONSTRUCTION IN THE SOUTH

I. TEMPERING THE BODY TOGETHER

I. "MEN OF EVERY TRIBE AND TONGUE AND PEOPLE AND NATION"

IF the band of *Mayflower* Pilgrims had been composed of the same stuff as the present nation, and in like proportions, it would have included twelve negroes, a Porto Rican mulatto, and a mongrel of mingled Indian, Chinese, Japanese, and Hawaiian blood. Thirteen of its number would have been Pilgrims by adoption only, and twenty more the children of at least one non-Pilgrim parent. Hardly one half would have remained of real Pilgrim stock. Picture this strangely varied group kneeling together in the cabin of the *Mayflower* to weld itself into a "civil body politick!" The task is not lighter now that Providence has taken millions for hundreds and scattered them unevenly over a vast land of imperial natural diversities.

The Earlier Struggle for the Union

The early struggle for the Union was an attempt to harmonize the interests of an essentially homogeneous stock. They brought, to be sure, some Old-World animosities to these new shores, born of class struggles or the competitions of mother-lands. To these were soon added differences created by the new environment. The scant population of the thirteen colonies occupied a fringe of seaboard, the widely varied physical resources of which were the basis of economic differences and conflicts. The North naturally became commercial and industrial, the South rural and agricultural. Intercommunication was difficult, and only the common danger to their frontier from the French and Indians, and the united struggle against England, taught the colonists cooperation. They were scarcely able at length to write their fateful compromises into a constitution. Yet they had all come from a very small region in northwestern Europe, where blood and traditions had been blended as in no other area. They were predominatingly middle-class people, and save for one colony were Protestants. Their temperamental differences, however deep, had been included in a common history and civilization.

But now the nation includes representatives of the entire human family in their whole range of physical and mental differences. The white, black, yellow, brown, red, are all Americans. Whatever sunderings untold centuries of diverse experience and contrasting environment have wrought between the most widely separated branches of mankind exist between us as fellow citizens and intrude as internal problems for our people. Men of every tribe, tongue, people, and nation have become members of our common life. Our national institutions were not made by them nor for them, but were founded upon the ideals of a very select human group and never fully applied even within that group. Consequently, unless the foundations of the Republic are to be changed, and the American of our faith ceases to be, the diverse human stuff of the present nation must be inwardly prepared for participation in a democratic order of society. Such an order irrevocably demands that men be fit for it.

American Institutions not made for Our Present Population

II. THE UNASSIMILATED POPULATIONS

The peoples for whom the Americanizing energy of the nation has hitherto failed may be considered in three groups:

1. *An old and neglected group.* In the triumphant march of American civilization from east to west across the continent there has been one striking failure. A fragment of an original colonial stock in the fastness of the Southern Appalachians remains fixed in the civilization of a hundred years ago. They represent the average American of Abraham Lincoln's boyhood and are our chief example of an "arrested frontier." One finds here

The Mountaineers of the Southern Appalachians

> the human type not to be met elsewhere in the United States. He is farmer, hunter, blacksmith, shopkeeper, or rude preacher. He is courageous, original, reads the sky and forest in lieu of books, and is little troubled by the outside world. He could not raise cotton, he did not own slaves, and his sympathies were with the North rather than with the South in the Civil War. His family lives as his great-grandfather's family lived, for change is almost unknown. Division of labor has little place in such society, where homespun still prevails. These men are the descendants of the backwoodsmen who came from the Old World, from Pennsylvania, from Virginia, and the Carolinas, to the Holston, the French Broad, the Kentucky, and the Cumberland. Retired from all the world, they reveal the effects of a stable environment in a remote region.[1]

Akin to the Appalachian mountaineer and of the same stock is much of the population of the Ozark re-

[1] Brigham, Geographical Influences in American History, p. 102.

gion, covering parts of Missouri, Arkansas, and Indian Territory.

The gross population of these regions is over three million, but one must deduct from the problem the inhabitants of those valleys with their fertile fields and prosperous cities through which civilization from the earliest time has run as through a funnel. There is no uniform isolation of the mountain population, and no accurate enumeration of its submerged element is possible. Yet it is clear that here is the largest and most valuable fragment of the original American stock not fully assimilated to the national life.

Under this same category of old and neglected peoples must be numbered the "Greaser" type — a product of the ancient mingling of Spaniard and Indian. Its chief seats are New Mexico and Arizona. Its proportion of illiteracy greatly exceeds that of any other part of our population classified as "white." It constitutes a small but appealing problem for national solution.

The Spanish-Indian Mongrel Population

2. *A new and unexpected group.* Our national complacency with reference to foreign immigration suffered a sudden check with the unforeseen change of the character of that immigration, dating from about 1882.

Immigration from Eastern and Southern Europe

This change was the rapid shifting of the sources of immigration from Western to Eastern and Southern Europe. A line drawn across the continent of Europe from northeast to southwest, separating the Scandinavian Peninsula, the British Isles, Germany, and France, from Russia, Austria-Hungary, Italy, and Turkey, separates countries not only of distinct races, but also of distinct civilizations. It separates Protestant Europe from Catholic Europe; it separates countries of representative institutions and popular government from absolute monarchies; it separates lands where education is universal from lands where illiteracy predominates; it separates manufacturing countries, progressive agriculture, and skilled labor from primitive hand industries, backward agriculture, and unskilled labor; it separates an educated, thrifty peasantry from a peasantry scarcely a single generation removed from serfdom; it separates Teutonic races from Latin, Slav, Semitic, and Mongolian races. When the sources of American immigration are shifted from the Western countries so nearly allied to our own, to Eastern countries so remote in the main attributes of Western civilization, the change is one that should challenge the attention of every citizen. Such a change has occurred, and it needs only a comparison of the statistics of immigration for the year 1882 with those of 1902 and 1906 to see its extent. While the total number of immigrants from Europe and Asiatic Turkey was approximately equal in 1882 and 1902, yet in 1882 Western Europe furnished 87 per cent of the immigrants, and in 1902 only 22 per cent, while the share of Southeastern Europe and Asiatic Turkey increased from 13 per cent in 1882 to 78 per cent in 1902. During twenty years the immigration of the Western races most nearly related to those which have fashioned American institutions declined more than 75 per cent, while the immigrants of Eastern and Southern races, untrained in self-government, increased nearly sixfold.[1]

In other words, for more than two-thirds of a century our incoming population came almost exclusively from those lands which were working out with us the great democratic tendency. Some had progressed more slowly

[1] Commons, Races and Immigrants in America, p. 69.

and less successfully than we, but the general tendency was the same, and their children came to these shores inwardly disposed to the ideals and institutions which we were creating. The newest comers are the victims of a too abrupt transition. There is a gulf to be bridged before they can be made worthy participants in our national life.

Another group of the new and unexpected peoples has come to us by annexation. It is the fruit of the so-called imperialistic tendency of our nation. Hawaii brought us about 154,000 people, occupying eight mid-Pacific islands, with a total area about that of New Jersey. No part of our territory shows so much ethnic variety. Natives and half-castes form a dwindling half of the population. Southern Europe is represented by 8000 Portuguese. The most aggressive element is Oriental, predominatingly Japanese, but including 25,000 Chinese, and latterly Koreans, and even Hindoos. As to religion, Buddhism is a close second to Christianity. The ruling and exploiting Anglo-Saxon minority shows little desire to equalize opportunity for these Americans of other blood.

The Fruits of Annexation: Hawaii

Porto Rico, which is three-fourths as large as Connecticut, is one of the most densely populated parts of our domain. Its people number nearly a million and consist of perhaps 100,000 pure Spaniards, 400,000 negroes and mulattoes, and 500,000 " Porto Ricans," which means people of Spanish and Indian mixed blood. Nowhere on the mainland is any such degree of illiteracy known as prevails here. The nominal Roman Catholic Christianity leaves almost everything to be desired. The superstition, illiteracy, poverty, and vice of the Porto Rican are all un-American and constitute a

Porto Rico

national problem which has come to us so unexpectedly that we have not yet properly appreciated it.

Alaska as a habitation for Americans and a possible seat of civilization is so recent a possibility that its population belongs to the unexpected group. As a national domain it dates back to 1867, but its mining camps are the newest example of a frontier waiting for complete Americanization, and its perhaps 25,000 Eskimos and Indians present our only remaining opportunity for justice to the original American.

Alaska

3. *An exceptional group.* He ignores the central clue to our history who forgets that for important elements of our people American democracy broke down from the beginning. To Jefferson, the most idealistic and thoroughgoing of the founders of the nation, it was a perplexity and grief that there existed a slave population which even his faith could not think of as included in equal citizenship. Though trembling " to think that God is just," he, with most good men of his day, comforted himself with the thought that the contradiction was for a brief time and that the negro would soon be emancipated and deported. Now every eighth American is black, and beside this dark and massive problem every other problem of assimilation dwindles to insignificance.

The Negro

The Indian presented no such original perplexity to conscience. New England had indeed attempted somewhat half-heartedly to evangelize him without much thought of how he was to be treated afterward, but the national policy from the beginning was to consider him an alien with whom treaties were to be made as with foreign nations. Those who tried to Christianize him were always counted as foreign missionaries. Words cannot tell the bitterness of the struggle

The Indian

that dispossessed him; and however benign and inevitable the result, the methods employed were unspeakably shameful and brutal. Fragments of his race were isolated and engulfed by, rather than received into, the nation — as one swallows a speck of dust with his food. The remnant of less than one hundred and twenty-five thousand remains on the reservation, but is rapidly being scattered among the nation by the distribution of lands in severalty. This means the sundering of all ancient ties — the social foundations of the Indian's higher life and aspirations. Forced to merge himself in a social order abhorrent to his deepest instincts, he presents to-day his most pathetic appeal for a tolerance tempered with pedagogic sense to ease his passing.

More than two hundred thousand Orientals, chiefly on our Pacific Coast, constitute another anomalous group, and the only one the treatment of which involves us in complication with foreign nations. Restriction of Chinese immigration was attempted as early as 1854 by the State of California, and the nation completely shut out the Chinaman as a competitor of American labor by the treaty of 1880 and law of 1888. This restriction goes far beyond and is radically different in principle from that practised toward any other nation. "In the case of European immigration, the burden of proof is upon the immigration authorities to show that the immigrant should be excluded. In the case of the Chinese, the burden of proof is on the immigrant to show that he should be admitted."[1] The recent influx of Japanese, which mounted to 14,000 in 1906, has been checked, temporarily at least, by the limitation of emigration on the part of their home government. A few Koreans and Hindoos have been imported as scouting par-

Orientals

[1] Commons, Races and Immigrants in America, p. 235.

ties of great industrial armies which will surely come unless our anomalous policy of exclusion is extended to them also. More than any other group the Orientals are feared as tending to depress the American standard of living. On the other hand no other is so quick to resent or so able to revenge by war or boycott the indignities put upon them. Thus facing the Pacific, American problems take on international scope and broaden into problems of the relation of all men upon the earth.

III. THE NEW STRUGGLE FOR THE UNION

It is against increasing odds that the nation to-day renews the task of creating a union out of diverse elements.

Pioneer Conditions made Assimilation Easy

If we had not the deeper problem of making men inwardly fit for our civilization, if we were confronted only by the older and easier problem of adjusting conflicting sectional interests, our task would still be harder; for the fathers of the Republic achieved political union and the nation assimilated its earlier immigrants under very unique conditions. To be sure, America continued European inequalities in the class-governments of Massachusetts, Virginia, and indeed most of the colonies; but social privilege largely melted away as men turned to face the West. They found there an empire of free land. The frontier knew no social advantage, and its temper came to dominate the Union. Men were not prejudged and socially placed according to a conventional scheme. All prizes were open to the primitive virtues. Men struggled against nature rather than with one another. As soon, however, as the land was occupied and they turned to human competition, it was seen that the dominant classes were not inwardly neighborly nor tolerant of men of other types. Our hospitable soil hitherto, and not our brotherly spirit, has Americanized the alien.

Now our absorbing power has certainly suffered diminution. Americanism — no matter whose — was of course bound to change under the pressure of changing social forces. But our departure from the original type has been abnormally rapid because of the " great dilution " of national character by alien blood and spirit. The prior question now is, Who shall Americanize the American? Witness the indispensable and highly successful attempt by the Hebrew Educational Alliance in New York City to prepare the incoming Jew for intelligent citizenship. No one can praise too highly its results; yet no one can pretend that the Americanism to which they are introduced is that of Puritan Massachusetts, or old Virginia, or even of the Teutonized Middle West. It may be better; it is certainly not identical.

<small>"The Great Dilution"</small>

The issue, moreover, is not whether we have passed the theoretical danger point in the saturation of the nation by alien stuff. It is that of its abnormal congestion at our weakest spots, namely, in the cities and in geographical regions of little assimilative vigor. The unassimilated masses will not and cannot be spread proportionately throughout the native population. The critical point of assimilation as a national problem relates to these areas of alien congestion.

<small>Congestion of Aliens at the Weak Spots of Civilization</small>

Again, as never before in America, the " ascensional energy of the individual " finds a check in a stratified social system of increasing rigidity. If Danish Hilda had immigrated to the prairies of North Dakota she would have sung in the choir of the

<small>Stratification of Society</small>

little white church with the son of an Iowa farmer, and their children would have gone to the Agricultural College and perhaps to Congress. Stopping in the suburbs of New York City, she must marry the iceman or the greengrocer. Everywhere throughout our older society the individual is forced back upon his own class, which only by the combined efforts of its strugglers can hope for great advancement. Hence our day has seen a great strengthening of these struggling groups within the nation. By his vocation, and often by his race, the newcomer is predestined to join one or another of them. He finds no easy opportunity to obtain the knowledge and sympathy which overcome artificial and even instinctive barriers and release in men their essential like-mindedness. Only in the South, to be sure, is the system of social caste professed and dogmatically defended, but it is actually in force almost everywhere in the Union and is the greatest and most deadly foe to the assimilation of the alien groups. Increasingly, therefore, it is the part of patriotism and statesmanship to endeavor to maintain the ideal of national unity on democratic terms and consciously to direct the assimilating forces. It is more complicated than it was yesterday; a vaster and more urgent contribution to national destiny, and a mightier challenge to the intelligence and energy of all good men. It is the new struggle for the Union.

Beyond all physical and social difficulties, present-day democracy involves a moral difficulty of its own creating. *Higher Ideals* We are asking ourselves to go further and do more than our fathers tried; namely, to carry democracy into detail and to extend it literally to all sorts and conditions of men. There is a rising standard and an enlarged definition of the American ideal. It means more to us, in our complex civilization must mean more varied and difficult adjustments of men, than Jefferson dreamed. And we have solemnly undertaken to solve the race problem on democratic terms — a task self-imposed by conscience and a sharpened sense of equity, and broader than any the former generations knew.

IV. THE RACE PROBLEM

The praise which has been lavished on the assimilative vigor of the American stock and on the triumph of their democratic institutions is justified only when one ignores the exceptional group — roughly, one-eighth of our mainland population. In spite of the odds above enumerated, we might look forward to the triumph of the American spirit over the social complications of the age except for the difficulty which lurks always in the background — the race problem. This cuts the nerve of our efforts for the most needy. It is the crux of democracy.
<small>The Crux of Democracy</small>

From the standpoint of the nation's duty of fitting its people for citizenship, the race problem is, as Prof. A. B. Hart has called it, the *Anglo-Saxon problem*. Its root is a wavering faith in democracy which makes us fail to use to the full our Americanizing vigor. If the inner transformation of all people of alien spirit could be undertaken by us in perfect equity and benevolence, and with the equal application of our ample resources, the result would show, of course, various degrees of resistance on the part of the unassimilated groups. Different capacities for speedy and perfect participation in our life would be revealed. This is the objective natural difficulty in the making over of those who are at present unfit for democracy. It must be fully
<small>"The Anglo-Saxon Problem"</small>

Tenants on School Farm
Brick School, Enfield, N. C.

Carnegie Building, Fessenden Academy, Fla.
Built entirely by negro labor

and frankly recognized and adequately measured before we close the case.

But such a statement of the case bears no resemblance to our actual problem. What we actually find and must reckon with is the deep-seated disposition to give up in advance, and on theoretical grounds, with respect to certain peoples called the "lower races." The common thought is that some peoples are only belated in the process of civilization, and could easily catch up under proper stimulus. The mountain people of the Southern Appalachian are ascribed to this class. Other peoples are supposed to be essentially inferior — as all the off-color races — and most of all, the negro.

Popular vs. "Scientific" Judgment

To be sure, popular judgment in the matter does not at all draw the line where the scientific judgment is thought to draw it. The supposed scientist is likely to say that the distinction between superior and inferior races is, at the bottom, that between the temperate and tropical zones. This makes the Chinaman and the American Indian belong to the superior races; but the trade-unionist of the Pacific coast and the Western ranchmen do not think so. In the Northern cities the negro indiscriminately occupies the same tenement as the recent emigrant from southern Europe, and "dago" and "nigger" tend to become interchangeable terms. Finally, although by his proportionate influence on history the Jew is the greatest of the human stocks, in American practise he is widely shut out from some of the privileges of other citizens. The point is that we have everywhere to deal with the spirit which draws a line against a greater or smaller part of our population and treats it as incapable of full Americanization under democratic ideals.

CHRISTIAN RECONSTRUCTION IN THE SOUTH

Now it is to be always insisted that our problem is not that of the natural equality of men, but of their successful preparation for participation in the common national life. There has been some actual practise of democracy in the world — less than we have sometimes thought, but still some successful association of men under self-government and with the will to equalize opportunity. Democracy has existed; equality never; therefore democracy does not depend on equality. Its success has not been based on the natural equipment of its members, but rather on their domination by common ideals. It is the vigor and health of spiritual forces of social control which makes democracy possible. " By one Spirit are we all baptized into one body."

<small>Democracy does not depend on Equality</small>

Again, it is clearly and positively to be stated that amalgamation of blood through intermarriage is not the necessary or desirable method of initiating and hastening the assimilation, at least of the more divergent stocks. The marrying of the white and negro in the South, for example, as a means of solving the race problem, is not seriously contemplated by anybody.

But this plain and explicit denial must in candor be accompanied by the denial also of that negative dogmatism which forbids amalgamation on the ground of an alleged natural barrier between the races. It is absolutely not proven that nature interposes or intends to interpose any physical or mental barrier. All supposed facts to the contrary miss the mark because conditions have never allowed a fair trial of the case. The half-breed has everywhere been the half-caste. His status and fate have been those of the underfed, the ill-housed, the socially

<small>Valid Objections to Amalgamation, Social and Psychical, not Physical</small>

unprivileged. His lack of a controlling and saving social tradition, and the conflicting impulses of his two worlds, have subjected him to mental overstrain. But his problem is social and psychological, not physical. No one knows whether under equal opportunity the half-breed would show less fecundity, less forcefulness, less physical stamina and moral balance than the basal stocks. The laboratory of civilization has not yet tried that experiment. No state has ever been great enough to do social justice to those human mixtures which are banned by race prejudice, or to care to find out their actual capacity.

None the less and partly for this reason amalgamation as a solvent of the race problem is definitely to be rejected as tending to confusion and aggravating the original difficulty. It is a mistaken social method, the possible profitable employment of which in some future is beyond the horizon of our practical choices. And it is not necessary. All the present European nations are indeed the products of amalgamation, but an amalgamation which " occurred at a time so remote that it has been ascribed to the Stone Age. The later inroads have either been but temporary and have left but slight impression, or they have resulted in a division of territory. Thus the conquest of Britain by the Teutons and the Normans has not produced amalgamation so much as it has caused a segregation of the Celts in Scotland, Wales, and Ireland, and of the Teutons, with their later but slight infusion of Normans, in England. On the continent of Europe this segregation has been even more strongly marked." [1] Now racial distinctiveness has not kept the Scotch and Welsh from full and loyal partnership in British nationality; and Ireland's

Amalgamation a Mistaken Solution; and Unnecessary

[1] Commons, Races and Immigrants in America, p. 17.

estrangement is due to flagrant social injustice based on race prejudice. There are plenty of analogies, then, to show that it is possible to include diverse races in the essential spiritual unity of the nation without the mingling of blood, and also plenty of warnings against the fatefully inevitable schisms and irrepressible conflicts which come when an included population of distinct race is denied equal opportunity in the nation.

Our actual business is assimilation. It is to make learners of all in the nation, teaching its members to observe all things which are characteristic of Americans. For " it is not physical amalgamation that unites mankind; it is mental community. To be great, a nation need not be of one blood; it must be of one mind. Racial inequality and inferiority are fundamental only to the extent that they prevent mental and moral assimilation." [1] Now no human mind can tell in advance of the event whether and to what extent mental and moral assimilation is impossible. To find out by actual trial is the nation's central task.

Limits of Assimilation to be discovered Only by Trial

V. THE UNDERLYING STRUGGLE FOR DEMOCRACY

In the problem of assimilating the various groups of incomplete Americans we touch an acute phase of the profoundest of human issues — the struggle for and against democracy. " In this warfare there is no discharge."

With the growth of wealth and luxury there are daily more people who do not anticipate nor desire the assimilation of alien groups into the national life on democratic terms. Many will thoughtlessly deny this, some will deliberately resist the charge, yet the fact remains: the democracy in which

Fundamental Democracy in Danger

[1] Commons, Races and Immigrants in America, p. 20.

we believe is rather a democracy of the descendants of the races of the temperate zone or of northern Europeans or of long-headed blondes — not the democracy of all Americans. This is positively not a sectional phenomenon. Its most outspoken profession is in the South, but its prevalent spirit is national.

We are not without explicit exhortations as well as subtle temptations to choose the easier task of tempering the diverse American groups together on a non-democratic basis. Mr. Alfred Holt Stone,[1] for example, recently warned and urged the assembled sociologists of the nation that the alleged lower races should be taught by precept, law, and social convention to accept a permanent caste status; that they should be left uncorrupted by the American spirit, content in the unalterable lot of the peasant. He thinks that the alternative is a devastating race war, the responsibility for which will be theirs who have taught the masses to aspire and to struggle. On the other hand, we have recently had many a persuasive setting forth of the beauty of the social system of the old South. Looking at it as it seems to those who hold it in memories mellowed and softened by time, it strongly appeals to those of us who are daily irritated by the struggle with household servants, or nagged into meanness by endless labor controversies. How natural the thought, "If we could only have a recognized servile class which knew and kept its place all would be peace"! Compared with this pleasing vision how stubborn the reality to which actual conditions destine us! How aggravating the incomplete American as neighbor or employee; how "uppity!" the new negro; how socially difficult any man who

The Temptation to adjust Groups within the Nation on a Non-democratic Basis

[1] Studies in the American Race Problem, ch. vi.

stumbles upward, but half appreciating the inner standards and sense of fitness of a more favored group! What lack of gratitude, what frequent contempt, repays him who would help! Against such difficulties shall we not cease to strive?

Well, democracy as a social policy is not likely long to continue unless reenforced by some profounder sanction. "It is a sort of religion," says Professor James, "and we are bound not to admit its failure." Specifically it is an expression of the characteristic Christian passion for "the more feeble, the less honorable, the unlovely." "God tempered the body together, giving more abundant honor to the part which lacked." The defense of this paradox is possible only on religious grounds, and intelligible only to those for whom these grounds are good. To be sure the political and economic tendencies of the present age have given vast opportunity to the democratic spirit. Many under favorable conditions are capable of accepting it imitatively. But its continued mastery of men depends upon its power to reproduce the inner certainty and incorruptible zeal of an original spiritual insight.

<small>Democracy "a Sort of Religion"</small>

Old Aunt Dinah died the other day down in Alabama. She was a delightful example of the old-fashioned negro type, numbers of which have survived in connection with almost all the older schools of the American Missionary Association in the South. They transferred the affection which they had for their former masters, unblemished and undiminished, and lavished it upon those who now stood to them for power and kindliness. They never comprehended what was sought in the freeing of their race. For themselves they passionately repudiated any act or sentiment which disturbed their inbred sense of inferiority.

They wanted only to serve, to cling, to fulfil life on the level of subjection to some white master. Few fulfil so appropriately the rôle which they inwardly accept. It is difficult for the mind without an innate democratic passion to see that all this is after all less beautiful than the too frequent representative of the new order — obnoxious in dress, in voice, in manners, an unsatisfactory worker and still less satisfactory enjoyer of the means of life, an irresponsible member of the state and a potential menace to it. Yet the most perfect slave is lower than the most imperfect freeman. However admirable the choice fruit of the old order, " he that is least in the new kingdom is greater than he."

May one count on the ratification of this judgment by men as the years fulfil their present tendencies and bring forth their certain surprises? We do believe so, and will risk the outcome. The inner springs of democracy may be trusted. There will not fail a line of men who have seen the vision of human brotherhood and who will storm the universe to make the vision good.

> "Speak it boldly, 'These are Gods,'
> All besides are ghosts."

VI. COMPETENCY OF MISSIONARY JUDGMENT ON NATIONAL PROBLEMS

It is the fashion to discount the testimony of the man on the hilltop in favor of that of the man on the ground. In judging the prospects of our unassimilated American groups the near view is preferred to the far view. " Their neighbors know them best," is the cry. The Coast understands the Chinaman; the Plains the Indian; the

The Man on the Ground vs. the Man on the Hilltop

South the negro. Especially in the latter case is there passionate insistence that the "outsider" keep his hands off and leave practical adjustments to the immediately responsible parties. Especially if the outsider be politician — or missionary! I do not doubt that the South has suffered at times from both.

It happens, therefore, that testimony proceeding from missionary sources, this book for example, has to meet a certain presumption of unreliability.

The Argument against Missionary Competency The missionary, it is first alleged, is not in contact with a full and representative range of facts. "The trouble is that in the schools they see the best specimens of the race, at an impressionable period of their lives, and under abnormal conditions."[1] Their good showing is possible because they "work only with stringently sifted material."[2] They do not touch the masses.

Again, the missionary is a sentimentalist. No more damning charge, it is assumed, can be laid against any man in this practical and scientific age.

In view of the first charge it will be illuminating to consider the range and character of the contacts which *Extent and Intimacy of Missionary Contacts with Significant Facts* a representative missionary organization has with the materials of its problem. The American Missionary Association has carried on religious or educational work for the negro at from two to three hundred points in twelve Southern states during a period of sixty years. During all this time it has touched the life of the race in all its phases and extremes.

Its work at Fessenden Academy in central Florida, for

---

[1] Kelsey, The Negro Farmer, p. 6.
[2] Tillinghast, The Negro in Africa and America, p. 214.

Two Congregational Deacons of Rural Churches

[Note striking contrasts of physiognomy between pure negro types]

example, began with a people nearer Africa than any other group of American negroes. In this semi-tropical climate, life was possible without stove or shoes. Cooking was done the year round in the open air. When at length capital came in to hew the forest, drain off the turpentine, and strip the phosphate beds, these lowest of negroes were the crude recruits who rushed blindly into the hardest of industrial fates — that of unskilled transient laborers, living in temporary camps and continually moving on as industry despoils one place after another. " North Carolina nigger " is a generic term for turpentine worker; and Principal Wiley of the Fessenden school finds out by statistical investigation that a large proportion of such workers in his community are actually immigrants from the " old North state." This shows what the exploiting industries do for their workers. Migration becomes a habit. The material product is lumber and naval stores; the human products irresponsible, homeless men, criminals, and vagrants.

The Negro of the Turpentine Camp

The typical camp consists of parallel rows of company houses, generally single-roomed, battened cabins, with tight shutters at the windows, and mud or brick fireplaces. Rarely they are whitewashed. A company commissary, aptly called " the grab " (where supplies are bought at upwards of thirty per cent above ordinary figures), and a turpentine-still complete the picture.

Now, " single men in barricks don't grow into plaster saints," nor ebony either. Turpentine workers are mostly young. Vice is their amusement — drinking, gambling, lewdness. Women camp-followers cook and wash for and live with successive men. There are always exceptions — decent men with families, who have caught the migratory habit but try to protect their wives and children. They seek to rent little cabins apart from the quarters. A few rise to be bosses or succeed financially by sub-letting turpentine rights, but wages are paid infrequently and often in checks on the company store, which contrives to keep the employee generally in debt. The " gentleman's agreement " between employers, and sometimes the rifle and bloodhound, keeps him from running away. It is not an attractive life. Yet the lure of it, its wandering and gregarious irresponsibility, attracts many a boy from the farm. Thus the turpentine, lumber, and phosphate industries are educational institutions. They teach successive generations of illiterates to know nothing better.

If these are exceptional negroes, the best specimens of their race, what is the average life? Yet, in spite of the fact that the saloon party enfranchised a thousand negroes in the county (by paying their poll-taxes), the influence of Fessenden Academy carried its precinct for no license in the late local option campaign; and now and then even from the turpentine huts a boy or girl and sometimes a family is redeemed to better things.

Recently there has been erected at Fessenden a modest Carnegie building. Not only was the gift secured by a negro principal, but the building was designed by a negro architect, whose professional training was had at a mission school, and erected entirely by negro labor at a cost of some $8000. The master builder acquired his trade under his slave-trained father, now a prosperous contractor in Alabama. Two industrial teachers — one trained at Hampton and one at Talledega — shared the direction of the work. The two other regular carpenters were products of the Brick School at Enfield, N. C. Their

Experience with the Negro in Industry

work was supplemented by that of the Fessenden schoolboys. The chief mason, a slave-trained artisan, was aided by a Baptist preacher and a nondescript who had "just picked up his trade." The mortar-maker was taught his job in the United States army. The plasterer, an Ohio negro and fine workman, regularly commanding $5 per day, stipulated that he be allowed two half-days per week to get drunk. His assistants had less ability but like habits. The painting contractor, the son of a free negro, and much above the average in ability and character, is one of the leading craftsmen in his line in a neighboring Florida city. He uses neither tobacco nor liquor, has a good education and genuine artistic gifts as a decorator. He employs at times as many as ten men, and his work on the Carnegie building was an excellent job. Indeed the building as a whole was the most satisfactory of some ten or a dozen built by the Association in various parts of the South during the same year, part under white contractors and a few with white labor exclusively. On most of the buildings white and negro laborers worked side by side at the same trades, making immediate comparison possible.

The fortunes of the work were not all joyous. The principal complained that most of the men continually asked to draw pay faster than it was earned and added:

> Some of my other workmen that had not been trained would go off after pay-day, and the next thing I would hear was that they were in the lock-up at Ocala charged with drunken brawls or fighting. One was charged with gambling and had to flee.
> The trouble with some was that they did not keep their word. I would scour the country for a man, and get his promise, and the promise would not be kept. I had more trouble and quite as much disap-

pointment in digging the basement as the United States will have in digging the canal.

Hot weather and hard work, even with good pay, did not mix. Of course we got the basement, but it was with the dis-operation of the ox, the nag, the boys, the physical labor, and planning of your servant, and, more than all, the power of God.

This certainly does not prove that negro labor is faultless; it does prove that a missionary agency in its industrial experience has opportunity to discover the faults of its average representatives. The Association erects ten or a dozen buildings every year. Negro hands have built property for it worth millions of dollars. The Association knows the agricultural negro through a dozen school farms and some scores of tenants, whose successes and failures are matters of record; and this experience happens to cover all the chief agricultural provinces of the South. It knows the negro in domestic service through the necessity of providing three meals each day and beds every night for two and a half regiments of colored pupils. It has employed many more artisans, farmers, and cooks than it ever has teachers and preachers. It knows the negro upper classes too, the educated and select. Edgar Gardner Murphy shows that the South's chief ignorance of the race is at this point.[1] Representatives of the Association are admitted into hearts and homes where only friends can enter. Thus through vital contacts at all significant parts of the race's life, in twelve states through forty years, it has been acquiring information. If it is ignorant, it is not because of aloofness from the heart of the problem.

Experience with the Negro in Other Lines

[1] Present South, p. 168.

TEMPERING THE BODY TOGETHER

On the contrary Mr. A. H. Stone, one of the meritorious and candid of recent Southern writers, illustrates the fact that the man on the ground may have his gaze fixed on his own feet. He expends considerable sarcasm on the assumption of a Northern radical editor that a man in New York may understand the negro better than a man in Mississippi. In many respects Mr. Stone's survey of negro conditions is very broad and illuminating, but no syllable in his voluminous book indicates that he at all recognizes the experience or attaches any weight to the testimony of another distinguished Mississippian, Major R. W. Millsaps. Mr. Stone's plantation experiment leaves him with a very poor impression of negro labor. Major Millsaps owns a plantation of five hundred acres *within a few miles of Mr. Stone's.* On it he has twenty negro families, including seventy-five people in all. With them he has tried the daring experiment of trusting tenants without an overseer. His own version of its results is thus reported by Mr. Baker:

The Negro's Critic the Original Muckrake

> "Did it work?" I asked.
> "I have never lost one cent," said Major Millsaps; "no negro has ever failed to pay up, and you could n't drive them off the place. When other farmers complain of shortage of labor and tenants, I never have had any trouble."
> Every negro on the place owns his own mules and wagons, and is out of debt. Nearly every family has bought or is buying a home in the little town of Leland, near by, some of which are comfortably furnished. They are all prosperous and contented.
> "How do you do it?" I asked.
> "The secret," he said, "is to treat the negro well

and give him a chance. I have found that a negro, like a white man, is most responsive to good treatment. Even a dog responds to kindness! The trouble is that most planters want to make too much money out of the negro; they charge him too much rent; they make too large profits on the supplies they furnish. I know merchants who expect a return of fifty per cent on supplies alone. The best negroes I have known are those who are educated. Negroes need more education of the right kind — not less — and it will repay us well if we give it to them. It makes better, not worse, workers.[1]

The contrast between Major Millsaps and Mr. Stone seems to suggest that the physical nearness of a fact does not guarantee its recognition. John Bunyan's original muck-raker was oblivious to the surrounding glory because his eyes were fixed upon the ground.

The charge that the missionary is a sentimentalist implies that there are different states of mind in which we approach facts; that different clues may be brought to their interpretation. Proximity is no guaranty of knowledge to him who lacks the clue.

Need of the Man with the Clue

Prof. G. N. Carver of the agricultural department of Tuskegee is one of the most competent graduates of a leading Northern agricultural college. In his professional capacity he is often called upon to advise Southern planters as to the development of their farms. Recently on such a tour of inspection the Colonel said, " Well, Professor, what should we do with such soil? " Sifting a little of it through his thin, black fingers, Carver replied, " You ought n't to plow this farm; you ought to can it! This

[1] Following the Color-Line, p. 103.

City Slum, Tradd St., Charleston, S. C.

Agricultural Peasant of the Black Belt

is mineral paint." Now the Southerner had been treading those clods for fifty years, yet he knew less about them than a negro found out in ten minutes. Fifty years more would n't have added wisdom. A glance sufficed the expert, the man with the clue.

Now there are experts in humanity. Of one such it was said, " He knew what was in man." Some have his clue and others lack it. Being geographically next to a human problem does not help the latter. Proximity ought to mean spiritual nearness. The missionary must indeed establish his adequate contact with the facts, and can. The unbeliever's actual difficulty is with the missionary point of view. The issue essentially involves the competency of the Christian solution of human problems. In having his judgment challenged the servant merely shares the lot of his Master.

II. THE SOUTH AS MISSIONARY GROUND

I. SECTIONAL *vs.* NATIONAL PROBLEMS

The Congestion of Incomplete Americans in the Least Favored Sections

THE primary responsibility for any unassimilated group within the nation belongs to whatever old and established American population happens to be its immediate neighbor. But this original Americanism varies greatly in different sections, both as to its material and institutional resources for assimilation and in mental attitude toward the whole problem. In fact the greatest masses of incomplete Americans are congested in those sections of the nation which in these respects are least favored.

The first question of practical policy must be, Can the geographical neighbors of an un-Americanized group reasonably assimilate it? Have they enough civilizing leaven within them to leaven the lump? Will the national need be equally and adequately met if each section builds " over against its own house "? The answer is emphatically, No. Because of vastly unequal local resources the Americanizing of each unassimilated group is a national problem, and all sections are missionary ground.

The East and North, where the new immigration is chiefly located, have largely succeeded, so far as education is concerned, and the children of the aliens congested in cities there are better provided with school facilities than the children of Americans throughout the country at large. Less than one per cent of their children, from ten to four-

THE SOUTH AS MISSIONARY GROUND

teen years of age, are illiterate, while the proportion of such illiterates of native parentage is over four per cent.

The East and North as Missionary Ground   But this urban success is largely counterbalanced by the rural failure. Away from the forcing process of city life the clan spirit of the newcomer yields slowly, and the substitution of foreign stock for American country population makes the maintenance of New England's rural institutions increasingly dependent upon money and leadership from more favored communities. Deserted farms and decaying churches create an acute problem. The burden of domestic missionary agencies is double that of fifty years ago. Two at least of the great Christian bodies have recently established national agencies to meet the problem of immigration, chiefly congested in this section. As never before the nation must help the East and North.

The West as Missionary Ground   The rural West with its thin population owes the vigor and tone of its civilization largely to the frontier missionary and college builder, supported by religious and educational Boards drawing their funds from the East. Even if they had not regarded the Indian as an enemy, the struggling pioneer population could not have done for him what the paternalism of the government and the zeal of the evangelist have rather blunderingly done. The Oriental immigrant bears an almost negligible proportion to the population of the Pacific coast, yet money is every year sent from other sections to teach him to read the primer and the Bible. By these tokens the West is missionary ground.

In the South, however, is massed the greatest number of incomplete Americans, with the fewest resources for making them fully fit for citizenship. In the geography of assimilation this is the unfavored section. It is im-

possible to make a statistical statement as to the backward whites of the South, but there were more illiterate white children there in 1900 than the total number of reservation Indians and of Orientals in the United States. Add the fact of more illiterate negroes than there were when the Emancipation Proclamation was penned! This measures the proportionate magnitude of sectional dependence upon the nation.

<small>Proportionate Magnitude of Sectional Dependence on the Nation</small>

II. THE SOUTH AS MISSIONARY GROUND

The main current of American civilization is based on the assumption that a common school education is the irreducible minimum of preparation for worthy citizenship. The South cannot adequately furnish even this to vast masses of her people.

The twelve proud Southern states are in a distinct class with New Mexico, Arizona, and what was Indian Territory, at the bottom of the illiteracy list, and they would still be there if there were no negro this side of Africa. Their native white illiteracy at the last census ranged from $8^1/_{10}$ per cent to $18^9/_{10}$ per cent, being greatest in North Carolina, where every sixth white child is illiterate. The average was 11 per cent. Negro illiteracy in the sixteen former slave states stood at 27 per cent in Missouri, then increased from 41 per cent in Arkansas to 61 per cent in Louisiana, or 51 per cent on the average. In the best state of the South thirteen men out of every one hundred cannot write their own names; in the worst state, thirty-eight. This is distinctly a sectional phenomenon; it marks the South off from the rest of the nation, and indeed from

<small>Southern Illiteracy and Educational Backwardness</small>

THE SOUTH AS MISSIONARY GROUND

all the more enlightened portions of Christendom.[1] The Southern child goes to school but a fraction over one-half as many days per year as the Northern child. There is no compulsory educational system except in Kentucky.[2] The enrolment is only 64 per cent of the school population (nearly 10 per cent less than in the North), and that part attends 10 per cent less regularly than school children do in the more advanced section. Male teachers get an average monthly salary of $16 less than in the North and female teachers $9 less; but the salary is not so much behind as the Southern teachers' preparation. The number of college or normal graduates among them is painfully small. Eighty per cent have had only a common-school education. They do their work with one dollar's worth of buildings and equipment where their Northern brethren have eight. This means overcrowded quarters, consequently relatively poor teaching.

The North spends $254,000,000 annually for schools as against the South's $39,000,000; or $17.65 per pupil against the South's $4.54 per pupil; or $4.65 per inhabitant against the South's $1.59. The extremes are Massachusetts spending $26.42 per pupil and Alabama but $2.39; yet the latter state, of its poverty, has sometimes devoted to education one-half of its total revenue. No one claims that the Massachusetts product is better in proportion to the money spent upon it. Yet the difference is not wholly due to the relative wealth of the sections, for, taking their general average, the South spends for

[1] The statistical comparisons of this chapter are chiefly based on the Report of the Commissioner of Education for 1906.
[2] A few cities elsewhere have compulsory education under special "local option" legislation.

education twenty cents on every $100 of taxable property; the North twenty-six cents.¹

Two generations ago a Scotch family separated itself from the parent clan on the Cumberland Plateau in Ten-
The Tennessee Child vs. his Iowa Cousin nessee and its children colonized in several Northern states, including Iowa. This state has a population slightly larger than Tennessee and of about the same relative density, but has somewhat fewer children, the Southern mountain stock being notoriously prolific. It is interesting to compare the lot of the cousins who grew up in Iowa with those who remained in the Tennessee cabins. Ten per cent more children of school age attend school in Iowa than in Tennessee. Teachers number 29,650 in Iowa to 9189 in Tennessee; schoolhouses number 13,947 against 7354. Teachers' salaries average nearly one-third more in Iowa, which expends $10,898,030 for education against $1,751,047 spent by Tennessee; this being $4.49 per inhabitant and $16.43 for each child of school age in Iowa against $1.49 per inhabitant and $4.52 per child of school age in Tennessee. In other words, Iowa's child has over three times as many teachers, and more than three times as much money spent on him as his Tennessee cousin. He always has two seats in school to the other's one; he goes to school more than twice as many days each year, and his state gives him double the training to fit him for citizenship which the other receives — and all this because of the accident of his birth north rather than south of Mason and Dixon's line. Yet Tennessee is by no means the least progressive state in the South.

¹ See Coon, Twenty-five Years' Progress of Public Education in North Carolina: A Comparative Statistical Study of School Maintenance in the South, etc. National Educational Association, Report of Committee on Taxation, 1905.

THE SOUTH AS MISSIONARY GROUND

These facts are indisputable, but it is delicate business to say why they exist. The most thorough diagnosis is that of a Southerner, Professor Rose, of the University of Tennessee.[1] He enumerates five reasons for the South's educational backwardness. Each of these reasons merits our comment.

1. An aristocratic tradition unfavorable to popular education.
2. Poverty.
3. Excessive individualism which sets narrow limits to public activity.
4. A scattered rural population.
5. The fact of the two races necessitating a double school system.

We noted above that the North has been successful in educating the foreigner because he lives chiefly in the cities with their magnificent school systems. Massachusetts alone had in 1900 forty-seven cities with above 10,000 inhabitants, their combined population being 2,050,862. The nine seaboard states of the South had only forty-nine such cities, with a population of but 1,525,564. Five-sixths of the Southern population is widely scattered over mountain and plain, through swamp and forest. Such a sparse population is difficult to gather into schools. This makes the physical problem of education serious, and helps to explain the low standing of the section.

The South Five-sixths Rural

Again, the South is poor. Its chief resource is agriculture, and its most natural comparison is with the agricultural portion of the North, namely, the North Central states. These have a wealth

Poverty

---

[1] Report of the Commissioner of Education for 1903, vol. i, pp. 359 ff.

in agricultural land and buildings of nine and a half billion dollars. The South Central states, of about equal area, have a similar wealth of but two billion dollars. Iowa alone, with an area and population about those of Tennessee, has farm values of over two billions, or more than that of all the South Central states. All this is graphically revealed on maps in the Special Report of the Census Office on Wealth, Debt, and Taxation. These show that no Southern state has relatively as much taxable real estate as the poorest Northern state, and that the taxable real estate per family is two and a half times as large in the North as in the South. Only rarely do taxable values in the South exceed $300 per acre; while in the North they fall below this only here and there.

The scientific study of national resources by our government has revealed almost unimaginable theoretical pos-
The South's Amazing Natural Resources sibilities of increased production of wealth in the South, as in every other part of the continent. Inflamed by this vision and dazzled by the marvelous absolute gains of their section in almost every line, recent Southern champions have talked as though the handicap of sectional poverty would be quickly overcome, and the South furnished equally with Americanizing forces, at least with respect to its white population. As President Alderman puts it, their jubilation of spirit at this prospect "verges on something like hilarity."

Now no one who has traveled the South so as to know its land and people intimately can doubt that many of
Will the South overtake the North? these dreams will come true along with many others yet undreamed. Other sections have their dreams of wealth. Probably under scientific objective measurement the South as a wealth pro-

ducing section would be discovered to be decidedly inferior in possibilities to an equal area of the great upper Mississippi plains. Materials for such an accurate comparison do not yet exist, and if they did they would be beside the point; for the effective wealth of any land depends upon the use which is made of it. We have to consider, therefore, whether, on other grounds, it is likely that the relative gap between the progress of the sections will soon be closed and the South cease to be missionary ground. Of course if the hare lies down to sleep the tortoise will overtake and pass him; but is the hare going to sleep?

The slightest reflection shows that proportionate gains of a section which is just beginning development along new lines cannot keep up. It is easy to improve on little or nothing. The educational progress of the South looms up impressively on the background of its previous lack. The same progress elsewhere would almost be taken for granted. Nor are the proportionate gains all on the side of the South. It is not increasing the number of its teachers in proportion to school population as fast as the North is.[1] Now effective teaching means individual teaching. The crying evil of the Southern schools is that they are overcrowded; there are too many pupils for each teacher. Consequently they do not progress in quality as fast as in numbers. Again, the common school was long ago pretty completely established in the North. This section already had universal elementary schools and could not possibly show great proportionate gains in that direction. The high school, on the contrary, as the " people's university " has almost limitless possibilities of development before it throughout the nation, but the proportion of high school enrolment

Rate of Educational Progress

---

[1] Report of Commissioner of Education, 1906, vol. ii, p. 696.

is increasing faster in the North than in the South.[1] Also there is a larger proportion of boys in the Northern high school, and a smaller proportion of its pupils are preparing for college. These are indications of a more democratic character of the secondary public education in the North. It is not only developing faster, but in a more promising direction.

Turning now to the probable increase of wealth — which is the ultimate guaranty of education — we find **Probable Increase of Wealth** that the farm values of the United States, according to the estimate of the Department of Agriculture, increased in the five years from 1900 to 1905 over six billions of dollars. Considerably over half of this gain was to the credit of the North Central states, with an average gain in value of $11.25 per acre. About one-fifth of the increased value was in the South Central states, with an average increase of $4.66 per acre. Values in the South Atlantic and Western states increased about equally. The increase is explained as follows: " Subject to some qualifications the general principle is that the land itself has become more highly capitalized by a larger amount of net profit per acre." [2]

Now net profit per acre does not depend upon the theoretical fertility of the soil, but upon population, markets, **Southern Agriculture caught in a Vicious Circle** transportation, and agriculture. In its efforts to help the South realize the best from its resources, the agents of the government repeatedly find and record two great difficulties — first, the character of the people; second, the social system under which they live. Reports in the *Year*

[1] Report of Commissioner of Education, 1902, p. 1651. Cf. *Ibid.*, 1906, p. 507.
[2] Year Book, Department of Agriculture, 1905, p. 512.

Book of the Department of Agriculture for 1905, while recording much progress, complain that the farmers of the South are conservative and the available agricultural labor not intelligent enough to use improved methods of agriculture. The conclusion is, " In order to make any radical change in the type of farming which prevails over most of the cotton growing section, it is necessary to train the available labor in new channels and to give it a sense of responsibility not heretofore necessary." [1] This does not refer solely to negro labor, for the reporter for Arkansas and Louisiana writes, " White labor is very scarce and much of it is looked on as inferior to negro labor." [2] Moreover most of the Southern farmers, white or black, are slaves to the credit system, which is based on cotton as the traditional " money crop " in the South. Only by agreeing to put a specified number of acres into cotton can a tenant get his " rashuns " advanced while his crop is growing; accordingly he could not diversify his produce if he would. Southern agriculture is thus caught in a vicious circle. To get out at all it must educate its people to better methods, but the money necessary to pay for that education cannot be had till the net profit per acre in the South is greatly increased, nor can the gap between the Americanizing forces of North and South be bridged till this profit increases very much faster in the South than in the North. Of this there is no immediate prospect.

Praises of the " South of to-morrow " invariably read: When all our land is brought into cultivation and our agriculture rationalized; when immigration has increased our numbers and given us a new laboring population; when the engineer has done his

"The South of To-morrow"

---
[1] Year Book, Department of Agriculture, 1905, p. 194.
[2] *Ibid.*, p. 211.

work for our forest and swamp, and when the prejudice which now prevents most of the civilized world from regarding the South as a desirable home is overcome, we shall be able to take care of our own problems. But how soon are these things likely to happen? The government expert sees that there are many handicaps to the speedy change of the Southern agricultural system. *The Charleston News and Courier* just now confesses, " There appears to be no present prospect of direct immigration to South Carolina or to any of the other Southern states." The Italian government has recently diverted all its immigration from the state of Mississippi to save them from what looks to it like peonage. Of the need of an Appalachian forest reserve, Professor Brigham wrote in 1903:

> More than $10,000,000 was the sum of flood losses in the Appalachian states during the year 1901. With the abundant rains, wherever a slope of any steepness is cleared, it is cropped but for a few years, the soil is washed into the streams, tillage is given up, and the field is abandoned to ever-deepening gullies. Meantime the rich bottom lands below are either excavated and removed bodily by the torrents, or they are deluged with five, eight, or ten feet of stony waste, and become as useless as a gravelly river-bed. Ten years of delay would be fatal. The single states cannot do the work.[1]

Now five of these years of grace have gone by and *The World's Work* says, " The problem is to save one of the most valuable and attractive parts of the nation — literally to save it; for it is going to waste with a rapidity which is fairly astounding." [2] That the South will catch

[1] Geographical Influences in American History, p. 285.
[2] The World's Work, vol. xvi, p. 10300.

THE SOUTH AS MISSIONARY GROUND

up is possibly one of the may-bes, but it is certainly still one of the not-yets.

Every other Southern handicap pales before the fact that a third of its population are negroes but forty years out of slavery and one-half of them illiterate. There are some eight millions of them, increasing from $13^3/_{10}$ per cent of the population of Kentucky to $58^5/_{10}$ per cent in Mississippi; they constitute a majority also in South Carolina. Though declining in numbers relative to the general population of the section they increased more rapidly in the last decade than did the whites in six Southern states. Their poverty does not permit them to bear a proportionate share of the burdens of taxation, and from the standpoint of the South their race must have separate educational and charitable institutions. It would be neither safe nor just to leave to so handicapped a section so massive a national problem.

The Burden of the Negro

Excessive individualism and the aristocratic tradition unfavorable to general education remain, but are waning factors in the South's attitude; especially they are no longer politically dominant. The achievement of her people in popularizing their institutions fairly merits President Alderman's words: "They have developed an overwhelming public sentiment, with the social and political agencies necessary to sustain that sentiment, in favor of the education of all the people at public expense, thus making a social system, semifeudal in nature, a democracy in social usage, as well as in political philosophy."[1] This is fully true as far as the white population is concerned. It is not true as relates to the black third of the South's children. Judged by deeds the prevailing sentiment favors giving them an in-

The South's Half Loaf Unevenly Divided

[1] The World's Work, "The Growing South," vol. xvi, p. 10375.

ferior and class type of education, unequally supported by public resources. Only $2.21 is spent on the negro child to $4.92 for the white, while the most catholic minds of the South are definitely committed to the prior claim of the belated white. The cry is, "Let the children first be fed." "The lot of the Piedmont and Appalachian white man has been forgetfulness and neglect. The world might as well understand that the Southerner is done with this neglect forever. He sees that the redemption of his community lies primarily in the restoration and development of the white population."[1] Now with the South's present and probable resources the broadest and heartiest democracy could not adequately supply the needs of all its people. The lack of such democracy means the uneven distribution of the half loaf, which is all the South has. The plain confession of this situation is the final demonstration that the South is missionary ground.

III. THE DIVISION OF LABOR BETWEEN ASSIMILATING FORCES

To insist that the congestion of unassimilated population in that section makes the Americanizing of the South a national problem is not to deny that the big end of the work belongs to the South. In the division of labor between cooperating forces, Southern agencies and resources have the greater burden and glory. To the very limit of his strength and will, the belated white man and the negro are each the Southerner's problem.

To be specific, there are five cooperating agencies trying to Americanize the South — three of which are Southern.

[1] The World's Work, "The Growing South," vol. xvi, p. 10378.

THE SOUTH AS MISSIONARY GROUND

Primarily the responsibility rests with the state as the agency of democratic society; and no amount of philanthropy from any source can undo the wrong of the state's failure in full and equal justice to its citizens. In judging the success or failure of the Southern states one must avoid two errors. Much fulsome praise has been lavished on them for belatedly undertaking what in the eyes of civilization is the plain and self-evident duty of the state, namely, the elementary education of all its citizens. But equally one must not fail to appreciate the grave handicap against which the Southern people have struggled even so far. They have "had the political patience and equipoise not to disturb the only good thing decreed to them by a carpet-bag government, namely, the provision for popular education placed in their organic law." Out of this they have developed a general school system "fairly complete as to its machinery and methods." They are now spending forty-five per cent of all their public revenue upon education; fifty-one per cent of negro children (a trifle more than one-half!) and sixty-seven per cent of white children are in school; and this without state compulsion. Twenty per cent of all educational spending goes to the negro. This is not equitable, for he comprises thirty-two per cent of the school population. Yet every attempt to limit the support of the negro school to what the negro himself pays in direct taxation has been defeated, and the South stands theoretically committed to elementary education for all its people.

Cooperating Agencies: The State

And all this is far less significant than the fact that a new spirit has possessed the Southern people. The building of their schools has had the character of a popular crusade, and constitutes one

The Educational Revival

of the most notable idealistic movements of the day. Nowhere else in the Union have recent public campaigns been waged and governors elected on educational issues. Nowhere has the vital connection so quickly been grasped between education and the deeper problems of social reform. In brief, educational enthusiasm and consecration is the South's peculiar response to that social spirit which is the most vital and creative movement of our time. There have been no greater heroes in American history than the little handful of educational zealots of Southern birth who fought their section single-handed to perpetuate the carpetbagger's common school. There has been no educational philanthropy half so praiseworthy as the Southern taxpayer's at its best. The whole movement merits the most exalted eulogy.

> "For that the leaders took the lead in Israel,
> For that the people offered themselves willingly,
> Bless ye the Lord."

Cooperating Agencies: The Church. The Southern church shares the recognized conservatism of ecclesiastical institutions and has an additional measure of its own. It is not to discredit its ardent piety to say that it has shown itself the least adaptive of the reconstructive factors of its section. With a few shining exceptions, leadership has not been in it.

Before the war education was chiefly in its hands, and afterward the intense denominational spirit kept alive too many poorly supported and struggling schools, under the burden of which the impoverished sects well-nigh sank. Add to this that its type of education was polite and aristocratic, not popular and democratic, and it is clear that little outreach could be expected toward the less privileged elements of society.

THE SOUTH AS MISSIONARY GROUND

As regards the negro, the church fell more deeply the prey to mingled resentment and despair than did the secular educational forces. From the standpoint of statesmanship some measure of education for him was under the new régime clearly inevitable; but the church did not rise even to that plane. It could not bring itself to teach the recent slave, and when the Northern teachers came (seemingly in the spirit of a new army of invasion bent rather on demonstrating the high capacities of the exceptional negro than on preparing the mass for practical and productive citizenship), Southern organized Christianity in the main withdrew from the task. This is not to forget nor minimize millions of helpful contacts with the negro in his upward struggle. Much personal sympathy, moral support, and advice, and even money in no small measure, was given him. Especially fruitful have been the traditions of responsibility carried over by those Southern churches which had a large colored membership before the war — notably the Southern Presbyterian, the Methodist Episcopal, South, and the Episcopal. Many faithful ministers have continued to preach to black Christians. But confessed, direct, and systematic efforts for the education and uplift of negroes have been largely lacking. The state has found less embarrassment, for its operations have been official and its contacts have not involved any social implications. But evangelization and education at first hand clearly involve a degree of personal Christian fellowship which the Southern church in the main has hitherto been unwilling to grant. It has therefore withheld its hand from the work, partly from pique that the Northerner had undertaken it from what was interpreted as a sectional standpoint, and partly because it was unwilling to do it from its own standpoint. This is truth in the large as the broadest Southern churchmen now confess. Thus Rev. Charles E. Bowman, D.D., of Georgia, recently said: "Assistance in the education of the negro has been practically monopolized by boards, societies, churches, and philanthropists of the North, and we have been disposed to let them have it, excusing ourselves with the claim that more is being done for the negro than for the poor white children of the South, and that we have more than we can do to look after our own." [1] There have been exceptions, and just now indications multiply of the coming of a better mind.

In admitting that the Americanizing of the South is primarily the Southerner's problem one must not forget the Southerner most deeply concerned; namely, the negro himself. The rise of this unprivileged race to bring salvation with its own arm is an unparalleled phenomenon. Beyond all its helpers it has helped itself. It has expended nearly ten million dollars for education besides its share of taxation. It has multiplied schools almost beyond number. The result in many details show great crudity and inexperience, though in inadequacy and wastefulness the educational policy of the negro churches is scarcely worse than that of sectarian education throughout the country at large. They have simply been imitating their supposed superiors. Both in bulk and in worthy accomplishment the negro's successes in elevating himself rise to colossal dimensions. If the South is to be praised for rapid progress in public education, how much more the negro for the zeal which has built his hundreds of schools! In the divi-

Cooperating Agencies: the Negro Himself

---

[1] Annual Report of the Board of Education for the M. E. Church, South, 1907, p. 128.

sion of labor between cooperating forces he bears not the least honorable and responsible part.

Long before either of the Southern forces was ready or able to do a dominant or central work for the redemption of the South, there had been in the field a group of great nationalizing agencies which originated the ideal of the Americanizing of all Americans and set a standard for all succeeding efforts for its realization. The relative place of their work to-day is smaller, but their absolute burden is greater; for, all told, the assimilating resources have not increased as fast as unassimilated population, especially in view of the sterner demands of life in this age of rapid social transitions. The money and personality which they are now putting into the situation were never more essential. Yet, after all, their chief contribution has been, and is, the maintenance of a national view-point. It has been their function to correct the emphasis of those who have attacked the problem with local prejudice, so that the general outcome should be balanced. They have not themselves been free from all provincialism of method, but they have viewed national problems steadily and viewed them as a whole. This is the spirit of prophecy.

<small>Cooperating Agencies: Northern Christian Philanthropy</small>

The prophet has a strange and moving rôle in human history. From his far hilltop he looks down on the marching and countermarching of nations. He does not immediately belong to their problem, and its outcome seems none of his business. Yet somehow he turns out to have a better grasp of the situation than any participant has. He has a more unhindered access to the deepest sources of information than the man who has a personal interest in the fray. The strange outcome is that " whom he curses is cursed and whom he blesses is blest." He thinks that his judgment of the tendencies of his day is based upon insight into the purposes of God.

Our nation has had such men, who have definitely attempted to realize the divine purpose in America. Out of the strange human stuff providentially gathered they have tried to temper the national body together as it pleases God. Sometimes the nationalizing agencies used by such prophetic hearts have disguised their true function by calling themselves denominational Boards. Sometimes the nominal character of these Boards has swamped their higher function; but at the worst they comprise the most single-hearted and Christian factor which has entered into the problem. They have been essentially popular agencies, administering chiefly the genuine and unostentatious philanthropy of the " common folk " of the North.

The American Missionary Association is typical of them. Founded in 1846, it gathered up several local organiza-
<small>The American Missionary Association</small> tions which had a common missionary impulse toward less privileged peoples. It had other work for the pioneer in the South and West; for the Indian tribes, then counted as foreign; for recently emancipated slaves in Jamaica and negro refugees in Canada, and for the heathen in half a dozen foreign lands. This shows the scope of the original idea as not sectional nor even exclusively national. Gradually, however, its foreign work was assigned to more specialized agencies, and the outcome of the Civil War gave the Association its chief burden in the persons of four and a half million of freedmen. Fraternal cooperation in the uplift of their nine million descendants still remains its first concern as also incomparably the greatest assimilating task before the nation. This Association discovered the Southern Highlander as a distinct type demanding a special Amer-

A. F. Beard, D.D.
Corresponding Secretary American Missionary Association, 1887–1903

THE SOUTH AS MISSIONARY GROUND

icanizing effort. Its essential national character is revealed by its successive assumptions of responsibility for new and unexpected peoples which have come to us by conquest or annexation. Its present work includes an evangelizing and educating ministry to all the non-European and mixed groups under our flag, and by a happy exception which proves the rule, to the largest group of unassimilated white population, the mountaineer of the Southern Appalachians. Thus it tries to perform its office in the midst of its brethren in a spirit of confessed cooperation.

A tragic misunderstanding, the fruit of decades of sectional conflict, embittered by war and made doubly diffi-
<small>Cooperating Agencies: Joint Educational Effort of North and South</small> cult by the blunders of Reconstruction, long sundered the forces of uplift in the South. The two sections were temporarily incapable of a mutual trust, while the conservative South, represented by the church, did not appreciate the ideals of the more advanced educators. The negro had aspirations sundering him even from his would-be helpers. It is a thrilling story how they all came together at last; how the carpetbag governments laid the foundation of popular education; how in every state there arose a little handful of educational zealots of Southern birth who fought incredibly lonely, heroic fights to make good, after so long, Jefferson's vision of a common school; how before, and especially after the disbanding of the Freedman's Bureau, Northern Christian philanthropy undertook the education of the negro and later of the poor white; how its teachers toiled in fearful isolation, often ostracized, slowly learning the true needs of both races as only time can teach them; how the joint administration by high-minded men of North and South, of the

splendid benefactions of George Peabody and others taught new possibilities of cooperation and raised philanthropy to the plane of constructive statesmanship; how finally it dawned on men that there was a great unity of aim underneath all the separate agencies, and they drew together in a practical cooperation and good understanding which is the dominant character of Southern educational effort to-day.

The chief platform on which this good understanding has been reached is the Conference for Education in the South, organized in 1898. Here representatives of all interests met through a series of years, face to face, and worked out a common policy. To an unprecedented degree it appealed to a varied constituency, to politicians, to the press, to women's clubs, and somewhat to the clergy, as well as to the philanthropist and the professional educator.

Conference for Education in the South

It initiated a great and successful educational campaign in behalf of education throughout the entire section. As a result of such cooperative effort a number of ideals may be counted as established in the South. First, the development of popular education as a function of a democratic state is at once the highest philanthropy and the simplest justice. Agitation and organization must not cease until this is fully accomplished throughout the section. To encourage this movement is the finest exercise of the nationalizing spirit. Its success is the basis for all other ministries to the unprivileged classes. On the other hand, the clear lack of sufficient resources in the South as a section, and the inevitable gaps in its educational program, must be met by help from the more favored sections operating through nationalizing agencies, the cooperative spirit of whose work is

Agreement on Ideals

THE SOUTH AS MISSIONARY GROUND

to be appreciated by all. The disorganization and waste of the past must cease. The well-meaning competition of half-starved institutions, ill-advised duplication of agencies, and congestion of unnecessary schools, especially for negroes (as in Atlanta), must give way to the great principles of order and efficiency. Benevolence must study each institution which appeals for aid; whether it is wisely founded, strategically located, well conducted. The auxiliary forces of Northern philanthropy must have a special strategy so as not to complicate injuriously the movement of the whole. Most of all, perhaps, the denominational education of the Southern sects needs readjusting to an era of dominant public education. This requires a self-denying merging or abandonment of many institutions, preliminary to the strategic development of all the others. The educational policy of the negro churches, made aggressive by race consciousness and ecclesiastical pride, especially needs tempering by a sense of the whole situation and expert direction. Such economizing of resources through the application of the "trust" idea to Southern education has recently been attempted by the General Educational Board, administering Mr. Rockefeller's endowments, and by affiliated agencies. These are by no means likely to be the controlling force of the future: neither the Southern states, the negro schools, nor the missionary Boards will submit to it. Yet their moral influence will be wide, and the lesson they emphasize is in hopeful process of being learned by all the educational forces concerned. A well-understood division of labor is thus being achieved. All agencies are submitting to the test of efficiency. There are backward eddies, but this is the direction of the main current.

III. THE SIFTING OF THE SOUTH

I. THE TWO SOUTHS AND THE TWO SOUTHERNERS

THE most outstanding fact about the South is that there are two Souths, lowland and highland. Once there was no South except the mountains. Beginning with New Jersey, the Atlantic seaboard south to Florida, the lower half of the Gulf states, and the Mississippi Valley as far north as the mouth of the Ohio, were at the bottom of the sea. The waters lapped the feet of the mountains on the west, covering what is now the Blue Grass regions of Kentucky. This most ancient highland South — the South of Lincoln and Judge Hargis — looked out upon the ocean. Its most southern point was what is now central Alabama. Later the characteristic lowland South — the South of Jefferson Davis and of Lee — rose out of the waters as a level coastal plain, through which the broad wedge of the mountains thrust its rough fist far down through soft stretches of recent sea bottom toward the present waters of the Gulf. In these two strikingly distinct geographic provinces the two great human problems of the South are congested. The problem of the belated white man is chiefly the problem of the highlands; the problem of the negro is almost exclusively one of the plains.

<small>Geographic Separation of the South's Two Problems</small>

From their first settlement these two sections of the South have differed in temper and been antagonistic in politics. Historically the earliest associations of the uplands were with the North. The movement of population was southwest rather than directly west. The bulk of their immigration,

<small>Highland vs. Lowland: Population</small>

Scotch-Irish by birth, entered by way of Philadelphia and Baltimore, and worked down the great Appalachian valley rather than across the coastal plain from Atlantic ports.

Cut off from tide-water not only by the falls of the rivers — the head of navigation — but also by a parallel strip of pine barrens through much of its length, this region was in many respects a projection of the Pennsylvania type into the very midst of the South. It was settled in the middle of the eighteenth century largely by migration from Pennsylvania of Scotch-Irish, Germans, and English pioneers, having little contact with, or resemblance at first to, the seaboard life, either economically, politically, or socially. It was the first distinctively western region, non-slaveholding, grain and cattle raising, a land of dissenting sects, of primitive democratic conditions, remote from the coast, and finding the connection with Baltimore, Philadelphia, and the Pennsylvania valley, both in spiritual and economic life, more intimate than with the tide-waters of Maryland, Virginia, North Carolina, and South Carolina, within whose boundary lines it chiefly lay.[1]

The diverse civilization of mountain and plain thus root in their different origins.

The first habitat of the upland Southerner was the Appalachian foot-hills rather than the true mountains. Later he was driven back into the mountains as a result of the unsuccessful struggle, political and economic, with the lowlands. This struggle of up-country against tide-water is a significant clue of the earlier history of the six southern states crossed

The Struggle for the Piedmont

[1] Turner, "Is Sectionalism in America Dying Away?" *American Journal of Sociology*, vol. xiii, p. 665.

by the Piedmont Belt. "In every one the tide-water minority area, where wealth and slaves preponderated, ruled the more populous primitive interior counties by apportionment of the legislatures so as to secure the effective majority of the representatives. Unjustly taxed, deprived of due participation in government, their rights neglected, they protested, vainly for the most part, in each of these colonies and states."[1] Central North Carolina, for example, previous to 1830, had a magnificent normal development as a region of small farms and diverse domestic industries supporting a prosperous yeomanry of Scotch-Irish, German, and Quaker descent. The plantation system crept up into it against the economic grain. The slaveholders wanted to rule the Piedmont more than they wanted to farm it. The uplands vainly resisted with an intense antislavery agitation. When finally they were overcome, their people emigrated wholesale, especially between 1830 and 1840, into the mountains and beyond. "During that decade the white population of the state increased only 2.54 per cent compared with 12.79 per cent for the preceding period."[2] Thus the most virile and democratic part of the population was dispossessed of the better land and forced back into the poor and thinly populated mountain region.

As a natural barrier the Southern Appalachians presented no such absolute physical difficulty as the Rocky Mountains, which civilization so triumphantly crossed later. But their great width — some three hundred miles — and the unbroken length of their parallel ranges, proved too much for the

The Fixing of the Mountain Type

[1] Turner, "Is Sectionalism in America Dying Away?" American Journal of Sociology, vol. xiii, p. 666.
[2] Thompson, From Cotton Field to Cotton Mill, p. 30.

slight resources of the earlier pioneer. Their coves and narrow valleys caught him, and still hold his children in the civilization of a hundred years ago. Meanwhile the militant slaveholding South followed the coastal plains, added the new empire of the Southwest to its domain, and developed the peculiar mental and social aggressiveness which hurried the two great sections of the nation toward irrepressible conflict. But it is never to be forgotten that the first conflict of the South was within itself, and that the North fought with and for a consistent Southern minority.

The crisis of war revealed still further the dominance of physiographic over political divisions. The lowlander *Highland vs. Lowland: the Civil War* stuck to his state against the nation; the mountaineer clung to his region against his state. West Virginia was rent from the mother state and became a separate commonwealth. North Carolina slowly and reluctantly seceded. Kentucky, though south of the Ohio, remained within the Union. Tennessee sent a larger proportion of soldiers into the Federal armies than any Union state. Even in Alabama the comparatively slight but rough upland region remained persistently Unionist, and contributed its regiments to the Northern cause. It is not too much to say that the mountains held the balance of power and turned the scales of war. Throughout the awful struggle the bitterest animosity and cruelest deeds were between Southerner and Southerner, — mountaineer and lowlander, — in the border states.

After the war the mountains remained stubbornly Republican in politics. After 1876 the negro vote disappeared and the South became seemingly solid. Yet through all political fluctuations the mountains stand fixed

and maintain the " geographical distribution of politics." [1]
Except in national politics the South has never been solid,
and there only by the arbitrary inclusion within common state bounds of radically diverse populations. I am often asked by curious Northern friends if I am not a Democrat in the South. My answer is that I have lived in the South for eight years, and in two different states, but always in a Republican county and in a congressional district which has been Republican most of the time since the war. State boundaries disregard physiographic barriers; and under our Federal system it is the fate of persistent minorities to be forgotten in national politics.

Highland vs. Lowland: Politics

Thus from the beginning to the present time the two Souths have sifted their peoples. There are and always have been two Southerners, — each a splendid and appealing type. Their characters have been molded by the interplay of influences from the land and the social institutions built upon it. The land originated, the institutions accelerated, their characteristic differences. Then the land and the institutions together fixed the respective types of mountain-men and lowlander. This distinction is the first clue to the understanding of the South.

II. THE VARIED SOUTH

By all natural rights the region of our country which ought to show sectional solidity in political opinion and typical civilization is that heart of the North, the thousand miles of plains which continue the gentle westward slope of the Alleghany plateau, across

The Land of Contrast

---

[1] See Plates II and III (1, 2, and 3) in Turner, "Is Sectionalism in America Dying Away?" American Journal of Sociology, vol. xiii, pp. 664 ff.

THE SIFTING OF THE SOUTH

the lake and prairie region, to where the great plains meet the bases of the Rocky Mountains. The ice-sheet anciently ground the soil of most of this region into virtual homogeneity. To-day it dominates the nation with that sameness of life which Mr. Bryce thinks characteristic of America. The South, on the contrary, exhibits a greater range of physical diversity than any other part of our domain. It is the geographically predestined land of contrasts. Not only does it present the great contrasts of mountain and plain, but within each of these characteristic areas it shows a most intricate variety — in the form and contour of the land, the quality and composition of the soil, and the consequent economic adaptations of its minor areas. This great variety of natural wealth means in the long run equal variety in human work and consequent diversity in population.

Illustrations of these physical varieties are endless. Our national Department of Agriculture recognizes thirteen physiographic belts between the Atlantic and the great plains. Five of these are crossed in going westward from New York, eleven in going westward from Charleston. The soil-augur and laboratory tell a like tale. Of the nine soil provinces west of the great plains discriminated by the Soil Survey, six are almost wholly within the South, while on the contrary nine-tenths of the area north of the Ohio and Missouri rivers belongs to a single soil province. So far as the soils of the North and South have been locally explored the results show greater unevenness of productivity in the characteristic Southern types. Detailed study of the widespread "Cotton Kingdom" discovers that it ought to be peculiarly a realm of diversified agriculture.

<small>Physiographic and Soil Provinces</small>

Again, the broad coastal plain from Virginia to Mississippi shows a virtually continuous division into parallel belts. The pine levels merge into the pine hills and an infertile ridge of sand hills interposes itself, for much of the distance, between them and the Piedmont. The influences of these minor physiographic regions are as clear and permanent as those of the mountains and lowlands themselves. Indeed the distribution of population is minutely determined by them. In every state the negroes are found mostly in the pine hills between the plains and the Piedmont. They also hold the narrow fringe of alluvial coast lands and the alluvial regions of the lower Mississippi valley.[1] Thus throughout its length the South is crossed by alternate population-belts of black and white. The familiar term "black belt" applied first to the black-colored soil of the landward portion of the "belted coastal plain" which crosses the center of Alabama. It was only secondarily applied to the massing of the negro population in this and similar regions of the South. In general it is the low-lying, moist and rich areas which are overwhelmingly colored, while the whites tend to the higher, dryer, and less fertile lands. These belts of population constitute a natural geographical basis for the further segregation of the races which is going on under social impetus.

<small>Black and White "Belts"</small>

Now there have been from the beginning throughout the South persistent differences of population, whether white or black, due to these diverse local environments; but only intimate study of local history, state by state, reveals them. Older discussions of Southern problems almost entirely ignore them, and only recently has the work of a notable group of Southern state historians enabled us to

<small>Differences in Population due to Local Environment</small>

[1] Kelsey, The Negro Farmer, pp. 14, 15.

THE SIFTING OF THE SOUTH

trace their influence.[1] The general truth is that the South has included many peculiar areas each with its peculiar people. This is interestingly illustrated in the difficulty which the American Missionary Association finds in classifying some of its institutions. In north central Alabama, for example, is an institution usually reckoned as a "mountain school." It is at the center of a group of Piedmont counties having less than one per cent of negro population, yet surrounded by others in which the negro population ranges from twenty-five to fifty per cent. This white island in the midst of a colored ocean is due to the fact that the Tennessee River cuts through the mountains at Chattanooga and isolates the lower end of the Piedmont region in the midst of surrounding lowlands. Its broken sand ridges are not too rough for the raising of cotton, which is the chief product. Yet there is scarcely a negro in the country. Many of the natives have never seen one. The driver who carries one over to the school comes from the "Valley." He is outraged to see white women and children picking cotton; this is "niggers'" work. Thus the lowlander does not recognize cotton without the negro. The mountaineer would not recognize cotton at all. In brief, the ordinary distinctions between southern types do not fit the people of this region. They are an intermediate group, representing many similar ones — the products of limited local environments.

The great physiographic groupings of population within the several states are easily discerned. North Carolina, Tennessee, and Georgia have each three clearly distinguishable sections of about equal area; but the more intricate diversities of this land of contrasts, which are

[1] E. g. Fleming, Civil War and Reconstruction in Alabama. See pp. 108 ff.

the true clue to Southern history, can only be realized by patient study. They have been almost totally concealed by the great struggle which compelled men to forego their minor differences and join together in great contending armies. Except for the negro, the South would be the least solid section of America; and in the long run geographical diversities will have their way, especially as industry and agriculture, following the lead of science, seek out the specific adaptation of each small area for the production of wealth.

The South Naturally the Least "Solid" Section

Only misunderstanding and injustice can result when this natural basis of persistent human differences is forgotten. There cannot be and there never was any uniformity of social conditions throughout the South — even under the immense pressure of its sectional institutions. The local character of slavery was economically determined, and the institution everywhere colored by the varying fortunes of the master class. The condition of the slave was not the same on the exhausted seaboard soils as in the still prosperous middle districts. It was still different on the frontier. The varying reports which vexed the nation through all the period of the antislavery agitation were due to varying facts. Within the slave population too there were distinct economic classes. The status of the field-hand was practically different from that of the skilled mechanic or of the household servant and petty overseer.[1] Then there was a considerable minority of freed negroes, many of whom had considerable wealth and some culture, and sometimes an organized and recognized distinction between the mulatto and the black negro. In Charleston a mu-

Social Institutions Colored by Local Environment

---

[1] Hart, Slavery and Abolition, pp. 96 ff.

latto society, the "Brown Fellowship," has existed for over a hundred years, maintaining its social exclusiveness and its private cemetery. For many years it operated select schools for mulattoes only. The public records of that city still recognize a distinction between the mulatto and negro. Naturally, too, there was a difference between city and country, affecting both races. Back of these antebellum distinctions stretch dim vistas of African history, the untold story of long mingled races whose varieties only the most recent writers are adequately recognizing.[1] The differences developed in the negro by these ancient siftings go far toward explaining his unequal response to the demands and needs of the present day. It is equally true that the ordinary versions of the state of white society in the South before the war are altogether more simple than the facts. It was the general tendency of slavery to push the non-slaveholding white man down into the "poor white" class, and out into the less fertile agricultural regions. Still, even in the lower South, the middle class did not wholly disappear, and considerable areas in every state maintained a characteristically democratic organization of society. If such differences could maintain themselves then, how little cause to expect uniform conditions now? The fact is that social conditions in the South are, like the land itself, infinitely complex.

There is, therefore, but one generalization which it is safe to make about the South; namely, that one must not generalize at all. This is particularly true of all attempted judgments upon its belated and unassimilated populations. The negro does not show any uniform "race tendency" throughout the South. He is not generally given to an abnormal death-rate or to ex-

The Evil of Generalization

[1] See Dowd, The Negro Races, p. 415.

cessive crime; neither is he uniformly successful in acquiring property or education. There is no equal development of race consciousness or pride. All attempts to show permanent race tendency in these matters are futile. Existing statistics are deceptive. They seem to admit of an accurate comparison of the negro with the white; but they are not compiled separately for that part of the white population with which it is fair to compare the negro, namely, that belonging to the same economic and social status; and therefore they are practically worthless unless corrected by a knowledge of the local conditions which they attempt to generalize. The newer sociology is righting itself in this matter. It is continually narrowing its "unit of investigation" and seeking to do justice to the many human varieties molded by the diversity of natural environment and of work.[1] Meanwhile the bitterest injustice of generalization still characterizes popular judgments. The mountaineer, newly sensitive to the world's opinion, is justly resentful of sweeping alien statements as to his condition and his needs. His group is by no means homogeneous. Where there are mountains there are valleys, and these have been the ancient routes of travel and early seats of civilization. At the head waters of the Clinch and Holston, Sevier and his companions founded the "State of Franklin," which was in 1790, and has always continued to be one of the most thickly populated regions in the Union. The "Prophet of the Great Smoky Mountains" can literally look down on the domes of colleges a hundred years old. The mountaineer of fiction and romance is but the most isolated and least progressive class within the larger mountain province. Highland as well as lowland, the South is a region of variety.

[1] See Ross, The Foundations of Sociology, ch. iv. Also pp. 79 and 311 ff.

And now under the mighty and exuberant forces of the freed and awakened South, the future tends to bring forth still greater variety of human life. Uniform progress is not to be expected either in the lowlands or in the highlands — on the part of the negro or of the backward white man.

III. THE CRISIS OF THE SIFTING

To-day finds the South at the crisis of its sifting. It is characteristically a " growing South." It has become part of a new age which is silently resifting all civilized peoples. Vast forces — with which none of us are quite at home, so suddenly have they come into play — have gripped the South with revolutionary violence. An anciently primitive, rural, and agricultural section, feudally organized, is rapidly becoming modern, urban, and industrial. For the first time its fatal preoccupation with the race problem has been broken in upon by a whole new group of urgent social questions. The rise of the industrial labor problem, with the gradual evolution of modern organized labor and of a new class of Southern industrial masters, compels in the whole section a new attitude toward *work*. The fact of woman as an economic producer in the mills of the South and as a competitor with men in its business offices challenges the whole Southern ideal of the relation of the sexes. With this totter a thousand social conventions of the old régime, beautiful but doomed. With the new growth of wealth the old aristocracy of birth is threatened and often submerged. The invasion of the South by the Hebrew merchant has been eventful almost beyond that of the Northern armies. In every Southern state dominant political power has come into the hands of the " poor whites." This

(The "Growing South")

is almost as revolutionary as was the carpetbag era.[1] Southern education, which was studiously polite and apart from the practicalities of life, has leaped to the other extreme and leads the nation in its industrial and vocational tendencies. More slowly, yet significantly, the new habit of scientific candor attacks the theological and social dogmas of the South. The struggle for independent judgment — a characteristic feature of this age of transition — against the peculiar tyranny of sectional traditionalism, creates a new type of Southern leaders, heroic beyond their peers. For the first time in a century the South is developing, not on a tangent to, but in direct line with the choicest currents of Western civilization. Yet however we may glorify the process we must remember and regret its human wreckage and débris — the thousand "men of yesterday" whom the age is sifting out as unequal to its strenuous demands and its speedy ascent.

These mighty changes cannot but be especially crucial for the backward and unassimilated peoples. To them they mean life or death. The belated mountaineer and the undeveloped negro stand to-day in an acute stage of what the sociologist calls the selective process. Never before and perhaps not again for a century will the test of fitness be so insistent and so searching. It is not to be expected that either group should come off whole. No race was ever saved wholesale, least of all the Anglo-Saxon. By migration, war, pestilence, and economic stress he has been sifted and resifted; he has been tried in a furnace seven times heated. His salvation is the salvation of the remnant. The negro lacks thousands of years of the Saxons' sifting. The selective forces, which have made the Ameri-

The Backward People's "Bad Quarter of an Hour"

---

[1] See Brown, Lower South in American History, p. 256.

OLD MEMPHIS

Negro tenants in attics and basements of white homes

NEW JACKSON

Real estate office and advertisement of negro residential subdivision

THE SIFTING OF THE SOUTH

can of to-day what he is, were suspended for the mountaineer a century ago. The test which the rest of the nation has gradually met, these must undergo suddenly and without preparation. Each is having just now his "bad quarter of an hour." Every so-called "problem" of these backward stocks is just some phase or other of this selective process and as such must be judged.

The participation of the mountains in the rapid transitions of the new South is manifest chiefly in three movements.

First, the exodus of mountain population to the cotton-mills and industrial cities. This is part of the world movement from country to city. In the case of the mountaineer it is particularly pathetic because of his ignorance, his ingrained individualism and his lack of moral preparedness for city life. Whole counties are being well-nigh depopulated by emigration, and the problem of some sections of the mountains is whether there will be any people left in them. This transition is in itself a radical sifting. Under urban conditions the incapable sink into a singularly inert and hopeless class, well known to the charity organizations of the Southern cities. The capable, on the other hand, with marvelous rapidity become complete Americans and themselves masters of material progress.

Exodus from the Mountains

Second, the invasion of the mountains by industry. When the mountaineer will not come to the mill the mill goes after the mountaineer. The insatiable demand of modern industry for new and unexploited labor power has resulted in a marvelously interesting movement of industrial enterprise into the mountains. Their inaccessibility was such that all of Europe and even Asia were ransacked for workers before

Invasion of the Mountains by Industry

their fastnesses were attacked; but now the most unlikely places are invaded. No more violent test can be forced upon a primitive population than this of becoming industrialized; and the mountaineer is bearing it unequally. To one man, or family, it means not only a better wage, but an enlarged outlook on life and an escape from petty and narrow tradition; to another it means only exploitation, degradation, and vice.

Third, the invasion of the mountains by leisure. Less massive, yet deeply significant, is the change coming over the mountaineer through the exploitation of his region by wealth in search of rest and recreation. Situated as the Southern Appalachians are between North and lowland South, their mild climate and beauty of scenery makes them increasingly the natural playground and the meeting-place of leisure for both sections. Not only are there much-frequented health resorts like Asheville, but new armies of invading tourists and seasonal residents keep breaking in upon the mountain people with alien customs and standards of life. They make an even more subtle and dangerous attack than industry does upon the essential genius and spirit of this our most democratic and peculiarly American remnant. The native is outclassed and is often reduced to servile attendance upon the pleasure-seeker, whose manners and dress set new fashions and whose freely-spent money rapidly overturns all local standards of value. The result is frequently a certain loss of independence and of that staunch self-respect which is the most wholesome and attractive heritage of the mountain people. Yet this same tourist invasion brings also ideals of culture and refinement and opens possibilities of life which create new worlds to many an aspiring mountain youth.

Invasion of the Mountains by Leisure

THE SIFTING OF THE SOUTH

Thus the sifting of the mountain goes on, and intensely, even as we read these lines.

The present crisis of the negro's sifting is outwardly shown in five significant aspects:

First, the redistribution of population.[1] The present movements of the negro are more general and massive than at any other time since his coming to America. They take two directions — first, to the Southern and, more recently, especially to the Northern cities. On the whole his city-ward movement is not as rapid as that of population in general, but he is less equal to city life, and the result of the urban sifting is terribly acute. Scarcely less important is the fact of the negro's massing in the Black Belt. In our previous discussion we have seen that he was carried up into the Appalachian foot-hills against the natural economic grain of that region. The present movement is a revulsion from the Piedmont and a massing in the valleys, the low prairies, and coast lands. From the standpoint of state boundaries this means that the ratio of negroes in several border states is rapidly diminishing with a corresponding increase in the lower South. Of ninety-seven counties in Virginia, sixty actually lost negro population between 1890 and 1900. The coming census will probably show still farther movements in this direction. Whatever may be the minor significance of this movement it in general indicates the affinity of the negro for the lower, hotter, and, as it happens, the more fertile regions of the South.

Two Movements of Negro Population

Second, the newly mobile negro population is increasingly subject to alarming social evils. Such transitional maladies always attack people who are undergoing violent

---

[1] Kelsey, The Negro Farmer, pp. 12 ff; Commons, Races and Immigrants in America, pp. 54 ff.

social changes. The negro seems to show new physical weakness. His death-rate is, roughly speaking, double that of the white population. On the face of the returns he seems to be far and away the least promising element of our people morally. His crime rate is especially excessive. Yet sociological insight pronounces these to be the usual traits of peoples in like circumstances. They are acute phases of the selective process.

<small>Transitional Maladies</small>

Third, there has come to be a marked differentiation of elements within the negro population. The negro has distributed himself throughout all of the economic activities of American civilization. A magazine writer puts the case rather jauntily as follows:

<small>Differentiation</small>

> A large city could be formed without a single white man in it, and yet lack for no trade or profession. There are 21,268 negro teachers and college professors in the United States, and 15,530 clergymen. The negroes could finance a railroad through their 82 bankers and brokers, lay it out with their 120 civil engineers and surveyors, condemn the right of way with their 728 lawyers, make the rails with their 12,327 iron and steel workers, build the road with their 545,980 laborers, construct its telegraph system with their 185 electricians and their 529 linemen, and operate it with their 55,327 railway employés.
>
> Colored people complain that they have to sit in the gallery in white theaters, but their 2043 actors and showmen might give them theaters of their own in which they could occupy the boxes in solitary grandeur. They have 52 architects, designers, and draftsmen, 236 artists and teachers of art, 1734 physicians and surgeons, 212 dentists, 210 journalists, 3921 musicians and teachers of music, and 99 literary

THE SIFTING OF THE SOUTH

and scientific persons. The colored baby can be introduced to the world by negro physicians and nurses, instructed in every accomplishment by negro teachers, supplied with every requisite of life by negro merchants, housed by negro builders, and buried by a negro undertaker.

There are negro bookkeepers and accountants, clerks and copyists, commercial travelers, merchants, salesmen, stenographers and telegraph operators. Negroes are in every manual trade, — carpenters, masons, painters, paper-hangers, plasterers, plumbers, steam-fitters, chemical workers, marble-cutters, glass-workers, fishermen, bakers, butchers, confectioners, millers, shoemakers, tanners, watchmakers, gold and silversmiths, bookbinders, engravers, printers, tailors, engineers, photographers, glove-makers,—everything that statisticians think it worth while to count. And the curious thing is that in whatever line a negro man is at work there also is a negro woman. The only occupation which the colored women have allowed their men folk to monopolize are those of the architect and banker and broker, the telegraph and telephone linemen, the boiler-maker, the trunk-maker, and the pattern-maker. You can hire a negro civil engineeress and an electricienne. There are 164 colored clergywomen, 262 black actresses, and 10 Afro-American female lawyers. One negro woman works as a roofer, another as a plumber, and 45 of them are blacksmiths, iron and steel workers, and machinists. Three are wholesale, and 860 are retail merchants. Others are journalists, literary persons, artists, musicians, government officials, and practitioners of an infinite variety of skilled and unskilled trades.

Such achievement is the result of a brief and imperfect sifting. There was an infinitely wider range of capacity and possible usefulness within the race than the most sanguine could have imagined when the slave was freed.

A full quota of social classes has also appeared, and the stratification of negro society has proceeded almost as fast as that of white. Every considerable Southern community now shows a complete and almost self-sufficient negro group life, with its separate institutions and ideals, within that of the general population. The organized life of the American negro is fast becoming an *imperium in imperio*.

Fourth, there is an increasing segregation of the negro population from the white. Its development from within and its new habit of self-dependence, results in a growing loss of contact with the general life. This is necessarily so in those geographically distinct Black Belts in which the negro is massing. Within the cities, too, the races tend increasingly to occupy separate sections; while the social ban and barrier on the whole certainly grow more rigid. This means the temporary withholding of great untouched masses of the race from the acute sifting which their city-going brethren are experiencing. It is certain to prolong indefinitely the problem of the complete assimilation of the negro. Cut off from the stimulus of white civilization, he frequently shows reversionary tendencies toward African conditions. On the other hand, segregation in the rural regions tends to hold in reserve the sounder element of the race, from which capacity and moral health may be supplied to the future. All peoples need such a reserve force from which recruits can come, not too rapidly, under the strenuous demands of civilization. Thus the withholding of the Black Belt from the acute sifting of the present has an important and favorable bearing on the ultimate prospects of the American negro.

Fifth, as a result of the partial and incomplete sifting of the immediate past, a negro minority has emerged fully prepared for participation in American civilization. This emerged class, the "talented tenth," is a new human type, bearing the characters of freedom and demonstrating the immense advantage of even the limited democratic opportunity which the race has had since emancipation. It had a certain historic basis in the attainments of the free negro of the old régime and the privileges of certain upper classes of slaves; yet its essential traits have never before been attained by the negro. For the first time in his history there is the firm establishment of monogamous marriage and the ideals of the Christian home. The first generation of children born of such homes are just entering upon independent life. This group, too, has developed a genuine culture, including distinctive esthetic and ethical marks of negro genius, which constitutes a yet unmeasured contribution to the ideal life of the world, yet sharing the best thought, feeling, and activity of Western civilization. It has developed manifold organs of social control and reached a magnificent place of leadership over the general negro mass. On the other hand there are manifest tendencies for the emerged class to break away from that mass. Hitherto it has consisted largely of mulattoes, and one of the most fateful questions for the American negro is whether the mulatto group will attempt to regard itself as an intermediate race between the white and black, or accept that identification with the negro to which white sentiment assigns it. This is the deepest issue within the higher negro classes to-day.[1] Upon this issue race leaders are divided and by it race sentiment is being sifted. Whatever

Emergence of the "New Negro"

---

[1] Baker, "Following the Color-Line," The Mulatto, ch. viii.

else the emergence of such a group signifies, it is clear that among those socially classified as negroes there was a considerable minority who are not unfit for the competitions and achievements of white civilization. Under slavery its members were socially suppressed. So far, at least, the inferior status of the race was not due to inferior capacity. Now that part — and only part — of the pressure has been removed their fitness manifests itself, and they take their natural place of successful leadership. The progress of the negro under this leadership has already been marvelous, and is a reliable indication of still wider capacity and potential worth awaiting to be revealed when opportunity is more perfectly equalized.

Such are some of the phases of the great process of social selection working in the South. To illustrate and interpretate them still further will be the work of subsequent discussions.

IV. STUDY OF THE WELL-SIFTED NEGRO COMMUNITY

What the process of selection concretely means and how it actually works out is best realized through the study of the particular population. Thomasville, Georgia, shows such a well-sifted negro community. The facts relating to it here summarized were gathered by Rev. William H. Holloway, pastor of the local Congregational church.

In 1900, Thomasville was a city of 3296 colored and 2026 white population. It has grown to probably 8000 people, about the same relative proportion between the races being maintained. The county had at the last census 17,450 negroes and 13,626 whites. It is part of the "Black Belt" lying in Southwestern Georgia, about twenty miles above the Florida line.

THE SIFTING OF THE SOUTH

An investigation of the distribution of the two races within the city limits of Thomasville shows clearly the tendency to segregation. The negroes occupy solidly four distinct areas lying in general toward the outskirts of the city. Some of their better homes are near the center, and, in fact, they are well represented on the best streets, but such property was acquired before the recent growth in population. Contiguity between the races is due largely to the filling in of population between. A negro would not now easily find a central location. There is a marked tendency, and one vigorously encouraged by both races, toward geographical separation.

Segregation of the Races

On this account the most extensive of recent movements of negro population have been suburban. Within five years three distinct sections beyond the city limits have been developed as exclusive residential sections for the race. In them the acquirement of property and the building of homes has gone on most extensively. These developments have been modern, furnished with streets and drainage. Trees have been planted, and in one of the new additions a children's playground established. The district adjoining the American Missionary Association school, called the Normal School Annex, has seen the erection of thirty-five comfortable little homes and half as many more lots sold to prospective builders. In "Dewey City" twenty or more cottages have been built, while in a single season over a hundred lots were bought and several homes built in Normal School Park. Similar developments of exclusive residential sections for negroes are going on in most of the South Georgia cities. They are partly due to the activity of real estate promoters

Suburban Development

but rest back upon the community building spirit of the race.

The development of these residential sections means not merely the geographical separation of the negro from the white population, but also the geographical separation of the better from the poorer classes of negroes. It means segregation within the race. Whole streets and blocks of negro homes stand in sharp contrast to equal areas of tenant property. The houses are invariably painted, the yards neatly fenced, the surroundings generally beautified by shrubs and flowers. Within these homes are mothers and daughters who are primarily home makers. Frequently they employ servants. Such negroes maintain their own social distinction as strictly as do any American group. The tenant quarters, on the other hand, show long rows of bare, decrepit, unkempt cabins where turbaned Amazons may be seen washing over fires built in the front yards, or cutting their own fuel from the log, fences and door-steps frequently being used for kindling. These external contrasts stand for deep differences between negro groups. They are evidences of the sifting of the race.

Segregation within the Negro Race

It has been found impossible to collect complete information as to the ownership of homes by Thomasville negroes. Large areas within the city limits have been built up, and the negroes almost invariably own the property which they occupy, while the suburban developments just described are virtually all extensions of home ownership. "It is rare," says Mr. Holloway, "to find a colored man who has lived any number of years in Thomasville, who does not wholly or in part own his own home." City taxes in 1907 were paid by negroes on $139,000 worth of property — undoubtedly a conservative estimate, for

HOME OF NEGRO LANDLORD, THOMASVILLE, GA.
Tenant houses adjoining

NEGRO ARTISAN AND STREET OF ARTISANS' HOMES, THOMASVILLE, GA.

THE SIFTING OF THE SOUTH

the colored man has learned from his white neighbor how to return as small a tax list as possible.

Eighteen business enterprises carried on by negroes are housed in property owned by members of the race. These **Business Property** range in value from $2500 to $7500 and are situated in all parts of the town. Near the business center on Broad Street is a two-story brick building in which the negro owner conducts a first-class shoe business. On Jackson Street, the second business street of Thomasville, is a $3000 building in which the negro owner carries on his own grocery business. Another negro owns unimproved property worth $3000.

The most surprising extension of ownership by Thomasville negroes is, however, in the line of property for rental **Rental Property** purposes. Mr. Holloway has tabulated 207 separate dwellings, valued at from $75 to $1000, owned and rented by them. Ten of them are rented to whites. The most extensive negro landlord is a widow, Mrs. Toomer Hamilton. In a single block she has sixteen tenements, and in all twenty-six pieces of rented property, bringing her in a comfortable monthly income. The property was first acquired by her late husband, a successful liveryman, but has been added to by the shrewdness of his widow. Another negro landlord has twelve rental houses, another seven, and many others own from one to five.

All told this makes an impressive showing of property ownership by the Thomasville negro. To be sure the value of his property averages much less than that of the whites, but as representing the acquirement of the race within forty years it is most creditable. Moreover, as indicating a *tendency* toward ownership it is highly significant. Probably as many negroes own property in Thomasville in proportion to their numbers as whites do, and according to the real estate agents they are now building homes twice as fast as the white population.

Appended to this paragraph is a table showing that there are eighty professional negroes in Thomasville, rep-
Occupations: resenting fifteen different professions. A
Professional very disproportionate number of them are preachers. The list indicates, however, that the Thomasville negro group is almost self-sufficient in the matter of professional service. It carefully limits itself, moreover, to those only whose professional standing is commonly called first-class. Thus there are many nurses able to command as much as $10 per week for their services, but only the two who are graduates of nurse-training schools are listed.

The two physicians have each an extensive practise. Both are graduates of reputable medical colleges and have licenses from the Georgia Medical Association. One has practised in Thomasville eight years, the other five. They receive all professional courtesies from the white physicians and have equal privileges in the use of the city hospital.

The colored dentist is also a graduate of a first-class institution. His well-appointed office has the latest type of pneumatic chair and a cabinet of modern instruments. The colored community gives him an almost exclusive patronage.

The entire force of mail-carriers, numbering four, is colored. All happen to be graduates of schools of the American Missionary Association and members of the Congregational church. The positions were of course secured by competitive examination.

Of the fourteen negro pastors of Thomasville, five are college graduates, two of whom hold also diplomas from

THE SIFTING OF THE SOUTH

Northern divinity schools. These five serve the largest and most intelligent congregations. In thoughtfulness and careful preparation their preaching is in striking contrast to the emotionalism of the old-fashioned negro exhorter. They are men of good character, whose chief shortcoming is parochial narrowness and blindness to the large mission of the church to the community.

The nine other preachers represent the older type. With one or two exceptions they are ignorant and most of them are immoral. Nowhere indeed is the moral sifting of the race more strongly marked than in its church life.

The Thomasville negro has an almost undisputed monopoly in skilled industry. The statistics of the appended
Occupations: table are compiled from the books of the
Industrial labor-unions and list only first-class workmen, who constitute only about one-fourth of the membership. In the Carpenters' Union, for example, out of a membership of seventy-four only about twenty command the highest wage, $2.50 to $3 per day. Many of the palatial winter homes of the Northerners, some costing upward of $100,000, were almost entirely built by Thomasville negro workmen. All the white contractors of the city have negro foremen and there are three licensed colored contractors.

At the time of Mr. Holloway's investigation the city had just given to a colored man a $30,000 contract for an addition to the sewer system. Negro contractors had also secured the brick work for the new city hall and for the two brick business buildings then being erected. The negroes say there are no first-class white carpenters or masons in Thomasville. The same question put to a white contractor brought the answer that perhaps three white carpenters were first-class and two masons. This shows the dominant place of the negro in the building industries.

Many of the skilled negro workmen live in comfortable homes and bear the highest reputation for character in the community.

The appended table shows that in the whole range of skilled industry the Thomasville negro holds a commanding position. There is not a single occupation in which he is not found, and in which he does not compete successfully with white workmen. This, however, has led to little industrial friction, white and colored laborers working side by side on almost all jobs. Indeed this is usual in the smaller places throughout the South. In a recent carpenters' strike for a nine-hour day, white and colored unions met in conference, and when their demands were refused all stuck together.

The three blocks of Jackson Street leading up from the railroad station to Broad Street are in importance the second business center of Thomasville; the street, a paved thoroughfare with electric lights, good water and sewerage facilities, and lined with substantial brick stores. In these three blocks there are twenty-six different enterprises conducted by negroes. Their patronage is, naturally, chiefly within the race, but the better firms have also considerable white trade. In fact whenever the negro store is believed to carry a high grade of stock and to furnish first-class service it is favorably regarded by a large number of Southern white patrons. This fact has been the means of raising the standard in a considerable number of enterprises. While many of the twenty-six are businesses with small stocks and poor fixtures, an increasing number are thoroughly equipped and in every way creditable. Mr. H. Daniels, for example, in

Occupations: Business

Negro Business Men's Homes, Thomasville, Ga.

Negro Drug Store and Proprietor, Thomasville, Ga.

twelve years of business, has come to own a fine grocery store, occupying his own two-story brick building. He also conducts a first-class colored restaurant and a barber shop, runs a woodyard, and has considerable real estate which he rents to whites as well as negroes. In ten years Robert Mitchell, formerly an itinerant fishmonger, has acquired the largest stock of general merchandise of any colored business man. He has a branch store in the suburbs and owns five rental houses. Of the seven grocery firms on Jackson Street, five have been in the business for over seven years and one boasts a fifteen years' record. In addition to the Jackson Street business center, there are fifteen suburban stores run by negroes. The Local Business Men's League claims that at least two-thirds of the colored grocery patronage of Thomasville is held by negro merchants.

The strong tendency thus revealed toward a self-sufficient group life is of comparatively recent origin. It is interesting to note the circumstances which have brought race consciousness to light and hastened its development. For example, the colored physician had but a precarious practise until a well-to-do negro called in a young white doctor to attend his wife. The doctor walked into the patient's room with his hat on and sat down on the bed with a smoking cigarette in his mouth. The husband leaned upon the bedside, as he said, "mad enough to fight a cross-cut saw." He made no remonstrance, but later tore up the white doctor's prescription and called in a colored doctor. Probably no other white doctor in Thomasville would have been guilty of such discourtesy; yet, under the strained condition of race feeling, the incident set the negro community against all white doctors.

Development of Race Consciousness

Now the tendency is strong to favor physicians of their own race.

The case of the negro dentist was similar. For years a prominent white dentist had held practically all the patronage of the negro population, making no discrimination in his treatment of them. Whites were made to wait their turn when negro patients were in the chair. When this man retired from active practise, new white dentists came in, who set up second-hand chairs for negroes in their back storerooms. The same prices, however, were charged, and in response to this discrimination, the negro community imported and now exclusively patronizes its own dentist.

Similarly a leading millinery store inaugurated the custom of not allowing any negro customer to try on a hat. She must be satisfied with viewing it on the head of the white clerk. When a colored minister's wife was refused this privilege the minister took the incident to his congregation. As a result the firm lost all its colored patronage and soon went into the hands of a receiver.

These incidents indicate two things: on the part of the negro, a new sensitiveness as to his rights and a new consciousness of racial resources; on the part of the later generation of whites, new tendencies to discrimination.

Between seven and ten colored insurance employees make daily rounds to the homes of the negro community, collecting the small dues which secure sick and accident benefits. They represent three companies, one with headquarters in New York, the other two large Georgia institutions, organized and operated by negroes. Three years ago the legislature enacted some undoubtedly necessary laws to regulate such companies. Probably, however, their immediate instigation was by white insurance companies in the hope of put-

Negro Institutions: Economic

ting their negro rivals out of business. The result was that a large number of local companies combined and three negro insurance enterprises were able to make the deposit of $5000 required by state law.

Almost every negro home in Thomasville carries policies in some one of these companies. A weekly premium of five cents secures a sick benefit of $2 per week and a death benefit of $10. Ten cents secures a sick benefit of $3 and a death benefit of $15. Twenty-five cents secures a sick benefit of $5 and a death benefit of $25. In addition to this humbler type of insurance, Mr. Holloway reports that a number of families carry policies in regular "old-line" companies. Georgia has also two negro fire insurance companies, one of which maintains an office in Thomasville and secures a large share of negro patronage.

Besides their churches already enumerated, the Thomasville negro community has a full quota of social institutions. An organization of colored women called the "How to Live Club" has a membership of about forty. Besides literary features, it has undertaken as its particular work the support of the colored ward in the city hospital. The Women's Federation is building a negro "Old Folks' Home." Some thousand dollars have been collected for this purpose, and the race is thus attempting to keep its aged members from the hardship of the county poorhouse.

Negro Institutions of the High Life

Besides a public school, poorly housed, and with almost no playground, there are two schools for Thomasville negroes supported by philanthropy. One is a small parochial enterprise attached to an Episcopal Church and taught by its minister. The other, Allen Normal Institute, a well-equipped and growing girls' seminary, admits boys also as day pupils. This institution is described at length in another connection. These private schools are patronized almost exclusively by the better class of negroes. Thus segregation within the race is expressed also in its education.

The relations between negro and white in Thomasville are on the whole kindly and mutually helpful. There are occasional frictions, but they have never been serious. Discriminations are met by the negroes by the withdrawal upon their own resources instead of by active resentment. There has never been a lynching in the city and only one in the county, which was universally condemned by the better element of white citizens. Mr. Holloway writes, "There seems to be a growing conviction among both races that not all negroes are bad and that not all white men are good. There are evidences on every hand that good white people are lending a helping hand to the good negro in his efforts to rise, and the negro in turn is striving to make good his citizenship in the community where his rights are so secure and his opportunities so numerous."

Race Contacts

The whole story means that the negroes of Thomasville constitute a fairly typical American group. If they do not quite reach it, they at least closely approximate the national average of attainment. Their deficiencies are mere backwardness, not abnormal or unwholesome. They are practising a relatively complete group economy, yet without bitterness or practical antagonism to or from the dominant white population. From every reasonable human standpoint the black citizens of this typical city have made good.

APPENDIX TO CHAPTER III
TABLE I
OCCUPATIONS (PROFESSIONAL)

Physicians	2
Pharmacist	1
Dentist	1
Chiropodists	2
Graduate Nurses	2
Graduate Hair Dresser	1
Preachers	15
Teachers (male)	5
Teachers (female)	30
Civil Service	5
Rural Free Delivery	3
Government Service	1
Insurance	9
Editors	2
Musician	1

TABLE II
OCCUPATIONS (INDUSTRIAL)

Licensed Contractors	4
Carpenters, first-class (Union-men)	20
Brick Masons, first-class (Union-men)	18
Plasterers	11
Painters	6
Tinners and Plumbers	4
Skilled Mechanists	2
Pressman	1
Wheelwrights	2
Blacksmiths	4
Bakers	2
Paper-hangers	2
Carriage Painter	1

TABLE III

NEGRO BUSINESS ENTERPRISES

NO.	KINDS OF BUSINESS	EACH VALUE	MEN EMPLOYED	OCCUPY OWN PROPERTY	YRS.	UP-TOWN	SUBURBS
1	Drugstore	$4000	3	..	2	1	..
1	Grocery	3000	2	..	8	1	..
2	Groceries	2000	5	1	10–11	2	..
4	Groceries	500	7	..	..	4	..
15	Groceries	....	22	15	1–8	..	15
1	Undertaker	2000	2	1	4	..	1
1	Harness shop	300	2	..	2	1	..
1	Tailor	200	2	..	10	1	..
6	Barber Shops	....	12	..	..	6	..
1	Hotel	....	3	..	8	1	..
3	Pressing Clubs	....	7	..	2–8	3	..
1	Butcher	250	3	..	2	1	..
3	First-class restaurant	....	8	1	3–5	1	..
1	Dairy	300	2	1	1	.	1

IV. THE SIFTING OF SOUTHERN SENTIMENT

I. SIFTING THE HEARTS OF MEN

HOW shall a dominant social group respond to the partial sifting of any backward population in its midst? How shall it treat the emerged minority of such a backward population which approximates its own normative standards?

The backward group simply cannot be treated according to any single policy; for its members are not alike, and its extremes lie far apart. This necessitates discriminative changes in the social policy of the dominant group. We found the Thomasville (Ga.) negro, for example, showing marked differentiation, physical, social, and moral, according to which segregation was progressing within the race. Shall the responsible, property owning, home making negro be treated as the transient, tenant, and pauper class? Manifestly not. But this introduces new complexity into the race problem; indeed, it raises the whole group of modern social problems. This the South vaguely feels and variously acknowledges. For the first time it is awake to the varying intellectual and moral moods of the age.

The hearts of men are being sifted for practical responses to the changing facts. Underneath the superficial unanimity of Southern sentiment surge currents of perplexing variety.

Border States vs. Lower South

The general causes of these varying attitudes and practises are easily traced. They are partly geographical.

Geographical Causes of Variation in Sentiment

The negro population, as we have shown, is by no means evenly distributed throughout the South. In the border states where his numbers are proportionately few, race pressure is less acute than in the lower South where he is felt to threaten white civilization by the sheer weight of numbers. In Lexington, Kentucky, for example, the cooperation of colored citizens was especially invited in recent movements for civic betterment. They were invited to public gatherings, announcement of which was made in the negro schools. As a result members of that race have been frequent prize winners in competitions for the neatest home garden or the best kept lawn. Louisville supports a public high school for negroes, in which the classics are taught. This public institution has been probably the chief feeder of Fisk University. Indeed almost the only decently sustained public secondary schools for negroes in the South are in these states. Nearly two-thirds of all pupils in public colored high schools are in the five border states and Texas. The other eight combined enroll but a trifle more than eleven hundred.[1] The recent attack upon the negro's franchise rights has been less violent in these states. North Carolina, for example, refused to extend the time limit of the " grandfather clause " for the benefit of the white in the very year that Georgia and Mississippi were planning the complete disfranchisement of the negro. Both North Carolina and Tennessee have with Kentucky been carried by the Republican party in recent years and

---
[1] Report of Com. of Education, 1906, vol. 2, p. 1151.

are by many regarded as among the permanently doubtful states of the near future. Jim Crow regulations, while not absent from the border states, are not carried out in their more rigorous detail. In other words, these states tend rather to treat the negro as part of the general population, as the North does, than to make him a separate class.

Old South vs. Southwest

There are clearly marked differences in the race situation between the old slavery regions and those settled since the war. On soil never stained by the sweat and blood of the slave, where men of both races have pioneered together, the inevitable democracy of the frontier has modified race contacts. The Texas and Oklahoma negro clearly shows a certain initiative and resourcefulness and an independence of spirit which are the marks of the West rather than the South. It is a proverb of the mission schools that elsewhere the negro boy will take a whipping from a white teacher more graciously than from one of his own race. He has been used to white whippings. In the West it is not so, and he resents them. There the negro teacher has an advantage in discipline. Within a few years a negro has been elected by a majority of white votes to the Texas legislature.[1] Public provision for the schooling of the race in these Western states tends to be equable and ample, and to include high schools. On the other hand the hustling Westerner is less patient with the negro's deficiencies than is the easy-going Southerner. The West puts him under sterner tests of fitness for economic competition.

The Negro as Pioneer

[1] See Smith, "Village Improvement," etc., The Outlook, Mar. 31, 1900.

Aristocrat vs. Poor White

Other divergence of practises have an historical explanation. The former slaveholder and his children generally put a far higher estimate upon negro capacity and social usefulness than do the descendants of the poor whites. The former knows that slave energy and intelligence, as well as slave muscle, conducted many an old plantation. He has intimate personal ties linking him to the freedman. He appreciates the virtues of the negro, depends upon his services and "likes to have him 'round." He continues largely his sense of responsibility for the negro in need. In hunger, sickness, grief, and struggle, the old-time Southerner has been the negro's most frequent friend, and has shown toward him a million kindnesses to every one which has come from the long-distance philanthropy of the North. And he takes his own superiority so much for granted that he feels no need of asserting it aggressively.

Historic Causes of Variations in Sentiment

The white masses, on the other hand, hate the negro, who anciently shared his master's contempt for them as a landless class. Now the tables are turned, and the poor whites of former days are in political power throughout almost the entire South. Tillman, Vardaman, and Jeff Davis of Arkansas are their prophets. Theirs are the policies which are now drawing the color-line more rigidly and are increasingly narrowing political privileges by law. The man who cannot get his superiority taken for granted feels that he must shake his fist in the negro's face and vociferate, "He's got to respect my color."

Racial Bitterness of "Poor Whites"

The conflicting practises of these two classes are everywhere apparent throughout the South. The daughter of

THE SIFTING OF SOUTHERN SENTIMENT

the "first family" may greet her colored maid with a kiss in the sight of the whole city. Athens, the seat of the State University of Georgia — a state which generally is degrading its colored schools — supports a negro high school with a curriculum identical with that of the white, including Latin. The Northern critic of Tillman will find nothing to add to what the Southern conservative journals say about him. Witness the following from the leading paper of South Carolina, *The Columbia State:*

> If there is more ill feeling between the races in South Carolina than there was ten years ago, those that have done most to create ill feeling and suspicion are responsible, and Tillman is chief of that class.
>
> The negroes have in ten years made no opposition, offered no resistance to the white man's absolute control of every department of government. None except Tillman fears that they will ever attempt to dominate in the South. But Tillman's speeches and Tom Dixon's play, "The Clansman," are breeders of race hatred. They incite the more ignorant and vicious of both races to greater antagonism. That real trouble has not resulted is that intelligent public sentiment condemns the agitation.
>
> John Sharp Williams says that ninety out of a hundred negroes are peaceable, law-abiding, and work. Is it unnatural that these should feel aggrieved and discouraged when classed, by men having the ear of the country, with vagrants, thieves, and ravishers? Injustice is certain to beget animosity. Do the people of the South in town or country court animosity between the races?

From the beginning the best friends and helpers of Northern missionary enterprise in the South have been men of such views, the choice representatives of its old régime, its "high men." The Southern churches most faithful to the negro's spiritual interest have been those reputed most aristocratic. To this day the Episcopal Church refuses to recognize the ecclesiastical segregation of the races. In conservative Charleston the colored patron may still occupy a seat anywhere in a street car if he gets it first. It is in the new cities developed by Northern capital and dominated by the laboring class that the color-line becomes brutally aggressive. I am personally familiar with a group of communities in the Southwest, where for years no negro has been allowed to stay over night: without exception they are railroad or mining centers or else Northern settlements.

This familiarity and liking between the old-time Southerner and the negro has its bad side, in that it is the continuing ground of permanent and systematic but illicit unions between white men and colored women. In the more conservative communities concubinage is still frequent. Of more than one great planter have I heard it said, "Why, he has children in every cabin on the place." Within a few years a distinguished Charlestonian — a member of the school board — died and was buried from the home of the negro mother of his children. It was the only domicile he had. The children were called out of the mission school to attend his death-bed, *but the white schools closed for his funeral.* The mission schools have hundreds of cases annually where white men recognize their responsibility for the children of their negro families and pay their educational bills. Not infrequently they send letters full of parental concern and admonition. Such relations are perfectly well known and widely condoned, the possession of a colored family

<small>Systematic Miscegenation</small>

often being no bar to honorable church-membership nor frequently to subsequent marriage into the best white families.

The one alien widely scattered throughout the South is the Jew. He lacks something of the Anglo-Saxon's strong race feeling and, partly for commercial reasons, often draws the color-line loosely. In a Mississippi negro school of three hundred pupils I found by actual count that a full tenth were manifestly of Hebrew blood. In regions settled by the Latin races too — notably New Orleans — race mixture has gone further than in the Anglo-Saxon South. The fear that Italian and other immigration from the South of Europe would lead to still more excessive admixture is one of the deepest grounds of Southern dread of their coming. In Charleston and New Orleans I have even seen Chinese negroes.

Race Mixture with Semite and Latin

Now animosity and dislike between the masses of both races is a bar to such miscegenation, and thus has its useful side. It makes rude place for those ideals of race purity which may come to have personal sanction and moral meaning both for negro and white. The clergy and press are plucking up new courage for bold speech on this matter. Mr. Ray Stannard Baker tells me that his recent searching treatment of sex relations between the races [1] has brought him commendation, especially from Southern correspondents. Thus though the stream of illicit blood mixture flows steadily on, it is somewhat checked by these new eddies and cross currents.

In indiscriminate bounty, too, and his lax patience with inefficient labor, the tender mercies of the old-time Southerner have been cruel to the negro. After all, the sterner

[1] See Following the Color-Line, p. 164 ff.

demands of the new South are more honorable to manhood. The hurling of the race back on itself by means of the tightly drawn color-line has taught it that great lesson of self-help. Within his own people the negro has made hopeful progress in capacity for leadership. He is beginning to catch the knack of cooperation and to learn the art of group strength, which, rather than individual capacity, is the secret of white race superiority. The plebeian South has imposed these tests upon him in no pedagogical spirit. In a thousand ways its demands are unequal, arbitrary, and too severe, yet the wrath of men still praises God. Each of the contradictory class policies toward the negro is contributing good as well as evil to the race problem.

The Color-line and the Lesson of Self-help

Employer vs. Competitor

These class attitudes are crossed and complicated by others of economic origin. It is the general law that race antagonism is bitterest between people on a common competitive level. The present landholder or employer not only frequently carries over the kindly spirit of the old master class, but he naturally regards the negro as an economic asset from which he derives profit. On the contrary, the white laborer frequently covets the negro's job on the farm or in the factory. He envies his rapidly acquired prosperity; or hates him as an industrial disturber and strike breaker. It has been frequently noted that the relations of the races are most amicable in the blackest belts where the white laboring class is totally absent. The political and social attitude of the poor whites described in the previous section has an historical origin. Its chief and growing root

Bitterness on a Common Competitive Level

of bitterness is the actual progress of the negro and his new importance as an economic factor receiving a coveted share of the wealth of the South. And this economic jealousy will grow tenser as the ambitions of either race are quickened.

Industrial Employer vs. Planter

There are also different attitudes within the master classes. A great struggle for labor is going on between the mine and factory and the Southern farm. The negro is a new industrial factor. His employer likes him because he is an able-bodied and good-natured laborer to whom the color-line permits the payment of less than current wages, and who can frequently be played against the labor unions. The negro laborer was defended by an overwhelming majority of speakers at the great Immigration Congress at Nashville as superior to any class of immigrants now available in America. Contractor Oliver declared that he could take the chain-gangs of the South and build the Panama Canal. The negro in agriculture on the other hand is an old factor. Now that he has heard the call of the city he demands more than the former agricultural wage. The demand for him in industry has seriously disturbed agricultural conditions. The planter resents this and tries to fix him to the soil by securing his perpetual ignorance, by intimidation and violence and repressive law; or else by unwilling, childish concessions, — extra holidays, a mule to ride, whisky — poor substitutes for the real betterment of rural conditions. Thus the feud between industry and agriculture over the negro is very deep and with the growth of Southern cities tends

Competition between Employers for Negro Labor

to merge into a permanent difference of opinion and policy between the urban and rural districts. Already it has taken deep hold of politics.

Business Interests vs. Politician

The money-making element in the South to-day strongly desires racial peace. It wants to exploit the natural and human resources of its section for its own profit undisturbed by sentimental considerations of any sort. Its class-consciousness subdues its race-consciousness. For its purpose the white laborer frequently is inferior to the colored and gets no superior treatment. As the manager of a Louisiana sugar plantation put it to me, "The white man who works down here is the same as the nigger."

The Money-maker's Denunciation of the Demagogue

On the contrary, the average politician gets office in the South by appealing to the race prejudice of the poor white who holds the power of the ballot. Negrophobia is his chief stock in trade. The ordinary political campaign is a contest to see who can best abuse the race. Frequently the political bark is worse than its bite, but generally the animosity stirred by it leads to some new anti-negro measure or other. The man of practical commercial interest detects the selfishness and insincerity of all this and resents the preoccupation of the South by it to the detriment of its material progress. One finds therefore the meetings of manufacturers' or commercial clubs loud with the denunciation of the "demagogue" as a chief disturber of Israel. Undoubtedly he has done much to aggravate and distort the race situation.

Yet the case has another side; for what is politics but

the natural and inevitable arena for the expression of the aspirations and struggles of any unprivileged group in a democracy? The poor white himself is such a struggler against the ancient aristocratic organization of Southern society. He has virtually won his victory, but has not yet got his eyes clear of the dust of battle, and in its brutal heat does not consider that it is unworthy to rise by crowding another class down. Yet his example to the negro to-day is wiser than the conciliatory counsel and somewhat faint praise of the employing and commercial classes. Class struggle must get into politics. It is futile to forbid it. The negro cannot long be kept out. Tillman's "Organize! organize!" applies to him, too. The poor white marks his upward struggle by asserting his superiority to the negro, but for all that he is fighting a common battle for democracy. Humanity, it seems, must go forward by detachments and the unprivileged Anglo-Saxon blazes the way for all.

Politics the Inevitable Arena of Race Struggle

Man vs. Woman

Women generally draw the color-line tighter than men. Perhaps one sex is temperamentally given to applying its convictions more rigidly than the other. In the South women have abundant motives for rigidity, as appeared in the discussion of miscegenation. At any rate the relations between white and colored men, in matters which do not involve the other sex, are surprisingly unrestrained and often intimate. All sorts of business dealings are everywhere recognized, and "business" frequently is made to cover the comradeship of minds and hearts in other com-

Only Formal Social Intercourse forbidden

mon interests. I have known a Southern gentleman who by preference frequently spends the evenings in his office in conversation with a colored friend. This companionship is manifestly more congenial than those of the society functions from which he gladly escapes. It is not called " social equality," but it goes deeper than much that is. In accordance with this tendency to limit the ban to formal social intercourse, I have heard a white Federal office-holder try to explain away the objectionable features of the famous White House luncheon. According to his version it occurred not in the White House proper but in the executive offices. Mr. Washington happened to be calling when the President's luncheon time came. Mr. Roosevelt accordingly sent out for two trays of food. The two ate simultaneously, but not at the same table! Now thousands of Southern working men and farmers daily sit on curbs or in fence corners and dine out of dinner-pails along with their negro fellow workers. The Washington incident was held to be a parallel case having no social implications.

The Rational vs. the Passionate

These are the familiar temperamental classes of any population, and the race issue has emphasized their divergence in the South. To the Northern stranger Southerners naturally fall into two classes — those who can discuss the negro rationally and those who cannot. The latter is much the larger class. An habitual tendency to look backward and an abnormal tension of mind, frequently bordering on hysteria, has characterized the popular attitude on this matter. It has been a prolonged case of nerves. Yet the other class is surely growing. With the cooling of passion and the fresh prac-

Temperamental Classes

tical achievements of the South a new type of leader is emerging.

He is marked by a certain scientific mindedness in intellectual approach and mental habit. I mean by the scientific minded man, one who observes closely, who has mental patience, who thinks with his brain and not with his emotions, who is satisfied with the whole truth and nothing less. His reverence is for the past, but it is tempered with the common-sense patriotism which gives him enthusiasm for the future. He is at home in the republic, and a sense of mastery of the methods of his age, and perception of his kinship to all the world, have freed his energies and widened his vision. He has not attained wholly the ideal mental condition. He would be rather lonesome in America, if he had reached it; but he is moving that way.[1]

This attitude is sometimes associated and sometimes confused with those preoccupations of the commercial spirit which cares little for any struggle for ideals. Yet it is itself essentially founded on ideals and supported by patient faith that time will show the right. Its broadest representatives confess its religious basis.

" Good " vs. Good

It is not fair to judge the South by those whom it already recognizes and repudiates as bad. The moral tragedy of the race situation is rather that the conscience of the average good man is two-colored. This is always the case when a " superior " group of population erects social barriers against

Conscience
draws the
Color-line

[1] Alderman, "The Growing South," The World's Work, June, 1908, p. 10382.

an "inferior" one; it is doubly serious when the inferior group also belongs to another and a despised race. A double moral standard is then inevitable. Right becomes one thing within and another without the racial pale. Sanctions which protect the members of one class fail for the other.

Thus in the South "Thou shalt not kill," "Thou shalt not commit adultery," "Thou shalt not steal," "Thou shalt not bear false witness against thy neighbor," mean one thing as between white and white and another as between white and black. The negro's misdemeanors become crimes; the white's crimes shrink into misdemeanors. Conscience itself fails to operate equally as between the races.

Worst of all, perhaps, the boasted Anglo-Saxon sense of fair play is largely obliterated by race prejudice. Bryce notes that

Blunting of Characteristic Anglo-Saxon Virtues

> Even between civilized peoples, such as Germans and Russians, or Spaniards and Frenchmen, there is a disposition to be unduly annoyed by traits and habits which are not so much culpable in themselves as distasteful to men constructed on different lines. This sense of annoyance is naturally more intense toward a race so widely removed from the modern European as the Kafirs are. Whoever has traveled among people of a race greatly weaker than his own must have sometimes been conscious of an impatience or irritation which arises when the native fails to understand or neglects to obey the command given. The sense of his superior intelligence and energy of will produces in the European a sort of tyrannous spirit, which will not condescend to argue with the native, but overbears him by sheer force, and is prone to resort to physical coercion. Even just men, who have the deepest theoretical re-

spect for human rights are apt to be carried away by the consciousness of superior strength, and to become despotic if not harsh.[1]

President Alderman claims that the South's dealings with the negro since the war have shown " a juster and larger policy than was ever before pursued by higher groups toward backward and lower groups in any civilization." This may be true. The fact remains that the South in the large has treated the negro *just as* other superior groups have treated their alleged inferiors, namely, according to a distinct and lower moral code than pertains between equals. Only the aggressive and vital goodness of a small minority has been able to make its moral practises universalistic and democratic.

I recall once being in conversation with a courteous gentleman on a Florida railway platform. A careless negro driver threw a horse in crossing the track. Instantly the courteous gentleman became a raging fiend. " If that was my horse I'd get a revolver and beat that nigger within an inch of his life, and if he resisted I'd shoot him." Note the moral splendor of it! He would take bodily vengeance for a casual error. The law calls that criminal assault. He would use the advantage of his weapon against an unarmed man. Anglo-Saxon instincts call that contemptible cowardice. He would kill the negro if he resisted. The Ten Commandments call that murder. Yet this is not an exceptional incident. It represents the attitude of thousands of Southern whites, particularly of the younger generation. That it allows and perpetuates such moral contradictions in the lives of average good men is probably the most disastrous thing about the Southern racial policy.

[1] Bryce, Impressions of South Africa, p. 442.

CHRISTIAN RECONSTRUCTION IN THE SOUTH

"The Negro a Beast" vs. "Our Brother in Black"

These divergent attitudes and practises naturally find formulation and justification in various theoretical esti-
<small>Divergent Views of Negro Capacity</small> mates of the negro and the ultimate meaning of his existence. Some seven years ago an agent brought a book to my door entitled "The Negro a Beast." Since then I have found it from Virginia to Texas. It is a strange mixture of Darwinism and Biblical arguments in justification of the most brutal racial antipathy. During the opening years of the twentieth century it has become the Scripture of tens of thousands of poor whites, and its doctrine is maintained with an appalling stubbornness and persistence. Of course this is not the traditional, nor is it by any means the dominant, Southern view of the negro. The commoner thought is that he is a man, but radically inferior to the white in certain crucial capacities, especially those for practical achievement and for ideal aspiration and fellowship. For the higher realms of culture, for the more refined contacts of human intercourse and for political authority he is held to be naturally unfit.

Probably few Southerners could be found willing to confess so favorable an estimate of negro racial capacity as that proclaimed by the typical Northern idealist and now defended by eminently respectable sociological authority. Nevertheless there is a group of men of commanding influence whose point of emphasis makes their statement of Southern doctrine take a radically new sound and significance. Whatever their conception of the negro's natural deficiencies, *in respect to the things which count for most* they assert his fitness for full participation in the highest life of man. He is religiously capable; his Christian experience entitles him to Christian fellowship. This is the true clue to any present or future policy toward him. Bishop Bratten puts it thus: "The negro is capable of development to a point whose limit I have not yet discovered"; while the late Bishop Galloway said, "As the negro is a man and a brother, embraced in the divine scheme of human redemption, we cannot exclude him from any of the privileges and agencies that may fit him for service in the Kingdom of God." Just because they are so sound on the main issue, it is possible for men of such views to accede to the popular practises of their section in non-essentials like formal racial recognition. Their essential rightness of spirit should be recognized — and is — both by negroes and their less hampered Northern friends. Dr. Du Bois certainly does not doubt that Bishop Galloway accorded him the full rights of spiritual manhood, freely and without condescension, and that the bishop showed it beyond peradventure — whatever his habits as to eating with negroes. No essential barrier separates the men of different color or section who view the race situation from the standpoint of this common emphasis. *Practically speaking, the emphasis is the doctrine.*

When all classifications are exhausted it remains to be said that the characteristic Southerner is full of surprising and often charming inconsistencies. Whatever his natural or theoretical attitude his color-line weaves itself into complex patterns which are the despair of the alien. I recall the perplexity of a Northern minister who had recently taken a Southern church. "They tell me," he complained, "that I must n't shake hands with a negro lest I lose caste; yet here comes Dr. B—— from Charleston and shakes hands with a colored woman in the middle of Main Street. He pinches her

<small>Individual Exceptions</small>

baby's cheeks and talks with her for ten minutes, and I don't understand it." Indeed it is just those aliens who lack the inner sense of fitness in interracial conduct who are most apt to fall back upon a rigid observance of an arbitrary code. Because they have no other guide to conduct, the "spoiled Yankee" and the poor white draw the color-line the tighter.

II. THE COLOR-LINE

We have persisted through the tedious story of how geographical, historical, economic, and vocational differences enter into the race situation; how sex, character, and theory make a difference in the practical attitudes of Southerners toward the negro.

<small>The Conventional Creed of the South</small>

This was necessary because it is loudly proclaimed that the South is absolutely unanimous on this subject. Nothing could be further from the truth. There is a conventional creed to which most Southerners subscribe. No legitimate blood mixture of the races is to be tolerated. There is to be complete non-intercourse between them in the ideal interests of life. In the home, the church, the school, which are the central shrines of these ideal interests, they are to remain separate. To enforce these separations political power must remain in the hands of the whites.

The vast practical authority of this creed is not to be denied. It makes an immense psychological impression on both races.

On the one hand there is that wide-spread loss of the white man's keener sense of justice and social purity in the presence of an inferior population, which has already been illustrated; on the other, the negro's "resultant self-contempt and

<small>The Negro's Subjective Handicap</small>

THE SIFTING OF SOUTHERN SENTIMENT

despair. In the presence of the arrogant white, flaunting insultingly his superior powers, the despised blacks degenerate into baser beings than they would otherwise become. 'Dirt in his eyes, they soon become as dirt in their own.' And they become positively enfeebled by their consciousness of inferiority."[1] This description of the South African situation absolutely fits our own color-line. Its existence is an insidious attack upon the foundations of manhood in the negro man and of virtue in the negro woman. For in spite of all denials a good part of the South's policy is not a single-hearted attempt at racial separation for the protection of white civilization, but a deliberate purpose to humiliate the negro. It is aimed all too accurately at his self-respect. Over against this the South sometimes pleads the negro's narrower economic opportunity in the North — as though the two things were comparable! "We will not play with him," it says; "you will not work with him." But man does not live by bread alone. It is just the refusal of fellowship in the ideal interests of life — symbolized by the social color-line — which is the bitterness of the negro's cup. The denial of equality in these spheres chokes the very breath of freedom and moral life. That it has not strangled it altogether; that indeed the negro's race pride has shown rapid and hopeful increase is due partly to his encouragement by individual Southerners, but chiefly to the fact that he knew that a great section of the nation was backing his struggle as a freeman. However Utopian its faith and practically remote its help, it has been an immeasurable reenforcement of the negro's inner resources *that the North believed in him* — that Abraham Lincoln's picture was looking down from the dark walls of his hundred thousand

[1] Alston, White Man's Work in Asia and Africa, p. 88.

cabins. The backing of the moral sentiment of the nation's idealists is psychologically crucial; and never more so than now.

Again, the unequal dealing of the state between the races in practical matters — a difference everywhere confessed and excused — puts an almost impossible handicap on the negro. Apart from all atrocities and exceptionally oppressive dealings — in the whole realm of social betterment, the color-line condemns the negro to take the leavings. What disadvantage has the negro? Much every way; chiefly perhaps in sewers and sidewalks; in schools and security. His health is socially penalized by a comparative and sometimes absolute lack of sanitary provision for him. His schools are " good enough for a nigger." His property and his life suffer a higher risk than that of the average white citizen. This goes deeper than the withholding of specially granted franchise privileges; it limits common justice. Now the sociologist teaches us that in a democratic state the little more and the little less of opportunity, working out their results through long periods, produce the vastest social changes.[1] The ultimate result of the Southerner's policy cannot but be fatal to millions of American negroes who might otherwise have been saved to the nation. These are matters, too, which the state alone can control. Private philanthropy, near or remote, is virtually helpless. Absolutely the only ground of hope for him is the conviction that the South's better spirit of justice and humanity will come to the kingdom in time to save him.

The Negro's Objective Handicap

Yet no creed is so practically significant as the behavior of those who hold it. In spite of the impressive sentimental

[1] Ross, Foundation of Sociology, p. 202.

unity of the South, the general race situation is actually dominated by profound and far-reaching differences in its conduct which our previous discussion has discovered. Here and there exceptions to the creed have become the local or individual rule; whole classes and areas have signally modified it; while almost everywhere it is so tempered in daily application as to leave wide margins of opportunity not admitted on the face of it.

A Margin of Opportunity

III. CLUES TO PROPHECY

These differences of conduct, moreover, are the working out of certain large tendencies which in turn are reliable clues to prophecy. Of course the omens are not all agreed. It would be at variance with human experience if they were. Indeed some of them are distinctively adverse to the hope of interracial prosperity and peace, and indicate that in many respects the situation will be worse before it is better.

On the one hand, time is rapidly sundering the kindlier ties brought over from the old régime and the good understanding based upon the past is dying out. Physical segregation and mental estrangement will certainly go further. Both races will develop an even more extreme measure of irritability and touchiness.

Segregation estranges the Races

Over against this evil tendency stands the prospect that national ideals will be more and more adequately interpreted to the negro masses by their own leaders. The negro's native capacity for loyalty and his splendid patriotism may then be relied on. In spite of the color-line he may still share

But creates a Demand for Negro Leaders

the inspirations and ideals of our best life through the intermediation of the exceptional minority of his race. We have noted a new willingness in the South to recognize the opportunity and responsibility of the exceptional negro and so to cooperate with him for social peace as to preserve his racial pride and self-respect. No social class nor struggling race " can reach equality with other classes and races until its leaders can meet theirs on equal terms." In all its substantial aspects this is being admitted. White men of standing are associated with negroes on the Jeanes Board and as trustees of many colored schools. The exceptional negro is widely accorded exceptional treatment, and his representative character is felt by his race. Recently a Southern guest protested at the presence of Booker Washington at the Belmont Hotel Café in New York. Reporters rushed to interview the head waiter. " No," he said, " negroes are not allowed to dine here, but with Mr. Washington it is different." This particular exception is not met with in the South, but others of more practical importance are. After all, the children of the mind are more important than the children of the body, as old Plato said. Thus the psychical assimilation of the negro to the national type is hopefully possible. By the maintenance of the moral and spiritual contacts of the races at the top, the masses need not fail of the better incentives of American life. Their hope and self-respect may feed on the recognition and privileges accorded to the exceptional few.

The negro must expect a waning of the favor of the employing classes just so far as he ceases as a race to be tractable under industrial exploitation. He has already shown remarkable mobility as a laborer and a capacity for quick response to economic opportunity. He has

shown some hopeful evidence of capacity for cooperation and organization. In other words, he gives evidence of
Economic Development will lose the Negro the Employer's Favor
two of the chief economic virtues. It is just his previous lack of these which has endeared him to the employer. Perhaps he has a permanent temperamental advantage in his characteristic good nature, and undoubtedly his superior adaptability to the climate of the lower and hotter regions of the South gives him a certain permanent advantage over white labor. Nevertheless, his newly learned virtues will lead the employer to seek to displace him with an alien labor force, helpless through its lack of economic experience. This means bitter competition between the negro and the newly awakened white masses of the South. Extensive foreign immigration, though not immediately probable, must be expected in the long run. The undeveloped areas of the lower South will become industrialized, and the whole labor problem reach the acute stage to which it has come in all the more progressive sections of civilization. Hitherto the negro has had a practical monopoly as a laborer in the South. President Alderman is now undoubtedly right in saying that " he is yet to undergo the fiercest trials that come to backward races striving to forge to the front in an old civilization."

What will be the outcome of this sterner competition? It seems inevitable that in the long run the negro must be recognized and enlisted on the side of labor.

As the class struggle proceeds, new lines will be drawn
But will force the White Laborer to unite with Him
which will include the negro on the side of the white masses. They will have to make common cause with him. They must or lose their battle. It will be easier than in the case of any other alien race; for the negro already approxi-

mates to the current standard of living of his section. He spends freely, like a good American, and readily expands his scale of wants. The chief economic difficulty to his inclusion on the side of labor is thus absent. When the gap between diverse standards of living is once surmounted, racial animosities have repeatedly given way before the mighty unifying force of class consciousness. Labor organization has been one of the most important assimilative agencies in American life and, in spite of its errors, a chief adjunct of democracy. Already it has marshaled thousands across the color-line. Socialism, too, has undertaken a distinct propaganda among negroes. I do not anticipate great practical results from it, but it shows how the wind blows. Thus the vastest movement of Southern civilization — the struggle of the white masses for equal opportunity, merges with the world-wide cause of the unprivileged. Sooner or later it will discover that it must include the negro as well.[1]

The further curtailment of negro political privileges in the South is to be expected. From the standpoint of white supremacy he is tenfold more dangerous now that he has acquired education and property, now that he has developed race conscience, competent leadership and organs of public opinion, than when he was first enfranchised. The cry is now widely raised that the older disqualifying legislation does not go far enough. For many years Georgia thought the negro sufficiently out of politics through moral suasion and the poll-tax requirement; but Hoke Smith became governor on the plea that legal disfranchisement was still necessary. Mr. Baker quotes an argument from the editor of the Huntsville, Alabama, *Tribune*.

Political Privileges will be Further Curtailed

[1] Cf. Commons, Races and Immigrants in America, p. 115.

THE SIFTING OF SOUTHERN SENTIMENT

> We thought (in 1901, when the new Alabama Constitution disfranchising the negro was under discussion), as we do now, that the menace to peace, the danger to society and white supremacy was not in the illiterate negro, but in the upper branches of negro society, the educated, the man who after ascertaining his political rights, forced the way to assert them.

He continues:

> We, the Southern people, entertain no prejudice toward the ignorant per se inoffensive negro. It is because we know him, and for him we entertain a compassion. But our blood boils when the educated negro asserts himself politically. We regard each assertion as an unfriendly encroachment upon our native superior rights, and a daredevil menace to our control of the affairs of the state. In this are we not speaking the truth? Does not every Southern Caucasian " to the manor born " bear witness to this version? Hence we present that the way to dampen racial prejudice, avert the impending horrors, is to emasculate the negro politically, by repealing the fifteenth amendment of the Constitution of the United States.

Now there is not the slightest likelihood that the fifteenth amendment will ever be repealed, yet there is a general desire throughout the nation to guard the suffrage more strictly, and under cover of this feeling the South will undoubtedly devise new legal barriers for the negro.

Yet even on this point the tides do not all run in one direction. There are elements in Southern life which may yet feel the need of the negro's political assistance. Even in Georgia the argument has recently been heard that disfranchisement may go too fast; it may take the negro's well-known conservatism to defeat the destructive radicalism of the poor whites at the ballot-box. The industrialization of the upland South and the decreasing proportion of negroes in it, already result in franker political divisions within its borders along the lines of economic interests, and promises its final detachment from the lower South in national politics. There will yet be selfish efforts there to get the negro into politics and to use him as a balance of power as in the North. There are Southerners, too, who rest the political future of the negro on deeper theoretical and moral grounds. Witness ex-Congressman Fleming's notable address at the University of Georgia. He said, " Without some access to the ballot, present or prospective, some participation in the government, no inferior race in an elective republic could long protect itself against reduction to slavery in many of its substantial forms." The present South is not wholly deaf to this appeal and time cannot fail to bring other recruits to its standard.

The Negro will yet be Called Back into Politics

With the increase of wealth and luxury comes a weakening of the democratic instincts and a new willingness to anticipate the existence of a permanently servile class in the Republic. We must frankly confess the fact that there are daily more people who want other human beings to be conveniences rather than men, and who are glad to use the race which traditionally bears the badge of servitude. In the South a new plutocratic version of social inequality puts rigidity and harshness into the color-line. One would indeed despair of his country if he saw this only; if he could not discern in varied phases the progress of democracy, of which the unifying work of organized labor noted above is

Plutocracy adds New Burdens

part. This movement is seen in the new interest in social questions, in the widespread awakening of social conscience and in manifold concrete reforms. So strong is its momentum in the South that that section finds itself educating the negro, in apparent contradiction to its deepest racial convictions. The more democratic conceptions of the present day in regard to the family and social intercourse will show their racial applications to-morrow. Already the organized womanhood of the South is showing great interest in social betterment. Movements like those of scientific charity, prison and sanitary reforms assume the solidarity of communities and ignore the color-line. The sphere of public activity constantly widens and brings the impersonal justice of the state more largely to bear; and these outweigh the new burden of plutocracy added to old prejudice.

But is Outweighed by a Widening Democracy

Finally, the present moral crisis of the race question is certain to discover the apostasy of some professed idealists. Secure in the sense of the negro's immense practical handicap, and the conviction of his inferior capacity, there were some who encouraged him to hope and virtually said, "Of course if you ever prove yourself our equal we will then recognize you as such." Time has brought these men face to face with negro success and has called upon them to pay up the debt of their previous professions. A negro minority has emerged which by all the white men's tests has demonstrated its fitness for full participation in human privilege. How should it be treated? What if all negroes were Booker Washingtons? That this issue is actually upon the South, Thomas Nelson Page confesses in a recent notable article. His answer is, "If all negroes were Booker T. Washingtons the color-line must exist unrelaxed." To

The Apostasy of some Idealists

moral diagnosis this looks curiously like what theologians have called a "sin against the light." It is a deliberate refusal to adjust conduct to admitted facts.

But there is another side. On the whole the most encouraging aspect of the situation is the driving of true idealists into the open by this very moral crisis and enforced separation of sheep and goats. There is "nothing covered that shall not be revealed" was first spoken as a word of confidence, and as such it is justified in this case. In the face of the rising tide of race animosity, of the growing bitterness of competition, of political self-seeking at the expense of the negro, of unworthy and cowardly willingness to surrender still further the fundamentals of democracy, the best men of the South simply cannot hold their peace. And they have not done so. The last five years have probably heard more brave and candid discussions of the race problem and seen more deliberate moral choices than the thirty-five previous. Thus the ultimate just solution of this vast issue was never so assured as now that conscience has exhausted its conventional excuses and is forced to meet the situation on ethical grounds.

The Separation of Sheep and Goats

Of the ultimate happy ending of the race problem there is no more assurance than there is that democracy will succeed or that any portion of the human race will find a "golden harbor"; but, also, no less. For the race problem is simply a bit of the human problem with the same solution, if there is any. We feel the doubtful ebb and flow of the tide, but the strongest currents of the present are not so adverse as to deny to the brave man all he asks — a fighting chance.

V. WHAT THE NEGRO HAS DONE FOR HIMSELF

1. SUCCESS WITH A MINIMUM OF ASSISTANCE

THEY will call this title question-begging who believe that the negro can do nothing for himself. That certain gains in the way of landownership, annual production of wealth, education, and organization are credited to him in the columns of the census is admitted.

Are the Negro's Gains His Own? It is explained, however, that these are not proper race achievements, because made under white stimulus. All the negro's substantial gains, it is said, have been compulsory. Necessity and the constant efforts of his neighbors have prodded him to work. For his worthy victories, thank the South. His showier achievements have been imitative, under artificial stimulus from his sentimental allies. For his beatings of the air, thank the North. The negro himself thank for nothing, or if for anything, thank only the white blood in his veins. His progress in America is not genuinely his own. The following is a typical utterance of this view:

> The civilization of any people is the slow and toilsome growth of centuries, an unfolding of the people's spirit itself. Its virtue, its essence lies in this very fact. How then shall such a product be imposed upon an alien and inferior race? They cannot receive it; they can put it on only as an outer garment; it can never become truly theirs, the efflorescence of their own souls. . . . Generation after generation of cod-

dling and sympathy in the North has not effaced a single racial trait nor raised by a single notch the average character, moral or mental or physical.[1]

He has had an abnormal degree of help. The good side of his record must therefore bear a heavy discount.

So far as this is true may it not apply to the bad side of his record as well?

But is it true? Has the negro experienced anything other than the ordinary conditions of progress in a backward race in the present age? He is petulantly counseled to develop his own civilization; yet the sociologist declares,

Misread Sociology; the Charge of Dependence

A true social evolution obeying resident forces has nearly disappeared from the face of the earth, seeing that to-day the germs of every new social arrangement are blown throughout the world, and peoples at the most diverse stages of culture are discarding their native institutions and eagerly adopting the jurisprudence, the laws, and the organization of the most advanced societies.[2]

The stimulus of a more advanced civilization, therefore, far from being unique, is the natural, normal, and inevitable condition of progress in any less favored race or group. So much for bad sociology.

The negro has also been the victim of equally bad psychology. The attempt to apply the principles of individual development to the case of a backward race has been one-sided and marred by loose thinking; besides it has not

[1] W. B. Smith, The Color-Line, pp. 259, 260.
[2] Ross, Foundations of Sociology, p. 234.

WHAT THE NEGRO HAS DONE FOR HIMSELF

allowed for the imperfect analogy between the two. It is perfectly true that culture must be the unfolding of inner capacities; but it is equally true that the means of their awakening is imitation. The child instinctively imitates the ways of his surroundings; only after he has done so is the sense of their inner significance aroused. He does not first learn why a thing should be done, and then do it; he first does it, and thereby becomes inwardly aware why it should be done. What the critic probably means to charge is that the negro, when he imitates the white man's ways, does not get an adequate inner sense of their meaning. But imitation itself as the means of mental progress is the only way for even the Caucasian genius to enter into the gains of his race. The most original and spontaneous of gifts comes this way. No people could be excessively imitative except as their imitation might fail to fructify in the awakening of a self-explanatory and justifying feeling.

<small>Misread Psychology; the Charge of Imitation</small>

Is there any evidence that the negro is deficient in such inner responsiveness? This is the heart of the issue. Undoubtedly some members of his race are; just as some of a company of ostensible worshipers of God or votaries of fashion manifestly do not enter into the meaning of the acts they share. We see nothing laughable when an Arizona millionaire painfully speaks by the book, although his spontaneous utterance is picturesquely ungrammatical; but the negro's gravity in speech stirs our risibilities. We suspect him of posing; possibly he is. It is not to be expected that a general inner responsiveness to lately imitated ways will be acquired by the majority of a race in one generation — especially by those of its number whose mental

<small>Inner Response to Things Imitated</small>

habits are no longer plastic. But that the negro as a race is in America following the ways of a civilization which is essentially meaningless to him, to which his outward conformity signifies no inner response, is sheer assumption. Whether he would ever have developed anything like it if left to himself is beside the issue. What he would now do if deprived of the social pressure of his nation and age is equally so. Forgotten, the pure American stock in the Southern Appalachians degenerated. Races were not meant to live in isolation. Civilizations have never been independent creations. This is a world of human intercourse and mutual service. Unnatural it is, and unnecessary, to suppose that the American negro will ever be called to take the part of a racial Robinson Crusoe. Who dares to call the sunderings of the Ice Age the law of Christian civilization?

But, it is said, after all the black man does not respond to the forms of our life with exactly the same sense of meaning that we get. Precisely; here the principle of originality comes in. We imitate; we are thereby initiated into the meaning of acts; but we are colorless souls if we do not read something unique in them. The individual is never a duplicate. Speaking of inner experience " the same " never means " just the same." The judgment which condemns the negro as imitative frequently adds, " But whatever he does, he still remains a ' nigger.' " There cannot be higher praise. To imitate, to become enlightened thereby, and to impart some large measure of one's own peculiar mental contour into shared experience is the formula for normal human growth. It is desirable that inner meanings have only enough generic resemblance to enable men to cooperate in the large. The meaning of religion, for ex-

The Selfsame Response not Desirable

WHAT THE NEGRO HAS DONE FOR HIMSELF

ample, to an average negro congregation is too remote from its meaning to certain types of whites to allow them to mix comfortably in a common service; it is not so remote as to put the negro church out of the fellowship of the churches of America.

If men are sufficiently alike to participate in a common civilization, it is well to have them sufficiently unlike to give that civilization interesting variety and esthetic and moral enrichment. This the negro and his institutions help to do.

Well, then, admit that the negro has genuinely acquired whatever the facts show him outwardly to possess. Has it not been disproportionately through others' efforts? Emphatically, No! Through slavery, it is said, the South "gave" the negro the English language, Christianity, the rudimentary arts. So it did — after a fashion. So it does to its white men of to-day. Each generation of children takes for granted that it should receive an inheritance of wealth, culture, and opportunity; of material and social capital. No one charges it with inordinate dependence on this account. The negro has never had a thousandth part of the help the more prosperous classes of whites have had. It is not the fact nor degree of assistance that causes remark, but the surprise that it should have been held out at all to a despised race. That race, too, is identified by its color, set apart by social barriers and advertised as an object of charity. But just this fact of its isolation enables us to measure its comparative achievement and to say positively that no group of contemporary Americans has so largely created its own successes as has the negro of the last two generations. Whatever service the nation renders her children has been reduced to the minimum for

No Contemporary American Has Done so Much for Himself

him. He has had less help and more hindrance than any other. Over the record of his gains we may justly write, *What the negro has done for himself.*

II. WITHIN THE NATIONAL LIFE

We are first to consider how largely the negro bulks in his more external relations to the nation as mere physical presence and as economic producer. Speaking numerically, first of all, he has doubled his numbers since emancipation and now comprises one-third of the population of the South and eleven per cent of that of the entire nation.

Comparative Place: Numerical

The negro has greatly extended his habitat and range. While only one-tenth of his people live outside of the South, there are to-day more negroes in New York than in Richmond; more in Chicago than in Charleston; while Washington, not New Orleans, is the negro metropolis. Mississippi has a town composed exclusively of negroes, but so has Iowa. Into Montana and Idaho, and even the Canadian northwest, the negro miner has gone. The students of missionary schools share in a systematic and periodic industrial movement of the race. There is an annual summer exodus of boys from Brick School, North Carolina, to the truck farms of Connecticut, and of Fisk students to city jobs in Chicago. A washerwoman in Montclair, New Jersey, turns out to be a graduate of an American Missionary Association school in Jonesboro, Tennessee. A barber in Florida will discourse familiarly of the Pacific coast cities. I know of Oklahoma cotton growers who return every winter to their old homes in North Carolina, and can afford to do it. Read at large in census statistics such facts indicate a gradual redistri-

Geographical

bution of negro population throughout the North and West, showing increasing capacity for long-distance migration in response to economic opportunity.

Occupational

The occupations of the American negro in 1900 were as follows:

Agriculture, fishing, and mining	1,757,403 or	57%
Domestic and personal service	963,080 or	31%
Manufacturing and mechanical industries	172,970 or	6%
Trade and transportation	145,717 or	5%
Professional service	22,994 or	1%

As compared with native born and foreign born whites the most striking contrast is the excessive proportion of negroes engaged in agriculture, and their great deficiency in trade, transportation, manufacturing, and mechanical industries. In these occupations their proportion is only about one-tenth that of the whites.

The census further divides these groups of occupations into twenty-seven special employments. In all but three of these the negro made absolute gains and in thirteen he made relative gains during the last census period. On the other hand he suffered slight losses in some of the skilled industries, the significance of which fact is considered in a later paragraph. In agriculture, to which over one-half of his productive energy is given, the negro operates one-third of the improved acreage of the South and produces one-third of the annual crop values. This is probably not because he is as good a farmer as the white man (his deficiency in the use of fertilizers, for example, shows that he is not), but because in the main he occupies the better land. Yet whatever his deficiencies he exercises a tremendous productive function in his section, and annually adds untold millions to the national wealth. If he is a problem he is also an economic asset to the South of immeasurable value.

Of the homes in which he lived in 1900 the negro owned 21.8 per cent, a gain of over 3 per cent in the decade.

Ownership of Property: Homes

The white population owns 50 per cent of its homes. But three-quarters of the negro's homes were owned unencumbered by mortgage against only two-thirds of the whites. Something like this ratio would hold for a row of negro business places. Because of the lack of credit facilities the negro merchant ordinarily owns a greater proportion and borrows less of an invested capital than does the white. Personal property is often bought on deferred payments, yet even the negro's spring suit or Easter bonnet is more likely to be paid for than if they were on white bodies.

Of the farms which he operated in 1900 the negro owned 25 per cent, numbering in all 173,552. Their combined

Farms

acreage was above 12,000,000 or more than the total area of Belgium and Holland. His proportionate ownership was lowest in Georgia where he owned but 14 per cent of the farms, but this had risen to 20 per cent in 1906. His holdings in that state then numbered 82,822 farms, the value of which had increased in the six years from $14,196,735 to $23,750,219 — an enormous gain of 67.3 per cent. These holdings are divided as follows:

> 72 negroes own more than 1000 acres each.
> 368 negroes own between 500 and 1000 acres each.
> 1475 negroes own between 200 and 500 acres each.
> 3540 negroes own between 175 and 260 acres each.
> 10,392 negroes own between 100 and 175 acres each.
> 19,076 negroes own between 50 and 100 acres each.
> 39,652 negroes own between 20 and 50 acres each.

Negro Rural Home, Piedmont Region

Negro Business Street, Thomasville, Ga.

WHAT THE NEGRO HAS DONE FOR HIMSELF

The highest proportion of farm ownership in 1900 was in Virginia, where the negro owns over 58 per cent of the farms he occupies. Prosperity perhaps reached its high-water mark in Gloucester County.[1] This county has a population of 12,832, more than one-half of which is colored. Here 90 per cent of negro farmers own their land, and there is probably the best housed negro rural community in America. Under these conditions the race shows somewhat less crime proportionally than do the whites of Gloucester County. The moral stimulus which has made such gains possible is due largely to the proximity of Hampton and to the presence at Cappahosic of the excellent Institute and model farm of the American Missionary Association.

The economic basis of Gloucester County prosperity is, however, the Chesapeake Bay oyster industry, furnishing the negro a winter occupation and a cash wage which has largely been put into property. It is not by the land that land was chiefly acquired; and this, according to my observation, is the rule throughout the South.

How then do negroes acquire land, and what sort do they ordinarily acquire? Is it an easy thing to do? There is, to be sure, plenty of unimproved and waste land in the South, yet Professor DuBois is quite right in insisting that it is not now easy for the negro to become an owner except of poor and agriculturally impossible land, which he gets because no one else wants it. The general law throughout the South is that the blacks own the poorer but rent and occupy the better land. For acquiring ownership five methods chiefly have been open to him:

How Negroes Acquire Land

---

[1] Williams, "Study of Local Conditions," etc., Southern Workman, vol. 35, pp. 103 ff.

(1) Through a supplementary income from industry. I have repeatedly investigated the communities adjacent to mission schools and found land ownership proportionate to the local opportunities for winter work at a cash wage. In Gloucester County it is oystering; elsewhere, lumbering, the turpentine industry, tie cutting or railroad and "public" work. Large areas of the Black Belt have no such opportunities, and this lack constitutes their peculiar hopelessness. The unique industrial settlement at Kowaliga, Alabama, has for its central idea the supplementing of agriculture by industrial opportunities. Often land is bought by a son or brother working for wages in the North; or a whole family migrates there, expecting to return to the South when enough money has been saved to acquire land. Only rarely by agriculture does ownership come without a cash wage supplementing, for at least part of the year, the system of advances.

(2) Of course exceptions are numerous. The exceptional man, or the average man in an exceptional year, has been able to show a cash surplus from the sale of his produce, usually, of course, cotton. A "bumper" crop or possibly a market manipulation like the famous Sully cotton corner will disarrange the landlord's plan to take all the tenant makes, and perhaps leave a balance which the negro is sometimes wise enough to invest in land.

(3) A small but appreciable amount of property has come to the negro by inheritance. This seems strange in a race whose fathers were all slaves. The explanation is that often its fathers were not slaves but masters, who started their newly emancipated or more recently born sons with a farm each. I know of many cases where such

inheritance has been the beginning of exceptional negro prosperity.

(4) Philanthropy, too, has had a part in helping the negro to acquire land. Sometimes the patron was not fulfiling blood obligations, but merely expressing the gratitude of a former master or present well-wisher. Naturally, however, the giving of farms as gifts outright has been rare.

(5) Endeavors on the part of Northern philanthropy to assist the negro to acquire land have generally involved a sense of the virtue of self-help. They have therefore tried to combine philanthropy and business. Land has been set apart and sold to negroes on easy terms. Frequently the method has been too easy. The reputation for philanthropy has doomed the enterprise in advance. Northern inexperience with the negro has complicated the problem. Such experiments in connection with many mission schools have given opportunity to hundreds of negro families, yet few of them have been conspicuous successes from the economic standpoint. Just now a carefully guarded experiment in connection with the Calhoun School, Alabama, is in process of successful consummation, and North Carolina furnishes a recent interesting example of a frankly commercial venture undertaken by a Southern lawyer, Hon. James E. Pou of Raleigh.

Mr. Pou's account of the experiment follows:

> In 1897 my brother and I bought a large tract of practically run-down and abandoned farm land in Johnston County about five miles from the railroad. This land was naturally good, but had been cultivated by tenants for a great many years, and was in a thoroughly run-down, dilapidated condition, fences, houses, and everything. Much of the land was grown up in broom sedge and second-growth pines.

We cut the land up into small farms, usually from 80 to 100 acres, trying to give each farm a road front, some upland, some forest and some meadow, running back to a creek. We then undertook to sell a portion of this land to colored people, as there had been a very large negro population on this land before; some still remained and were attached to the old farm. When they heard it was to be cut up and sold, they seemed very anxious to acquire a foothold.

My brother and I found that not one could pay cash for the land, but we decided to give them a chance. We said to them that if they would go to work on the land, we would give them a chance to work it out. A considerable number accepted the proposition, and they began trying to work out their land in the year 1898. At the present time nearly all of them have paid for their land, and I do not know of a single one who has not either entirely paid for his land or so nearly done so that the debt against it is a small proportion of its cash value.

Besides paying for this land, in most instances, and paying nearly all for it in other instances, these people have greatly improved their farms. They have all built comparatively comfortable houses, some with four or more rooms. They have cleared land, and a large number have good live stock. They all live comfortably and their credit with the stores is good. Besides the land they bought from us, I understand that some have bought land from other people. I understand that Hezekiah Watson and his boys own land easily worth from three to five thousand dollars, and it is nearly, if not quite, all paid for. These men were tenants in 1897, and hardly ever expected to own land.

I have taken a great deal of interest in the out-

WHAT THE NEGRO HAS DONE FOR HIMSELF

come of this experiment (for it was an experiment to sell land on credit to colored people) and I have watched the conduct of these people closely. I do not think that one of these men has been in court since they bargained for the land. I have heard of no trouble in their community. Their white neighbors speak well of them and they are regarded by everybody as a useful addition to the community. I think the determination to own their homes has nerved these people up to unusual effort and their success shows what an industrious man can do when he tries.

I do not think that a single person that bought land from us has thrown his part up. One of these men moved away, but some other colored man of the community took his trade and carried it out. I think every one of the men now lives on his own land, most of them clear of incumbrance. This community has its own church and schoolhouse and the young ones can generally read and write.

No general or complete statistics of negro ownership of city property exists, but their assessments in many Southern communities are impressive and their rent-rolls long. Some indication is furnished by the results of recent investigation of the property holdings of ninety former students of Tougaloo University. Forty-nine own 5,896 acres of land valued at $26,430; seventy-two own 239 houses, mostly in towns and cities, valued at $118,075, and sixty-eight own town and city lots valued at $101,040. The ninety persons investigated represented thirty-six occupations. Such a widespread holding of moderate property, showing success in such varied lines of livelihood, is more significant of race progress than large acquirements on the part of a few.

City Property

Naturally no definite information is available as to the wealth of the negro business and professional classes. We are assured that the wealth of the thirty-six delegates at the 1908 meeting of the Negro Business Men's League, who gave talks on how they had succeeded, as well as of most of the five hundred delegates on the convention floor, would have to be represented by five and six figures. A superficial acquaintance with the professional negro in any of the larger Southern cities will discover not a few whose incomes are upwards of $5000. In other words, a fair proportion of the race is, financially speaking, successful beyond the average American.

<small>Wealth of Business and Professional Classes</small>

Statistics of government employment show a number of negroes enjoying comfortable Federal salaries. In the District of Columbia alone two hundred and ninety-two receive more than $1000 per year. The total number of Federal employees of the race is over 5500. All over the South the "Africanization of the post-office" is a familiar cry. Such Africanization can only take place after competitive examinations shared by white candidates. In so large a city as Mobile, recently, the entire force of mail-carriers was black, as were a large number of other post-office employees. For a series of years this service absorbed all the male graduates of Emerson Institute in that city.

<small>Government Service</small>

III. WITHIN RACIAL LINES

However impressive the exhibit of the negro's material progress, the most important thing which he has yet done for himself is to create social agencies and institutions. We shall follow out the story of his quantitative gains,

REPRESENTATIVE NEGROES

GEORGE W. CRAWFORD,
    Attorney, New Haven, Conn.

A. C. GARNER,
    Pastor, Washington, D. C.

H. H. PROCTOR, D.D.,
    Pastor, Atlanta, Ga.

J. W. WORK,
    Professor, Fisk University

WM. N. DEBERRY,
    Pastor, Springfield, Mass.

GEO. W. MOORE, D.D.,
    Supt. of Negro Church Work, American Missionary Association

but shall from this point attempt to accompany it with an interpretation of that qualitative development within the race which has made them possible. For a study of negro institutional progress reveals a type of organizing ability and instinctive social genius which prophesy immeasurable results.

A lady from Virginia, new to a border city, afforded her friends much innocent amusement by the inquiry whether the wife of a negro janitor could be engaged to wash dishes on a special occasion. She was dismayed to be told that she herself would be as likely to go out washing dishes as would the janitor's wife. This status of the negro woman as mistress of her own home the Virginian had never met before.

<small>Domestic Institutions</small>

Now the transfer of black mothers and daughters since emancipation from the kitchen or field to the fireside, with its privacy, sanctities, and graces, is perhaps the most radical revolution in the structure of negro society. That the creation of the home is a moral gain, all recognize. But popular thought fails to see in it a type of social organization new to the race, an unaccustomed division and specialization of labor. In view of this novelty, the conjugal statistics of the census ought not to be taken just for granted. It is a tremendous fact that the race has adjusted itself to civilized marriage. This adjustment is indeed imperfect. But, as we shall later discover, its weakness is due less to wickedness than to economic conditions. As compared with Africa and slavery, the gain is immeasurable, and a complete transition is hopefully assured by the material and moral progress of the past. All told, the domestic reorganization of his life is the American negro's most magnificent achievement.

The prosperous citizen who chances to overhear his

cook converse with her kitchen neighbor about "lodge"
and "ten-cent dues"; who finds that his wife
cannot go to the theater to-night because
"Caroline wants to go to the initiation," or
discovers his own way blocked by a procession
of a colored "Sir Knights," may dismiss such "nigger
organizations" with a smile of indifference and contempt.
Not so with the sociological expert. He sees in them profound economic originality and wisdom. "The first practical shelter," says Prof. Simon N. Patten, "of every man just over the subsistence line is in a fund for sick, death, or strike benefits, or in building and loan associations." On his humble levels of fraternalism the negro is developing social capacity and husbanding material resources; the results already add greatly to his group-strength, both economic and moral. His institutions of savings and insurance are yet chaotic in character. The strongest bear the names and assume to be legitimate offshoots of the older secret orders, like Masons, Odd Fellows, and Pythians. All told, they own from four to five millions of dollars' worth of property, and collect a million and a half annually from their members. The more significant institutions, however, are local. Secret society halls dot the rural South and cities are honeycombed with lodge rooms. Much of the motive behind these enterprises is naïve and primitive — a half superstitious desire to be "buried right," a childish love of display, the convivial instinct; but along with these goes a sound, economic instinct directed to substantial group ends. To be sure, the financial management of the local societies is often lamentably lax, and in some of the popular insurance orders a scientific basis of operations is lacking, yet both are learning by their mistakes and are

Economic Institutions: Fraternal and Insurance

slowly correcting them. As an administrator of charities in a border city, I frequently found low-grade negroes fortified through their lodges against loss through sickness and death as the corresponding white class was not.

The secret of much of the negro's success in acquiring property lies in modest organizations of the savings and loan type. A typical example is that of the Gloucester, Virginia, Land, Loan and Building Association. It was organized under the inspiration of Principal Price of the Cappahosic Institute. It endeavors to aid its members to secure homes or to establish themselves in business, and to provide a profitable investment for savings. Its charter is an instrument carefully drawn in the light of the best experience and conforming to the state law. Shares are $10 each on a capital stock of $25,000. They are acquired by an advanced payment of $1, which covers the first ten months' dues and ten cents per month thereafter till the entire amount is paid. The expenses of administration are carried by an entrance fee of twenty-five cents and a charge of ten cents on each loan, sale, or transfer. All such transactions must have the approval of a lawyer. Loans pay eight per cent interest. The membership is now over one hundred and seventy, owning from one to twenty-five shares of stock each. Seven per cent annual dividends have been paid for the last three years. Hundreds of similar institutions of thrift exist throughout negro society.
<small>Building and Loan Associations</small>

In many other lines the cooperative impulse has expressed itself. Productive cooperation has been tried in enterprises as diverse as cotton-mills, coal-mines, iron-foundries, brick and tile-work, turpentine plants, and farms. Negroes have even established
<small>Other Forms of Cooperation</small>

three street railways to compete with lines which showed race discrimination. In distribution, hundreds of enterprises have been established, especially in grocery and drug-stores and in publishing companies. Many of these attempts have been financial failures or at least have not been permanently profitable, but even these have had great educative value. It is not known whether or not the percentage of failures has been in excess of those of the business world at large. They simply repeat the story of the first cooperative efforts of any commercially inexperienced group with small capital. But the discovery of a widespread will to try such methods is deeply significant. They do not impress us because few recognize the possibilities of the cooperative system for anybody. It does not seem to harmonize with the general tendencies of the age. Yet the forces of the world never go all in the same direction at once. Varied principles of economic association may coincide and thrive. In organizing his group resources on lowly levels the negro points the way for other handicapped classes. The ships of Lancashire weavers who began cooperation on these levels now sail all the Seven Seas. Belgian peasants build cooperative palaces of marble. It is an American weakness to despise the day of small things. We ourselves do not succeed that way; therefore it is not a worthy pathway to success. This attitude shuts the door to comprehensive and just judgment of the negro's race-gift of group organization.

There are no up-to-date statistics on negro trade unionism. In 1902, however, 40,000 negroes were members of a group of trade-unions aggregating 500,000 members. These were most largely miners, tobacco-workers, longshoremen, masons, painters, and carpenters. The larger group of unions aggregating

Trade Unions

WHAT THE NEGRO HAS DONE FOR HIMSELF

700,000 members had in all only 1000 scattered negro exceptions; and in many cases, no negro members at all. This shows on the face of it the comparatively limited part of the race in labor organization. Even in unions where the negro is numerically strong, his practical opportunities are not uniform. In the South, "locals" are generally, though not invariably, organized separately. In spite of his union card, prejudice often keeps the negro out of opportunity which his white brother receives. Where he has been accepted it is generally because he has fought his way in. He has begun as a strike-breaker and has been afterwards unionized in self-defense by the white trade. Trade unionism, like all idealistic movements, finds it extremely hard to make its practises square with its theories. In practise its organization is too often selfish, using every prejudice to keep its own monopoly. It is to be confessed, too, that the inferior efficiency of the negro has often been a heavy load for the union to carry. The leaders of the movement have undoubtedly tried not to draw the color-line. Nevertheless the actual working attitude of organized labor is decidedly adverse to the negro, especially in the North.

The situation is not without signs more favorable to him. The recent unparalleled immigration of unskilled laborers has compelled the unionist movement to adopt a more democratic spirit. "The man who has joined one of the unions formed within the last six years learns 'that his lot is bound with that of the whole working class' and 'that he can no longer advance by building a monopoly of labor within his trade.' The lines of industrial caste must break in order to give the class which has the numerical power, free admission into the ranks above it."[1]

[1] Patten, New Basis of Civilization, p. 104.

This new attitude gives organized labor a fresh vantage-ground in moral principle and its working out and percolation into the South may be counted on as one of the most certain and massive forces against race prejudice in the future.

The foregoing is an inadequate treatment of the grave problem of the relation of the negro to organized labor.

Other Forms of Labor Organization — It is a sufficient answer, however, to the charge that he has shown himself lacking in organizing capacity. Up to the full measure allowed him, he has used the resource of industrial organization in its highest form. Beyond that he has devised original forms of cooperation, especially to affect agricultural wages. Said a Virginia clergyman to me, " The niggers down here are ruining the country. They've got a secret agreement not to work for less than a dollar a day. We cannot get a man for less." Similar laments fill the South. In the early winter of 1908 a number of negro society halls in southwestern Georgia were dynamited by whites. Local press despatches, explaining the occurrence, showed significant variations. Some charged the secret societies with harboring criminals, others with effecting combinations to raise wages. On September 27, 1908, in the same region (Calhoun, Baker, and Miller Counties) eighteen colored churches and schoolhouses were burned. Again two causes were alleged: that negroes plotted assaults, and that they had decided to sell cotton at a lower figure than that at which the white planters' association was holding the crop.[1] Thus outside of conventional labor organization, and in the field of agriculture where such organization ordinarily has proved least successful, negro group-action is a grim and mighty fact.

---

[1] See dispatch, New York Times, September 28, 1908.

WHAT THE NEGRO HAS DONE FOR HIMSELF

Banks

With the growth of negro city groups in wealth and race consciousness a system of regular banks, now numbering over forty in the United States, has arisen to furnish the facilities of commercial credit to the rapidly increasing business and investing classes. One of the oldest and strongest of these is the *Dime Savings Bank* in Birmingham, Alabama. Starting with $500 deposits in 1890, it has grown to hold $1,097,224 in 1906–7. This considerable sum belonged to 9112 depositors.

Combination of Activities by the True Reformers

Probably the most remarkable negro economic institution is, however, the United Order of the True Reformers with headquarters at Richmond, Virginia. It is a national organization combining an insurance company with 80,000 members, a central bank which has done a total business of $16,000,000 (and the only one in Richmond which continually paid specie during the panic of 1893), and a real estate enterprise owning twenty-seven income-bringing buildings, most of which are rented to local lodges. The Washington building cost $100,000 and contains a theater, a dozen lodge rooms, an armory, two stores, several offices, and a barber shop. The truly remarkable record of the Order is summarized as follows:[1]

1881. The Grand Fountain organized with 100 members and $150 cash.
1907. The Grand Fountain membership increased to 80,000.
   Sick and death benefits paid to date $2,340,389
   Paid up capital of the savings-bank 100,000
   Deposits in the savings-bank 336,272

[1] The World's Work, June, 1908, pp. 10, 348.

Real estate department's holdings	388,000
Value of property of Old Folks' Home	36,495
The yearly business of five stores	496,373

The negro church is an intricate and impressive social organization, as well as an institution of the higher life.

Institutions of the Higher Life: the Church

It is indeed the chief institutional creation of the race and its success is a vast economic achievement. Its proportionate membership greatly exceeds that of the white churches, including probably thirty-six per cent of the total negro population and of the population above ten years of age over fifty per cent. This number is distributed through about 25,000 local churches, of which more than four-fifths are in ecclesiastical connections exclusively under negro control. Ninety-eight per cent of all negro church members belong to various Baptist and Methodist bodies.

It is noteworthy that, while in the Methodist Episcopal polity authority is highly centralized, the Baptist system is extremely democratic.

Evidence of Administrative Capacity

Socially this is significant as showing the negro's capacity to use widely divergent governmental types. He has succeeded about equally well under the two ecclesiastical extremes. Thirteen bishops of the African Methodist Episcopal church, for example, are said to

> wield the power directly over 750,000 American negroes, and indirectly over two or more millions, administer $10,000,000 worth of property and an annual budget of $500,000.
>
> These bishops are elected for life by a General Conference meeting every four years. The membership of the General Conference consists of ministerial and lay delegates: the clerical delegates are elected

Ingram Chapel, J. K. Brick School, N. C.
Largest A. M. A. school under negro control

First Congregational Church, Atlanta, Ga.
Pioneer in the South in institutional work for the race

from the 'Annual Conferences, one for every thirty ministers. Two lay delegates for each Annual Conference are selected by the representatives of the official church boards in the Conference. Thus we have a peculiar case of negro government, with elaborate machinery and the experience of a hundred years. How has it succeeded? Its financial and numerical success has been remarkable, as has been shown. Moreover, the bishops elected form a remarkable series of personalities. Together the assembled bishops are perhaps the most striking body of negroes in the world in personal appearance: men of massive physique, clear-cut faces, and undoubted intelligence. Altogether the church has elected about thirty bishops. These men fall into about five classes. First, there were those who represented the old type of negro preacher — men of little learning, honest and of fair character, capable of following other leaders. Perhaps five or six of the African Methodist Episcopal bishops have been of this type, but they have nearly all passed away. From them developed, on the one hand, four men of aggressive, almost riotous energy, who by their personality thrust the church forward. While such men did much for the physical growth of the church, they were often men of questionable character, and in one or two instances ought never to have been raised to the bishopric. On the other hand, in the case of four other bishops, the goodness of the older class developed toward intense, almost ascetic piety, represented preeminently in the late Daniel Payne, a man of almost fanatic enthusiasm, of simple and pure life and unstained reputation, and of great intellectual ability. The African Methodist Episcopal Church owes more to him than to any single man, and the class of bishops he represents is the salt of the organization. Such a business plant naturally has called to the front many men of business ability, and perhaps five bishops may be classed as financiers and overseers. The rest of the men who have sat on the bench rose for various reasons as popular leaders — by powerful preaching, by pleasing manners, by impressive personal appearance. They have usually been men of ordinary attainment, with characters neither better nor worse than the middle classes of their race. Once in office they have usually grown in efficiency and character. On the whole, then, this experiment in negro government has been distinctly encouraging. It has brought forward men varying in character, some good and some bad, but on the whole decency and ability have been decidedly in the ascendancy, and the church has prospered.[1]

Equally significant of administrative capacity are the multifarious denominational activities of the Baptists through their local and state bodies and their General Convention and Missionary Boards. In short, these enormous and complicated social engines actually work under exclusively black control.

As human institutions, the churches have made most astounding strides. On the material side, they count some 25,000 church edifices. Frequently, as in representative cities like Macon and Mobile, these rank in quality with the better public buildings. The total property of the negro denominations is probably worth $40,000,000. Their combined annual expenditure approaches $10,000,000, at least $250,000 of which goes to education under church control. Negro Baptists support eighty schools, and the largest of the Methodist bodies twenty-five.

Material Holdings and Business Activities

---

[1] "The Negro Church," Atlanta University Publications, No. 8, p. 130.

WHAT THE NEGRO HAS DONE FOR HIMSELF

Many of these are of extremely low grade, doing but crudely work which the state ought to be doing for its citizens. On the contrary, the best, like Wilberforce University, Ohio, rank with the first negro schools in the country. The educational work of the negro churches has of course had much help from white philanthropy, especially that of the North. To counterbalance this, however, it should be noted that many schools supported by Northern missionary agencies show a large tuition income from their negro pupils.

About twenty official periodicals of standing and a horde of local sectarian papers constitute probably the most widely influential religious press of America. The Baptist Publication House for the diffusion of religious and denominational literature is one of the most extensive of race enterprises. It occupies four brick buildings on one of the chief business thoroughfares of Nashville, Tennessee.

> The plant consists of a large first-class steam-boiler, two engines, a complete electric plant, a complete system of telephones, with a well-regulated set of the most improved power printing-presses, a well-regulated bindery, with all the machinery and equipment that is commonly attached to the most modern printing and publishing plant, together with a complete composing room, with all of the modern paraphernalia, including linotype machines. This plant, with its stock, is fully worth to the denomination $100,000 and if it were in a stock company its stock, if placed at $100,000, would sell in the market at par, and its income would pay a creditable dividend.[1]

The annual circulation of religious publications through this agency exceeds five and one-half million copies, while

[1] "The Negro Church," Atlanta University Publications, No. 8, p. 114.

as employers of labor this and similar ecclesiastical enterprises furnish a means of support to thousands of negroes.

Working Status of the Negro Church
Descriptions of the working status of typical negro churches, for the rural district, the town and the city respectively, are borrowed from competent first-hand studies by the Atlanta Conference.

The Rural Church
Thomas County is situated in extreme southwest Georgia, within twenty miles of the northern boundary line of Florida. According to the census of 1900, the negro population was 17,450. Among this population there are ninety-eight churches. These churches represent all denominations, Baptist predominating, there being only one Episcopal and two Congregational churches. This number gives the actual churches which we have been able to learn of. It will be a safe estimate to affirm that about twenty per cent of this number may be added, of which we failed to learn.

This will give a church for every one hundred and fifty persons, and here it might be said that, unlike much of our American population, the negro is well churched. It is his only institution and forms the center of his public life. He turns to it not only for his spiritual wants, but looks toward it as the center of his civilization. Here he learns the price of cotton or the date of the next circus; here is given the latest fashion-plates or the announcement for candidates for justice of the peace. In fact, the white office-seeker has long since learned that his campaign among the negroes must be begun in the negro church, and by a negro preacher.

These ninety-eight institutions in Thomas County, like those of many other counties, have interesting his-

The Yamacraw Section, Savannah, Ga.

Negro Tenements, Charleston, S. C.

These and twenty more have as sole water-supply an open dipping well

tories. About half this number represent the churches whose beginning has been normal, the natural outgrowth of expansion. The other half's history is checkered. Their rise can almost invariably be traced to one or two methods. First, there is the proverbial split. A careful study of the roll of membership in many of the churches will reveal the second method. Some brother is called to preach. This call is so thunderous, and the confidence that he can make a better preacher than the present pastor so obtrusive, that he soon finds that there is little welcome in the sacred rostrum of the old church. He therefore takes his family and his nearest relatives and moves away. Study the rolls, therefore, of many of the churches, and you will find that they are largely family churches, and that the first preacher was some venerable patriarch. I think one will be perfectly safe in concluding that two-thirds of the growth in churches of the various denominations has been made in this way; and that little has been accomplished by the church executives as the result of direct effort at church extension.

It will be readily seen that churches having their origin in this way merely duplicate the old institution; often it is not a creditable duplicate. I know of no rural church in Thomas County whose inception had the careful nursing of an educated, cultured leader. Others have labored and we have entered into their labors. The largest churches and the biggest preachers in Thomas County do little home missionary work and organize no new churches.[1]

The Village Church
Contrasted with its feeble and socially divisive rural influence is the typically central place of the church in the small town, as revealed by a study of Farmville, Virginia.

[1] "The Negro Church," Atlanta University Publications, No. 8, p. 57.

The church is much more than a religious organization; it is the chief organ of social and intellectual intercourse. As such it naturally finds the free democratic organizations of the Baptists and Methodists better suited to its purpose than the strict bonds of the Presbyterians or the more aristocratic and ceremonious Episcopalians. Of the 262 families of Farmville, only one is Episcopalian and three are Presbyterian; of the rest, twenty-six are Methodist and 218 Baptist. In the town of Farmville there are three colored church edifices, and in the surrounding country there are three or four others.

The chief and overshadowing organization is the First Baptist Church of Farmville. It owns a large brick edifice on Main Street. The auditorium, which seats about 500 people, is tastefully furnished in light wood, with carpet, small organ, and stained-glass windows. Beneath this is a large assembly room with benches. This building is really the central club-house of the community, and in greater degree than is true of the country church in New England or the West. Various organizations meet here, entertainments and lectures take place here, the church collects and distributes considerable sums of money, and the whole social life of the town centers here. The unifying and directing force is, however, religious exercises of some sort. The result of this is not so much that recreation and social life have become stiff and austere, but rather that religious exercises have acquired a free and easy expression and in some respects serve as amusement-giving agencies. For instance, the camp-meeting is simply a picnic, with incidental sermon and singing; the rally of the country churches, called the "big meeting," is the occasion of the pleasantest social intercourse, with a free barbecue; the Sunday-school convention and the various preachers' conventions are occasions of reunions and festivities. Even the weekly Sunday service serves as a pleasant meeting and greeting place for working-people, who find little time for visiting during the week.

From such facts, however, one must not hastily form the conclusion that the religion of such churches is hollow or their spiritual influence bad. While under present circumstances the negro church cannot be simply a spiritual agency, but must also be a social, intellectual, and economic center, it nevertheless is a spiritual center of wide influence; and in Farmville its influence carries nothing immoral or baneful.[1]

The City Church
Atlanta, with a colored population in 1900 of 35,727, had fifty-four negro churches, twenty-nine of which were Baptist, twenty-one Methodist, while four belonged to other denominations. The total membership was upwards of 16,000, of which the Baptists had over 10,000. The combined value of church property was upwards of $250,000, and their annual income nearly $52,000. The most significant thing about the statistics was the fact that the reported active membership averaged little more than one-half the total membership claimed.

Detailed investigations discover that the Methodist membership is the most homogenous. It consists of the families of laborers with a sprinkling from the business and professional classes. In education they rank from fair to poor. Most of its ministers are men of character with moderate degrees of education. The Baptist churches, on the contrary, seem to fall into two extremes. They are either composed of an extremely poor and de-

[1] "The Negro Church," Atlanta University Publications, No. 8, pp. 81–82.

graded membership, with unclean, miserably lighted, and unhealthy places of worship, and with pastors to match; or of the more influential classes. Some of the Baptist pastors are men of commanding popular gifts, but they generally tend to display rather than to solid attainment. A small and select minority, the intellectual and moral elite of Atlanta, are in the Congregational, Episcopal, and Northern Methodist churches.[1]

Passing from its social and economic phases to the central question of the negro churches' efficiency as a moral and spiritual power, we need in fairness to confess the shortcomings of most white churches in these directions. Human brotherhood is undeniably a chief corner-stone of the Christian religion, but race antipathy has not yet been overcome by the white churches, either South or North. The religious shortcomings of the negro churches have been merely at somewhat different points from those of the white. These points are chiefly five:

Moral and Spiritual Efficiency

(1) They have frequently subordinated worship to amusement. This is partly due to the poverty of the race in social institutions. The church, in order to serve its people, has had to be a substitute for theater, lyceum, political club, and general social center. It has truly served in these things as well as in its spiritual ministries, but it has proportionately overdone them.

(2) Frequently the negro church has tolerated lax moral standards both among ministry and membership, particularly in financial and sexual matters. This deep stain is as bitterly confessed by the better negroes as it is bitterly charged by the white South. Direct evidence

[1] See "The Negro Church," Atlanta University Publications, No. 8, pp. 78, 79.

An "Uncle" "Auntie Peg-Leg"

AGED BREADWINNERS

from a wide field of investigation shows that slow gains are being made in these matters.

(3) The negro church has been to a sad degree the field of selfish exploitation by unprincipled leaders, who sought financial or political gains through ecclesiastical power. Success has more largely centered upon the personality of the pastor than in any white denomination. Churches have been known to gain as many as a thousand members under one pastor, only to lose them all when he left. But institutional stability is rapidly growing and is curbing such abnormal individual control.

(4) Sometimes the negro church has not only failed to sense the best tendencies of race development, but has obstinately opposed and subordinated them. Neither Mr. Washington nor the friends of higher education have found much genuine sympathy in the negro ecclesiastics. The leadership of the race in its larger, more fundamental, and, especially, its national relations has been with the schools rather than with the church.

(5) Finally, the negro church has been almost entirely blind to the fundamental social problems of the varied and rapidly developing groups within the race. It has been of very little service in the adjustment of the negro to his peculiar and trying city conditions. The crucial problems of health, for example, and of social betterment in general, have remained almost untouched. Neither has the church been an agent of rural progress. At no point has it led in the more serious attempts to adjust the race to the new conditions of its life in America.

The Atlanta Conference collected hundreds of opinions from representative negro laymen and Southern whites on these problems of the moral status of the negro church.

In general they indicated hopeful progress at all the weak points.

A striking feature of them was the frequent recognition of the exceptional character of the small but growing group of negro churches affiliated with Northern denominations. These constitute but two per cent or less of the negro church membership of America, but the testimony to their greatly disproportionate influence was decisive. A Southern planter, for example, answering " No " to all questions of general improvement in the negro church, made the following exception:

Exceptional Character of Churches Affiliated with Northern Denominations

> We have one good, honest, and reliable negro preacher in our community, and he is trying to raise the standard of living among his race. But he has an up-hill business to do so. The old negroes, as a whole, are a long ways better than the young ones. The negro preacher that I refer to is O. Faduma.[1]

Mr. Faduma is principal of the American Missionary Association school at Troy, North Carolina, and pastor of the Congregational Church. Naturally the type of church life which appeals to the masses of the race repels the cultured negro minority which is fully abreast with American civilization. These have largely affiliated themselves with the Northern denominations which have done the most for negro uplift and education. As class institutions, the churches of this select group have their peculiar weaknesses and temptations. They lack contact with the community, the masses of which, in turn, denounce them as " stuck up "; they tend to forget patience and sympathy.

Limitation to and within the City

---

[1] "The Negro Church," Atlanta University Publications, No. 8, p. 168.

WHAT THE NEGRO HAS DONE FOR HIMSELF

I am acquainted with a considerable number of such churches — small, cultured, sober congregations, but non-aggressive, and tending to be selfish. This is the central difficulty with all exceptional groups. On the other hand, it is absolutely necessary for the negro church to develop standard-bearers, and the tonic effect of the two per cent has been deeply felt by the 98 per cent. Thus Professor Kelly Miller writes:

> Presbyterian and Congregational missionary societies have spent many millions of dollars among the freedmen of the South, but the result is seen rather in the intellectual and moral uplift than in religious proselytism. The real advantage consists largely in the reflex influence upon the Methodist and Baptist denominations.[1]

When therefore the leaders of such select churches happen to be men of popular ability, outreaching zeal and social insight, they frequently reach places of commanding influence. To them both white and black turn in the hour of clash and crisis, and the higher race-statesmenship is largely of their making. Their memberships are small, their salaries meager; they are lonely men and the color-line draws cruelly across their hearts, yet many a high-salaried white preacher may well envy them their power. They have social authority such as is rarely given to men of equal ability, and many a Southern community sleeps peacefully to-night because a poorly paid but fully trained and great-hearted negro preacher stands as a daysman between the races.

In the interest and esteem of some of the Northern missionary boards this select type of negro church has been

[1] Race Adjustment, p. 137.

rather an adjunct to educational institutions or an effort to aid groups of graduates to maintain their ideals in the midst of a low-grade society, than an attempt at a general denominational propaganda among the race. This is confessed by the Congregationalists, the attitude of whose missionary agency has been the occasion of sharp dissatisfaction on the part of the more aggressive of their colored ministry. These feel the sting of ecclesiastical littleness and are ambitious that the best should minister to the average life of the race. Depending ordinarily, as these churches have done, upon the presence of sufficient groups of cultured negroes, they have chiefly been limited to the city.

Within a few years, however, the extension of educational influences combined with general rural progress has created a demand in many country places for a more intelligent type of religious leadership. Movements of revolt from the domination of the old illiterate and immoral ministers have turned to the churches which, under Northern auspices, have always maintained the higher standards. Thus there has developed a number of thriving groups of strictly rural Congregational churches. This body has probably the most select membership of any, yet its success with the rank and file of the race has been proved in limited areas. Such enterprises could now be infinitely multiplied if financial support were provided. Their general race significance will be more largely proved in the future.

Exceptional Cases of Rural Success

The story of almost any one of these rural enterprises shows splendid devotion. Recently, near Rockingham, North Carolina, a little church of eight adult members built a thousand dollar edifice. The pastor, trained in a

Servants' Quarters in Rear of a Modern Memphis Home

The Cotton Levee, New Orleans, with Negro Longshoremen

mission school, was chief carpenter, and every member had some physical share in the construction. They worked three or four days in each week. A deacon gave forty days' labor, besides working at night till midnight or after. His wife and daughters hauled the lumber from the sawmill. At night the women sawed boards, held lights, and cheered the men at their task by singing plantation melodies. A widow, living by washing and ironing, contributed in work and cash $20. The pastor's share was $110. It was a labor of apostolic simplicity and sacrifice. Out of church extension funds, a great denomination gave $200 of the cost, yet the building essentially represents what the negro is doing for himself, and shows how he does it. Since its erection the white neighbors, in appreciative and friendly emulation, have repaired and painted their inferior church.

Typical of the transmission of influence to the country through the products of the higher schools is the story of a Louisiana pastor, Rev. M. W. Whitt, of Belle Place Congregational Church, New Iberia, Louisiana, as given by Pres. Frank G. Woodworth:

> Mr. Whitt is a graduate of the Normal Department of Tougaloo and of Howard Theological Seminary. Fifteen years ago he went to Belle Place as pastor of an American Missionary Association church. The record of his early days there is of profound interest, but is another story. So also is the history of the religious transformations wrought, though they have economic consequences and value. It is only with the more strictly economic side that we have present concern. When he reached Belle Place in 1892 the church organization was a complete wreck, having gone from one hundred members to three, and

two of the three were not in regular standing. The church building was little more than a cow shed, with no ceiling or sashes. There was only one home owner in the parish. To-day there is an edifice that would be an honor to any town or city in the state, paid for, every dollar paid by the people themselves, who keep the property well insured. The church has now eighty-five members — no slight achievement for colored Congregationalism, which with its standards must at present grow slowly among the negroes. The families number thirty, and fifteen of these, stimulated by Mr. Whitt's teaching and example, now own their own places. Three of the home owners have about $3000 of property each. Mr. Whitt has a home that cost $1500, owns twenty shares in a building and loan association (valued at $200 dollars a share), paying in twenty dollars a month for nearly the past ten years to secure it, and he and his wife own three lots in New Orleans, for one of which he has refused $650. It is doubtful if many ministers have been of more economic value to the community than this American Missionary Association product, whose thrift has in no wise lessened the earnestness of his study or of his religious life and teaching. The work which he has done in the suppression of vice and intemperance has been of very definite economic value. To cite but one example: said a deacon of a neighboring church, " I have been in the church eighteen years, and it seemed to me that if I did n't get drunk Christmas I had n't done my duty. I was brought up so. But one Sunday night just before Christmas I went to Brother Whitt's church. I left my flask of whisky under the steps and went in. I listened to him telling what Christmas meant, how it should be kept, and how almost everybody about, including Christians, desecrated the day by drinking and getting beastly drunk and how families are made to suffer. I said in that church I would go home and stop drinking and stop renting land. To-day I have a home that cost $1000, paid for, and Elder Whitt is the cause of it." This is typical of the economic value of the Association's work through the men it has trained.

To the rule of social complacency and non-aggressiveness on the part of the select city churches there are brilliant exceptions. The most notable in the Congregational fellowship is the First Church, Atlanta. It is recognized as including the best negroes of the city, and probably no colored church anywhere has a higher average of character and intelligence in its ranks. At the same time it has long maintained a slum mission and other persistent activities for the uplift of the more degraded classes. Its pastor, the Rev. H. H. Proctor, D.D., a Fisk University and Yale graduate, is a man of race-wide influence. He has served as assistant moderator of the national body of his denomination. He rendered eminent service in interracial efforts for order and justice after the Atlanta riot. The church property occupies a central location in the city, and its main edifice has just been added to the existing chapel. The completed property is worth toward $70,000, and the equipment for institutional work makes the church unique among negro religious enterprises.

An Exceptional City Church

Such an attempt to meet the social problems of negro city populations in an outreaching spirit of service, besides being eminently Christian, is of fundamental importance to a race which is popularly judged by its worst, for whom its best are held accountable. Indeed, the deepest moral problem before the better negro classes is whether they will withhold themselves from an energizing fellowship

CHRISTIAN RECONSTRUCTION IN THE SOUTH

with their weaker brethren, or whether they will put their own strength under the need of those whose fate they so often have to share.

Most of the organized philanthropic efforts of the American negro have been in connection with his churches; though outside of church influence co-operative efforts have established many and varied institutions. In all, the negro is supporting some sixty homes and orphanages, more than thirty hospitals, besides hundreds of cemeteries. Recently a number of commendable enterprises for the protection and redemption of the child-criminal have been undertaken by negro women's clubs in various states.

Negro Philanthropy

Among the select city groups flourish manifold other institutions of the higher life, expressing its interest in literature, music, art, philanthropy, polite intercourse and race ideals. The message of such a negro poet as Dunbar, of a painter like Tanner, a composer like Coleridge Taylor, actors like Walker and Williams, a scholar and essayist like Professor DuBois or a statesman like Mr. Washington is, of course, far wider than the race. It appeals to the whole nation and indeed to the world. But its first appeal is to the negro minority, their peers. There are thousands of negroes who honor and appreciate the works of eminent genius which their race has produced. There are women's clubs with complete national and state organizations; dignified associations for the discussion of public questions, such as the Sumner Club of Charleston, which has a history of thirty years. The annual musical festivals of the Coleridge Taylor Club of Washington are superb artistic events. At a banquet of the Strieby Congregational Club one might shut his eyes and never be conscious that he was not

Other Institutions of the Higher Life

WHAT THE NEGRO HAS DONE FOR HIMSELF

attending a similar occasion in Boston. The tone of service and preaching in the First Congregational Church of Atlanta would appeal to the most exacting mind. In other words, there are select negro groups which not only equal but actually exceed the average of national attainment in many of the ideal realms. They think and feel and enjoy as do other select groups of Americans and live accordingly.

To crown all this varied social evolution the negro has developed organs for the control of his further growth.
Evolution of Organized Group Control These appear as two temperamental parties, — radicals and conservatives — whose chief respective exponents are the "Niagara Movement" led by Dr. DuBois over against Mr. Washington and his followers. These parties have found multiform agencies of expression and appeal both to the race and to the nation; a vigorous press, an extremely able controversial literature, devices for public agitation and for bringing political pressure. One may laugh if he will at the squabbles of the negro on his side of the color-line. Yet through them the race is beating into shape a disciplined and well-officered army, under experienced leadership. It is following the universal method of learning democratic efficiency. The temperamental extremes in any group must find themselves, organize, and fight out a balance between themselves. Thus the seethings of negro sentiment are a deep factor in present American history. This "ostracized race in ferment" is fitting itself to play a larger part in the common life. It is forging weapons of group consciousness and control which will some day give its now voiceless power, wisdom, dignity, and weight in the counsels of the Republic.

VI. A BACKGROUND FOR BLACK

I. DUBIOUS VERDICTS FROM CONFLICTING FACTS

ONE whose lot it is sometimes to address Northern churches in behalf of negro education soon learns to his sorrow to distinguish between an audience interested and an audience convinced, a distinction which often registers itself in the size of the collection. Such a description of varied missionary activities as we have attempted in the earlier chapter appeals to those who are chiefly moved by concrete situations, but in the minds of the more judicious there frequently remain thoughts like this — and sometimes they speak them forth. What is the average daily attendance of these schools you have been telling about? Probably ten thousand. How many negroes are at present under the direct influence of your whole group of missionary activities? Possibly one hundred thousand. What proportion of American negroes have reached a normal standard of character and civilization? We speak roughly of the "talented tenth" — possibly one million. And how many negroes are there in America? Nearly ten million. Are the things which are true of the ten thousand, the hundred thousand, and the million, true also of the ten million? However promising the exception, however successful the agencies of uplift with the few, however interesting and worthy the work for which support is asked, what about general race tendencies? Assure us, if you can, that your hopeful story is not related to a mere fragment of the race — say, that which shares white blood — while the main currents of the American negro's life

marginal note: Ten Thousand *vs.* Ten Million

A BACKGROUND FOR BLACK

plunge down toward the abyss. In answer to such just and inevitable questions, it is the purpose of this chapter to declare the things which are true of the ten million.

The critics and the defenders of the American negro have fought a drawn battle hitherto, and chiefly because of defective tactics on both sides. On the one hand there is the Booker T. Washington school of optimists, whose chief resource has been the cataloguing of case after case of negro success. Here is this man and that man and another negro who have made good. Every time Mr. Washington comes North he has a new lot of men. Every article he writes has new cases. Stubbornly and truthfully he reiterates from year to year the story of thousands upon thousands of successful negroes. The trouble with this method is that over against it one can bring a case of failure to offset each case of success, and probably the failures are in one's own kitchen or barnyard, while the successful ones are far away. The outcome is that this method does not convince. It has not convinced the South where most of the successful negroes are, and the nation at large, though impressed, is unsatisfied. The mere enumeration of hopeful facts, however massive, cannot justify optimism. It is not enough to enumerate; one must weigh the facts.
_{Unconvincing Optimism}

If it be true that no people less than half a century out of bondage ever made such magnificent gains as the American negro has, it is just as true of Americans in general. There is no such human record as that which our country has made since the Civil War. Has the progress of the negro been in proportion to the general progress? In spite of his tremendous absolute gains, has he really kept pace with the rest of the nation? I confess that I am not so
_{Doubts as to Relative Progress}

sure. When, thinking of the negro, we proclaim: "Saul has slain his thousands," must we not also add: "And David his ten thousands"? As things are now going, would not white America gradually pull ahead of negro America, and forever increase the gap between?

But optimism faces a still deeper difficulty, namely: That the present deficiencies of the negro — which his best friends must measure and confess — are in matters so serious and so fundamental that if present tendencies hold, he is certainly doomed. No amount of progress on other lines could possibly overcome his deep failure in these fundamental respects. When the dark charges against him are formulated, they are found to be chiefly three:

1. He is deficient in physical stamina;
2. He lacks the fundamental economic virtues;
3. He is excessively immoral.

Whoever is deficient in these things is doomed, if his deficiencies continue.

A Fighting Chance For the first and third charges there exists what looks like authoritative proof. According to the census statistics, the American negro's death-rate is twice that of the white population; and his prison population is two and one-half times as great as his proportion in the general population. His economic weakness is supposed to be established by the facts that his numbers have absolutely decreased in some of the skilled trades and relatively decreased in others; that, especially in the Northern cities, skilled negro workmen are frequently forced out of trades into janitor's and porter's work; and that the South widely testifies that as a laborer the negro is deteriorating. These are grave charges and supported by ugly facts. They are frequently and unnecessarily overstated. At best they are bad enough, and nothing but the most adequate answer to them will avail to save popular faith in the negro. No critic of the race can be more anxious to have the nation know how precarious the negro's future is, than his friends should be. It is no easy battle he has before him; therefore he needs our help the more desperately. The most any one dare contend for him is that he has a fighting chance.

II. NEED OF A SOCIOLOGICAL BACKGROUND

Whether such a fighting chance will be allowed depends ultimately not upon the naked facts, nor even upon the discovery that some of them are seriously adverse to the negro, but upon their interpretation. For, after all is said and done, every thinker on the race problem, however scientific and unbiased, consciously or unconsciously brings a social philosophy to the interpretation of his facts. He puts them on a certain background, and the background gives them their color. Any woman can testify that a piece of dress goods in the shops does not look as it will when it is made up and worn. Its appearance changes with its setting. In the laboratory, patches of different colors are put upon different backgrounds and are found to take on complementary hues. I recall a story with a plot like this: A woman desiring to humiliate her social rival set about it by discovering the color of her rival's best frock. Then she invited her to a place of ostensible honor at a social function and set her over against a background which turned her charms into horrors. This is what the popular judgment, and frequently social investigators as well, have done for the negro. They have put the distressing facts of his present deficiencies upon the background

Philosophy always Present in the Interpretation of Facts

of a racial interpretation which makes them look blacker than they are.

The real issue is whether the negro's present deficiencies — which certainly doom him if like tendencies hold — are The Real Issue inevitable and necessarily permanent, or remediable and only temporary. Do they belong to the negro as a negro? Are they due to hereditary traits, predestined or unescapable tendencies of blood; or to social handicaps, to conditions which men can control? If the latter the negro has a fighting chance, and it is the duty of just men to help him in his fight.

The dominant social doctrine of yesterday held the former view and recent champions of the South, with much The Failure of Race as an Explanation show of belated learning, still reiterate it. But a revolutionary change meanwhile has come over the science of sociology by which an ever-narrowing sphere is allotted to heredity, and an ever-increasing sphere ascribed to social control. One of the brilliant younger sociologists, Prof. E. A. Ross of Wisconsin University (the man who coined the term "race suicide," and started a President a-preaching to the nation on that evil), summarizing a world-wide survey of recent tendencies in sociology, puts the case thus: —

> The superiorities that, at a given time, one people may display over other peoples, are not necessarily racial.[1]
>
> More and more the time-honored appeal to race is looked upon as the resource of ignorance or indolence. To the scholar the attributing of the mental and moral traits of a population to heredity is a confession of defeat, not to be thought of until he has

[1] Ross, Foundations of Sociology, p. 353.

wrung from every factor of life its last drop of explanation.[1]

Note the order of explanation; for this is the kernel of the thought. *We are to cry " race " last of all, after we have reckoned with every other factor, every nearer and more obvious cause.* Then if there is something left of the negro's deficiency, which belongs to him as a negro, one must confess it; but not until from every social factor has been wrung its last drop of significance.

In the present issue, merely to set the negro's deficiencies against their specific sociological background is to steal away much of their sharpness. This does not mean that the race factor has no influence, but that, when the general charge of malign race traits is forced to become explicit, when each alleged hereditary shortcoming is isolated and the nearest and most obvious explanation applied to it, the racial residuum, if any, is harmless.

III. ALLEGED RACIAL TRAITS AND THEIR SOCIOLOGICAL EXPLANATIONS

1. *The Negro's Inferior Physical Stamina*

Black Americans have a double death-rate. Waiving the facts that the statistics on which this conclusion is based are inadequate (and the census confesses as much), the best conclusion available is that, though the death-rates of both are declining, black Americans are now dying nearly if not quite twice as fast as white.[2] This

---

[1] Ross, Foundations of Sociology, p. 309.
[2] Census Bulletin 8, Negroes in the United States, p. 64; Willcox, "Census Statistics of the American Negro," in Stone, Studies in the American Race Problem, pp. 490 ff.

proportion holds for the total population and also for infants.

In such cities as Savannah, Georgia, five negroes die to every three whites. Considering the most fatal diseases, it is found that the negro proportion of death from tuberculosis is three to one; from marasmus — a wasting disease, generally of children — five to three; from malarial fever, five to three; from pneumonia, two to one. On the other hand, it is to be noted that in recent United States army examinations of candidates for enlistment negroes have made a slightly better showing than whites. A Southern commentator thinks this is because military service appeals to the best class of negroes, but only to the poorer class of whites. Again, it is most pertinent to note that extra-excessive mortality is chiefly a city phenomenon. Nothing, however, at present known can obviate the conclusion that the negro's outlook for health, though not hopeless, is extremely dubious.

This excessive death-rate is by no means overcome, as some suppose, by the still more excessive negro birth-rate. The birth-rate of both races is declining, but that of the negro much more rapidly.

The Negro's Double Death-rate

During the last twenty years of the nineteenth century the decline in the proportion of Southern negro children was 160 and that in the proportion of Southern white children only 75.[1]

While the black population of the South has doubled since the Civil War, the white population, virtually without

[1] Willcox, "Census Statistics of the Negro," in Stone, Studies in the American Race Problem, p. 507.

A BACKGROUND FOR BLACK

the aid of immigration, has tripled. If this ratio continues the negro is doomed to be an ever-diminishing fraction of the population. Between 1890 and 1900 the relative increase in the South Atlantic states was, negro 14 per cent, white 20 per cent; in the South Central states, negro 20 per cent, whites 30 per cent.

The final result, as shown in the relative proportion of the race in the South, is, therefore, that the negro is losing ground. What now is the significance of these facts? Is it that the negro has an inferior constitution, that nature made him a weakling, that God is responsible and no one can help it? On the assumption that inferior physical stamina is a racial trait, Southern oracles, following a Northerner, Prof. W. F. Willcox of Cornell, have prophesied the ultimate extinction of the negro in America. It is interesting, however, to note how vastly the ardor of a prophet enlarges the cautious conclusion of the statistician. Should the present ratio of increase in the two races prevail until 2000 A.D. there would then be in the South thirty-three million negroes to one hundred and fifty-five million whites, but the negro would constitute only 17.6 per cent of the population of which he now constitutes 32.4 per cent. Two thousand A.D. is a long way off, and a negro population of 17.6 per cent might still constitute a race problem of considerable difficulty. No one can safely prophesy whether or not the present ratio of increase will continue. A good many things are likely to happen to modify it. Yet to the author of " The Color-Line " it seems certain that " the general movement of the life of a continent is toward the elimination of the African-American."[1] Dr. Smith's jubilation at such a

Racial Interpretation of the Death-rate

---

[1] Smith, The Color-Line, p. 215.

CHRISTIAN RECONSTRUCTION IN THE SOUTH

divinely ordained result is both sincere and ludicrous; and even a just and generous mind like President Alderman's cannot forbear to utter a note of sectional exaltation at the alleged prospect.

Are Professor Smith and President Alderman willing to undertake and to work to their legitimate finish perfectly obvious measures tending to defeat their own prophesies? A considerable part, at least, of the negro's present death-rate is absolutely unnecessary; its present causes are very largely environmental, such as bad sanitation, poor housing, lack of proper clothing and food.

In the mayor's report of the city of Savannah for 1906, one reads something like this: "Ours is one of the most crowded cities in the South. Its oldest districts, especially, furnish too little light and air for the health of the people. It is now recognized also that the furnishing of means of recreation to its citizens is part of the function of a modern city. We need more parks both for the physical and the moral good of the people." But who occupies the more crowded quarters of old Savannah? The negro. Is he allowed to use the present municipal parks, and will he be admitted to the new ones? No. A negro or two may pass through a park of Savannah, but by unwritten law the negro population is forbidden to make the parks places of recreation. They cannot use them for any purpose for which they are ordained and supported, partly by negro taxes. Are parks for the majority? Then they are for the negro. Are they for the more needy? He is most needy. A Savannah negro mother cannot take her child to a park as a relief from her stifling alley; she may take a white child. The new municipal playgrounds, for which the mayor pleads, will not be available for black boys. A group of colored young people cannot enjoy a picnic there under the swaying moss of the live-oaks; a gang of colored laborers cannot rest there at noontime. Yet the alleys of Savannah are lined with negro houses. The block in which Beach Institute is located, and every block in that region, has long rows of disreputable alley tenements, where filth and bad sanitation contaminate the air, and menace the crowded and rapidly increasing colored population. A visitor writes,

> The last time I was entertained at the Mission Home my colored next-door neighbor emptied her dish-water from a window less than six feet from my own down into a sunless place between buildings. What does Savannah expect? Why should not the Savannah negro die?

Social investigators have explored such alley homes time and time again, and probation officers have followed the records of children who come out of them. There is no obscurity about their fruits. It is a suggestive fact that the municipal jail is not far away.

Dr. W. F. Brunner, the city health officer, understands the case perfectly well and puts it thus:

> We face the following issues: First, one set of people, the Caucasian, with a normal death-rate of less than sixteen per thousand per annum, and right alongside of them is the negro race with a death-rate of twenty-five to thirty per thousand. Second: The first named race furnishing a normal amount of criminals and paupers, and the second race of people furnishing an abnormal percentage of lawbreakers and paupers.

Is the negro receiving a square deal? Let a commission investigate the houses he lives in: Why, in his race, is tuberculosis increasing; why furnishes he his enormous quota to the chain-gang and the penitentiary; investigate the industrial insurance companies, the money lenders, the instalment furniture dealers, and, finally, the matter of the surplus population, which is a most potent factor in producing that class of persons which is dangerous to this community and must contaminate its health and prosperity. . . .

The negro is with you for all time. He is what you will make him, and it is " up " to the white people to prevent him from becoming a criminal and to guard him against tuberculosis, syphilis, etc. If he is tainted with disease you will suffer; if he develops criminal tendencies you will be affected. You cannot observe these things without going where he lives in colonies in this city. Investigate them, and you will soon learn that *if he desired to improve his sanitary condition he could not do it.* Observe the house he must live in; the food that he must eat, and learn of all his environments.

This is no sentimental dissertation; it is a statement of cold-blooded facts that is of as much value to the whites as it is to the negroes.[1]

The cemetery is open. The mayor's report takes pains to say that, whereas the white portion has been beautified with trees and shrubs, the negro portion has been kept clean and in good condition, and fenced off and separated from the other by a new barbed wire fence, " making each portion distinctive." Here the Savannah negro's body is laid away after being poisoned to death. There is noth-

---

[1] Mayor's Report, 1907, pp. 162–164.

ing racial about it. Any one would die who had the same kind of experience.

I know a Charleston alley lined with thirty-two negro tenement houses. In the midst of the alley, its sole source of water supply, is an open dipping well, surrounded by a sixteen-inch curb. On this curb all the people of the thirty-two houses do their washing. They dip into the well any dish that comes to hand, and any contaminated cup from any one of the thirty-two families might give disease to all; but specific contamination would not make much difference, for the water in the well all leaches in from the near-by marshes which are dumping-grounds for the city filth. Further interesting facts about Charleston are set forth with rather muckrakish fervor in a recent article by Samuel Hopkins Adams:

Charleston

> In the matter of the cisterns, for instance. Charleston now has a good city water supply fairly free from contamination where it starts, and safely filtered before it reaches the city. But a great many of " our best citizens " prefer their own cisterns, on the grandfather principle. These are underground, for most part, and are regularly supplied from the roof drainage. Also they are intermittently supplied by leakage from adjacent privy vaults, Charleston having a very rudimentary and fractional sewerage system. Therefore typhoid is not only logical but inevitable. I have no such revolutionary contempt for private rights as to deny the privilege of any gentleman to drink such form of sewage as best pleases him; but when it comes to supplying the public schools with this poison, the affair is somewhat different. Yet, as far as the Charleston Board of School Commissioners has felt constrained to go, up to date, is this: They

have written to the city physician asking that "occasional inspection" of the cisterns be made, and decorating their absurd request with ornamental platitudes.

With sewage it is the same situation. There is, indeed, a primitive sewer system in part of the city, but any attempt to extend it meets with a determined and time-rooted opposition. The Charlestonians are afraid of sewer gas, but apparently have no fear of the filth which generates sewer gas; said filth accumulated in Charleston's streets subject only to the attention of the dissipated-looking buzzards, which are one of the conservative and local features of the place. I have seen these winged scavengers at work. It is not an appetizing sight. . . .

Throughout the South figures and conditions alike are complicated by the negro problem. Southern cities keep a separate roster of mortalities, one for the whites, one for the blacks. In so far as they expect to be judged by the white rate alone, this is a manifestly unfair procedure, since, allowing for a certain racial excess of liability to disease, the negro in the South corresponds, in vital statistics, to the tenement dweller in the great cities. If New Orleans is to set aside its negro mortality, the death-rate among those living in the least favorable environment, New York should set apart the deaths in the teeming rookeries east of the Bowery, the most crowded district in the world, and ask to be judged on the basis of what remains after that exclusion. New York, however, would be glad to diminish the mortality in its tenements. New Orleans, Atlanta, Charleston, or Savannah would be loath to diminish their negro mortality. That is the frank statement of what may seem a brutal fact.[1]

[1] McClure's Magazine, vol. xxxi, pp. 250-251.

A BACKGROUND FOR BLACK

If your mother, going out to work by the day, left you, an infant in the cradle, and a clumsy father, a careless elder sister, or a none too thoughtful neighbor, had the care of you, you might not get proper things to eat, nor at the proper time. You might die. You would then ornament a statistical table, and be pointed out as a racial tendency; perhaps even charged up to the divine decrees. In proportion to population, more white women work in Fall River, Massachusetts, and more white babies die than anywhere else in the Union. The negro married woman is a breadwinner eight times as frequently as a white married woman, and her infants but follow the white's example. Thus the negro's phenomenal death-rate is largely a necessary consequence of the economic condition of his family.

Working Mothers and Dying Infants

Part of the negro's excessive death-rate must certainly be credited to the mental effect of the sharp social transition which he has undergone since his emancipation. Freedom brought new responsibilities to which the race was unwonted, and the nation made no provision for the economic future of the ex-slave. He ceased to be a chattel only to become a pauper; but the death that he suffers as a poor man must not be credited to him as a negro. Its causes are social rather than racial. The nation needs to learn that men, including negroes, die for lack of hope. Depressed by their unequal struggle against poverty and social prejudices, many a black man loses all heart to live. Any one who has observed the feeble hold on life frequently exhibited by negro students will be convinced that the causes of death are largely mental. Life simply does not hold out sufficient incentive to keep breath in the body. Southern observers have fre-

The Effects of Sudden Transition, and of Discouragement

quently noted the loss of cheerfulness since the emancipation, and have credited it to the negro's incapacity to meet the responsibilities of freedom. To me it seems rather an unnecessary tragedy growing out of social prejudice. It is the rebuff of his aspiration by the white man which discourages the negro to death.

The part which vice plays in the death-rate is by no means to be minimized, and it has not been either by the negro or his Northern friends. A majority of the rejections of candidates for enlistment in the army was on account of venereal diseases. Immorality is an arch enemy of the race. Nevertheless, the zeal of the moral teacher may easily overstate the fact and miss the remedy. It will not do to assume that vice is a racial trait. Perhaps, like death, it may be traced to specific causes. However ominous, it is still preventable.

Vice and the Death-rate

Now when one subtracts the deaths which are due to poverty, to bad sanitation and to preventable diseases; those which are due to social hardships which brotherliness may overcome; and those which are due to vice which the race may conquer, how much is left as a general racial residuum indicating inferior physical stamina in the negro as such?

The Racial Residuum

With respect to America as a physical environment, I believe we should admit that his deficiency is partially racial, in that the negro is only partially adapted to it. The mouth of the Mississippi is eighteen hundred miles north of the mouth of the Niger — as far as from New Orleans to Manitoba. When any people cross an ocean, even on the same isotherm, the new country puts it through a physical sifting. There are new diseases as well as new social conditions. Every migration is a selective crisis; how much more a migration accompanied by an extreme climatic change as that from Africa to America? The race as a whole has not been here long enough to complete its physical sifting. Slaves still filtered in even to the outbreak of the Civil War, and slavery, which sifted its victims barbarously along other lines, screened them somewhat from nature's stern work.[1] No people has ever been saved wholesale, and the negro cannot expect to be, especially as he expands his geographical range, as in his present rapid migrations. In the cities of the North, he is subject to a fierce climatic sifting. Thus his death-rate in Chicago and Newark is almost as bad as it is in the less sanitary Southern cities. Social causes of mortality are reenforced by geographical causes there. On the other hand, the negro already has a physical advantage in the hotter, moister, and lower parts of the South. With respect to these environments, it is the white man who is subject to a climatic sifting; and, of the two, the negro has probably the greater capacity for acclimatization. Ross thinks "lack of adaptability a handicap, which the white man must ever bear in competing with black, yellow, or brown men,"[2] and calls our race "physiologically inelastic."

Again, the sifting of the negro by his new responsibilities as freedman is equally inevitable. Brotherliness, we argue, could prevent some of the deaths from hopelessness, but no one can guarantee, nor should be led to expect, that the whole race should be able to adapt itself to the part of freemen in a strenuous civilization. Of Israel's captivity also it was written, "A remnant shall return." The conclusion would seem to be that social justice could cut down the excessive negro death-rate largely, but not entirely.

[1] See Tillinghast, The Negro in Africa and America, ch. iv.
[2] Ross, The Foundations of Sociology, p. 358.

CHRISTIAN RECONSTRUCTION IN THE SOUTH

I am afraid that social justice, which is still lacking for the poor white, will not reach the negro very soon. Assuming only a slow and gradual improvement of conditions, what do the facts suggest as to the probable future of his race in America? Do they necessarily indicate the negro's extinction here? Will justice *come too late* to save him? I do not think so. The present excessive death-rate might mean the creation of a new racial variety through natural selection and the survival of the stronger. If one alternative is extinction, another equally good is the emergence from this sifting of a better negro than the world ever saw before.[1] Why is the Anglo-Saxon stronger than other races? What is the secret of his superiority? It is that so many of his race are dead. At some time in the past, and more than once, he had a highly excessive death-rate which killed off weaklings and left a stock stronger than the original variety. We have been sifted more frequently and more sternly than any other people; consequently we, the remnant, are in some respects better than they. We could still be improved by the same grim method. Our race would be stronger if more of us were dead, but the conscience of Christendom revolts from such a policy of improvement. By sanitation, medicine, philanthropy, the moral sense insists upon keeping alive the otherwise unfit. Enough suffering remains to wring our hearts but not enough to better our stock. From the negro alone, hitherto, have been withheld the remedial resources of American civilization; consequently his is probably the only American group which is getting any constitutional good out of his tragedy. Its death-rate is actually so excessive that it may well be physically selective. Perhaps we should

Side note: The Physical Future of the Negro

[1] Giddings, Independent, February 14, 1906, p. 383.

read in its grim statistics a story of the evolution of a more resistant type which, instead of being exterminated, will help to people the nation with a posterity adapted both to our climate and to our civilization. This is at least as safe a prophecy as that of extinction. Add to this, too, that, if the white population continues to prosper more rapidly than the negro, it will continue to be more subject to the decreased birth-rate which always follows upon an advancing standard of living. With the increasing wealth of their section, Southern whites, who hitherto have had large families, will commit race suicide, — and faster than the negro does. Thus the more resistant negro of the future may for a time multiply faster than the white and his race continue to bear as large a proportion in the general population as at present. At any rate, it is the part of common justice to eliminate all preventable social factors of the negro's physical inferiority, and with faith in both races to allow Providence to provide for the future.

2. *The Negro's Precarious Economic Position*

A fair and conservative statement of the facts as statistically indicated is given by Prof. W. F. Willcox:

> In the industrial competition thus begun, the negro seems during the last decade to have slightly lost ground in most of those higher occupations in which the services are rendered largely to whites. He has gained in the two so-called learned professions of teachers and clergymen. He has gained in the two skilled occupations of miner or quarryman and iron or steel-worker. He has gained in the occupations, somewhat ill-defined so far as the degree of skill required is indicated, as sawing-mill or planing-mill em-

ployee, and nurse or midwife. He has gained in the class of servants and waiters. On the other side of the balance sheet he has lost ground in the South as a whole in the following skilled occupations: carpenter, barber, tobacco and cigar factory operative, fisherman, engineer or fireman (not locomotive), and probably blacksmith. He has lost ground also in the following industries, in which the degree of skill implied seems somewhat uncertain: laundry work, hackman or teamster, steam railroad employee, housekeeper or steward. The balance seems not favorable. It suggests that in the competition with white labor to which the negro is being subjected he has not quite held his own.[1]

The racial interpretation of these facts is that the inborn indolence of Africa sleeps in the negro's blood. Laziness is a virtue in the tropics. Nature there selects the languid to survive. The negro simply lacks the inborn impulse to work with the degree of energy which is normal for the white man. A table of economic vices and virtues may thus be drawn out as racial contrasts. The white worker is energetic; the negro lazy. The white worker is self-reliant; the negro servile. The white worker is reliable; the negro is childishly unaccountable. The white worker is thrifty; the negro utterly lacks a "compelling vision of the future." This contrast, it should be noted, incidentally takes grave liberties with the facts about Africa. That great continent does not all lie in the banana belt. It has temperate table-lands which conduce to energy and it has millions by no means living without working.[2] Prof. N. S. Shaler,

Racial Interpretation

[1] American Race Problems, pp. 493–494.
[2] See Dowd, Negro Races, ch. xxxix, for a description and comparison of the different African "zones."

A BACKGROUND FOR BLACK

Kentuckian and Harvard professor, and Judge Emory Speer, of Georgia, justify their relatively high estimate of certain American negro types on the very ground of heredity. Some, they think, are descended from superior African groups whose native environment made for vigor and foresight. It seems likely, however, that the majority of the forbears of the American negro came from less favorable parts of Africa. Following the clue of inborn laziness into the future, many reputable Southern theorists, and with them some notable Northern authorities, predict his complete economic displacement. President Alderman, following Hoffman, argues that the negro cannot long hold the land which he already owns, while Alfred Holt Stone is convinced that immigrant labor, whenever it comes, will displace him as tenant farmer in the South. The prejudice and increasing competition of organized white labor is said to narrow and threaten his hold on industry even where he has hitherto had an undisputed labor monopoly. Thus, on all sides, his outlook is dark. " Whosoever hath not, from him shall be taken away even that he hath."

We will fall back upon the racial explanation if we must; but remembering Professor Ross' warning, we would not
<small>Social Alternatives</small> be so cowardly or indolent as to resort to it before we have exhausted the meaning of more obvious causes. We must first wring from every social explanation its last drop of significance.

Since this man is dying twice as fast as we, it would be natural that the physical weakness which is killing him should make him drag before he dies. He who is about to die with a double death-rate will not be able to work with normal energy. So much is self-evident.

And whether the negro is a good worker or not, he is a

worker in larger proportion than any other race. The ratio of breadwinners among Southern negroes exceeds that among Southern whites by 15 per cent and chiefly in three classes, women, children, and old men, the excessive labor of women accounting for three-quarters of the difference. In proportion twice as many colored boys are breadwinners as white, five times as many colored girls as white, four times as many colored women as white, eight times as many colored married women as white, while 25 per cent more old negro men drag out their working lives after the years at which white men retire.

<small>Effects of Child and Mother Labor</small>

Now when such things are true, the outcome is obvious. The child laborer is one who robs his own manhood of energy. He uses up vitality now which should have been reserved to make his maturity strong. All of the sluggishness and much of the mental deficiency of the negro is due to the too heavy burdens put upon his childhood. What happens when mothers work? Their children are robbed. Unborn children come into the world weakened and continue undernourished. Both the mother who must be the breadwinner, and also feed and attend her child, and the child who is born of that working mother, will drag their ways through life. The labor of white mothers and children is recognized as a social evil which stirs the conscience and arouses sympathy. Its result are perfectly well understood. The labor of negro women and children is taken for granted as part of their divinely ordained law and the results charged to racial deficiency. The old man who drags his decaying body through the forms of work is an additional example of the negro's alleged indolence.

But the physical aspect of the case is not the chief one. The social opportunity allowed the negro has not furnished him with adequate motive to labor. Why do we, who possess normal energies, work? Because prizes are set before us. Experience, sociology, and common sense unite to declare that the real incentives to make men effective laborers are incentives of possible promotion, of social gain. A ladder is set before us and we are told that if we climb there is something for us at the top. The appeal may be to a sordid earthly ambition or to a high and noble ambition; it must be to some sort of ambition. Only for a prize set before him will a man contend with all his might.

<small>Lack of Social Incentive</small>

Why is it that the peasantry of Europe do not work as those very peasants do when they come to America? Here they receive miraculous new energy. They keep step with our best progress; their children rise to the highest places — to governorships, and seats in Congress, and the Cabinet — and why? Simply because the social system in the Old World gave the peasant no opportunity, while the New World fills him with inspiration. Now the lot of the negro in the South, as of the peasant in Europe, is one of repression through social prejudice. He is pushed on the far side of a color-line, within which there is no adequate incentive. Man does not live nor strive for bread alone. His full manhood will hear nothing less than some high calling.

To make the case specific, the most damaging complaints about the negro as a laborer relate to the plantation hand of the lower South. Why is he worse than other negroes? Because he lives under a worse economic system, a system of forced labor, while in the cities, the factories, and in the agricultural uplands the negro is under the ordinary wage system.

<small>The Case of the Plantation Negro</small>

The South declares that the negro will not work without compulsion and has shaped its policy accordingly. Isolated cases of men kept at forced labor by the bloodhound and the shotgun are of small moment compared with laws denying the fundamental principles of the relation of free labor to its employers. The proof of peonage is not a matter of convicting this or that planter, but of analyzing the economic legislation of the South. The mass of negroes there live under a system expressly devised and intended to hold them to the soil. Their debts are legally collectable through forced labor, as no poor man's debts are collected anywhere else under civilization. Running away from one's job, which in the North would be called "striking," a privilege guarded as the laborer's most essential prerogative, is in the South made a crime punishable by compulsory service.[1]

A special report on the Federal peonage investigations, made in December, 1907, by Assistant Attorney-General Russell, characterizes the legal basis of these oppressions as follows:

<small>Peonage Investigations</small>

> These state laws take various forms and are used in various ways to uphold peonage and other kinds of involuntary servitude. Some of them are vagrancy laws, some contract labor or employment laws, some fraudulent pretense or false promise laws, and there are divers others. Some few of them in question, such as absconding debtor laws, labor enticing, and board-bill laws, were not originally intended to enslave workmen, but in view of the uses to which they are put they need amendment in order that they cannot be so abused.
>
> These laws are used to threaten workmen, who,

[1] See Commons, Races and Immigrants in America, pp. 135–136.

having been defrauded into going to an employer by false reports as to the conditions of employment and the surroundings, naturally become dissatisfied. They are used before juries and the local public to hold peons up as lawbreakers and dishonest persons seeking to avoid their "just obligations," and to convince patriotic juries that the persons accused of peonage should not be convicted for enforcing, still less for threatening to enforce, the laws of their state.

Whether constitutional or unconstitutional, they should all be wiped out or amended so as to be harmless for the purpose of enslaving workmen.

In view of this report a Florida representative shrieked in Congress:

My God, what an affliction! Charles W. Russell, a Southern man and a Democrat. "It is a dirty bird which befouls its own nest."

Perhaps the Supreme Court of South Carolina is also an "affliction." It recently pronounced unconstitutional the labor contract laws of its state, declaring that the laborer cannot legally be punished for mere evasion of debt, but only if it can be proved that he entered into debt with "intent to defraud." A considerable part of the legislative session of 1908 was given to devising a new bill which should be "proof against Federal laws" and also "meet the demands of the farmers, who were considerably upset by the recent decision of Judge Brawley of said Supreme Court."[1] To this sectional attempt to secure his labor by compulsion rather than by incentive, the

[1] Columbia State, February 4, 1908.

laborer has responded exactly as he should, by poor and grudging service. Hence the economic condemnation of the plantation negro.

On the other hand, if one should actually take a poll to-day of the industrial employers of the South, they would vote in favor of the negro as the best laborer that they have, or think they could get. The negro on the farm is very widely condemned; in the industries very largely approved, as every investigation by Southerners has borne witness. Comprehensive inquiries were made in 1899, 1900, and 1901 by a leading industrial journal, *The Chattanooga Tradesman*, the results of which (as even Hoffman grudgingly admits [1]) were " on the whole favorable to the negro as an industrial worker." He adds: " The significance of it is that so many should favor the negro as an industrial worker in view of the fault that is found with him as an agricultural laborer." [2] But the employer simply declares the facts as he knows them. Mr. O. J. Hill, of the Barrel Trust, tells me that their single plant, operated exclusively by negro labor, runs more days in the year than any plant operated by white employees. I attended in Nashville the great Immigration Conference, along with six or seven Southern governors and representatives from every state and industry of that section. The burden of proof in that conference was upon the partisans of white, and especially of Italian immigrant labor as against negro labor; and the South was not convinced. A mass of testimony and the great preponderance of opinion was that the negro is the very best laborer available for the South to-day. In fact, I never before

(marginal note: Industrial Employers favor the Negro)

[1] "Race Traits and Tendencies of the American Negro," p. 278.
[2] *Ibid.*, p. 273.

found the race in danger of the woe which impends "when all men speak well of you."

Mr. A. H. Stone, the great advocate of the Italian as a substitute for the negro in agriculture, confesses that he does not expect "any sudden revolution in Southern agricultural and industrial conditions. ... Thousands, I might say hundreds of thousands, of Southern white men prefer the negro under any and all circumstances to any class of white labor."[1] But this attitude Mr. Stone thinks is mere inertia. He himself has had very poor luck with negro labor on a Mississippi plantation. It does not occur to him that the conflicting conclusions of agricultural and industrial employers may be due to the fact that negroes respond differently to a system of compulsion and a system of incentive. Yet it seems perfectly clear that wherever the black man has escaped from the old, oppressive, feudalistic system of forced labor and come under the plain and none too perfect wage-system, the result has been a quality of laborer who on the testimony of his employers is very satisfactory.

The Reason Why

Yet even in the industries much is lacking of normal incentive to the negro. He frequently re-receives unequal wage for equal work. Thus Prof. John R. Commons writes:

Incomplete Incentive in Industry

> I have made comparisons of the pay-rolls of two gas works in Southern cities — one employing negro stokers at eleven cents an hour and the other whites at twenty-two cents an hour, and both working twelve hours a day seven days a week. The negroes put in as many hours between pay-days as did the whites, and if they "laid off" after pay-day, it is no more than any class of white workmen would do after two

[1] American Race Problems, p. 175.

weeks of such exhausting work. The negro in the Southern cities can scarcely hope to rise above twelve cents an hour, and white mechanics have a way of working with negro helpers at ten cents an hour in order to lift their own wages to twenty cents an hour. White wage-earners and white employers in the South speak of the negro's efforts to get higher wages in the same words and tones as employers in the North speak of white wage-earners who have organized unions and demanded more pay. A foreman condemned his "niggers" for instability when they were leaving him at ten cents an hour for a railroad job at twelve and one-half cents an hour. Praising the Italians in comparison with the negro, he could not think of paying seventeen and one-half cents an hour for pick and shovel work, which Italians were said to be getting in another section of the state. The right to quit work is the right to get higher wages. If the higher wages are paid and proper treatment accorded, a process of natural selection ensues. The industrious and steady workmen of all races retain the jobs. The gas company referred to above, by a system of graded pay advancing with years of service, had sorted out a more steady and reliable force of negroes than they could have secured of whites at the rate of wages paid. The test is indeed a severe one where a race has always been looked upon as servile. With high wages regarded as "white man's wages," the process of individual selection does not work out, and the dominant race excuses its resort to whipping, beating, and peonage on the ground of the laziness which its methods of remuneration have not learned to counterbalance. Even the industrious Italians treated in this way would not be industrious — they would leave for other states.[1]

[1] Races and Immigrants in America, pp. 139–140.

Manifestly, then, there is a good deal to be subtracted from the negro's reputation as a poor worker before it can justly be charged to racial tendencies.

What is true of the charge of laziness is true of every other charge of economic deficiency. The negro does not The Negro not Servile tend by racial instinct to enter servile callings. Numerically speaking, the representative of the race in America is not a menial but a farmer. Its proved losses in some of the skilled trades and alleged gravitation to the lower forms of service is directly traceable to a peculiar economic situation. On the one hand, the old independent, all-round artisan, white or black, is gradually disappearing. His work is taken over by the factory and done by machinery under a minute specialization of processes. White as well as negro carpenters have decreased during the last decade. The white artisan's son, however, follows his father's job into the factory and does part of the old work there under another name. But the factory is the stronghold of organized labor, and when a negro makes the same attempt he is repulsed by the color-line in the union. This does not prove that with a fair field, as a man and a producer, he also might not have achieved his economic transformation. If he now falls back on the servile callings, it is because he is pushed down by man, not pulled down by his own nature.

Then, on the other hand, with the remarkable growth of American wealth and luxury, there has been a vast increase in the demand for personal service. Competition of the Low-grade Immigrant It is no discredit to the negro that he enters these open doors when others are shut to him. As a matter of fact, he is not entering them so fast as foreign whites are. They are actually ousting him from janitor's, bootblack's, and pedler's work.[1] Another evidence, then, of the negro's economic incapacity? Well, when immigrants come over to compete with our white labor, the cry goes up that the sacred American standard of living is attacked. It is not considered an economic virtue to be able to compete with men on a lower scale of subsistence. The displacement of successive races in the New England mills is regarded as a fall upward. But when a Mississippi planter, studying the Italian in his own land as a possible substitute for the negro on the Southern farm, reports, "Their diet was simple and inexpensive — a Southern plantation negro would scorn to accept a similar ration," [2] the negro is condemned in the next breath as lacking economic strength because they drive him from his job. So would they drive the white American were he not bulwarked by organization and public sentiment. Denied these defenses, *the skilled negro has been underlived, precisely because he had the prime economic virtue, a relatively high standard of subsistence.*

In his turning this way and that to escape his economic handicaps and to find or make a chance, the negro has exhibited a mobility and resourcefulness which completely overthrow the charge of servility. He is called a "slave to local attachments"; when he disproves it by coming to the city in increasing numbers and by scattering over the continent in search of work, he is blamed for instability and a childish taking of risks. The fact is that he has developed what all theorists hold to be another of the chief economic virtues, namely, a wide industrial outlook and a quick command

<small>Gains in Mobility</small>

---

[1] Stone, American Race Problems, p. 157.
[2] Manufacturer's Record, November 9, 1905, quoted by Stone in American Race Problems, p. 194.

of the entire country as his labor market. This new migrant habit exposes him to numerous moral dangers, but it expresses practical good sense.

In addition to this new economic mobility the great resources of group economy, previously discussed, have been most skilfully used by the negro as an escape from ruinous competition of low-standard whites. On his own side of the color-line he has proved himself capable of well-nigh limitless expansion. His dominant mood is anything but servile. Latter-day efforts at self-development even tend to be too impatient of friendly guidance. Already the outstanding characteristics of the American negro are not dependence but growing racial pride and purpose.

Growing Racial Pride

We have called mobility a virtue; yet it is just the younger generation of American city-going negroes which is credited with the most vexatious of economic vices, unreliability, and inefficiency. The experience of the North with this class tends to make it sympathetic with the South's injured, discouraging wail, "As a worker the negro is deteriorating." It is an easy, but also a cheap, explanation to ascribe this alleged tendency to malign African characteristics, the essential unaccountability of a childish race, temperamentally unfit for freedom. The South is the less to blame for such a view because it is economically provincial; it lacks experience with any other laboring class than the negro. The North, however, has only to compare him with other immigrants to discover that he exhibits identical traits with theirs. Every group undergoing violent industrial transition and newly entered upon enlarged opportunity experiences transitional maladies. They belong to the immigrant as an economic type

The Psychology of Inefficiency

whether he be white or black. The psychology of the unsatisfactory worker has been keenly analyzed by Prof. Simon N. Patten:

> It is composed of the hundreds of thousands of workers who have reached with a bound the line of full nutrition, the way having been cleared for them by the insatiable demand for men to handle the inrushing wealth of America's resources. Placed in a young, industrial civilization, their advance has been so swift and urgent that social restraints have fallen from them; they have broken old habits of fealty to bonds; they have forgotten the sympathies that made good service to employers a virtue to be sought, and they have not attained new industrial traits that make work enjoyable. They have been changed from drilled and dutiful beings to raw recruits of an economic freedom, which to them is complete because in the exercise of it they for the first time gratify their wants and keep pace with their material desires. Their employers and other observers characterize them as having an unreliable, undisciplined independence in their industrial relationships — these half-skilled mechanics, grocers, clerks, butchers, barbers, household cooks, domestics, and the rest of the army of the wasteful, ineffective, and indifferent. It is said of them that they render unsatisfactory service and shirk the equivalent of their wages because they can find new places with less effort than they can do their work in the old ones. They are generally inefficient, yet always in demand, unskilful, yet reasonably sure of employment; and thus fortified they have become the peripatetics of industry. Their obvious value to society gives them an independence which is not justified by their power of initiative, and a mobility which is without thoughtful far-seeing purpose; they have

fallen into a period of arrest because they are satisfied with a status in which their gratifications are flush with their wants. They are for the moment without motives to work well; in the first place they " owe nothing," they say, to the chance stranger who bespeaks them; and in the second, their conscious and simple needs are so amply met that reasons for working well are lacking.

Of this class was a woman who took a position as highly paid cook in a family of two. When she proved to be frankly untrained and incapable, and was taxed with false pretenses, she said with hurt dignity, " You got a pair of hands to wash some of your dishes for you, and I have seen ladies waiting a long time for that." [1]

The above-mentioned cook may well have been a negro; but Professor Patten is not thinking about negroes. He points out everywhere a class of economically disappointing laborers who have broken away from old standards and not yet become adjusted to a new freedom. This is a world problem, and the South would find such alleged " nigger " traits in any laboring race which it might import in any numbers.

The presence of hordes of negro vagrants in its streets is one of the South's chief complaints. Upon retiring from twelve years' service on the police bench of Savannah, Judge Norwood made one of the bitterest of recent attacks on the colored race. He charged that Savannah had from five to eight thousand of such vagrants, whose shiftlessness and immorality he attempted to explain by a detailed statement of the condition of the negro in Africa. Apparently he

Economic Origin of the Negro Vagrant

[1] The New Basis of Civilization, pp. 80-81.

knew more about Africa than about Savannah. Here is the third greatest seaport in the South and the world's greatest center for the shipment of naval stores. To-day it requires thousands of unskilled laborers to load and unload the cars and ships. Should one or two hundred be lacking they would be telegraphed for and brought down from Atlanta before dinner. To-morrow they will need but one half as many — for such are the irregularities of industry — and the rest must stand idle in the market-place because no man has hired them. On Sunday they will all be in the streets and alleys — the parks being closed to them — homeless, irresponsible, idle men. Compared with London dockers and Hong Kong coolies they may be quite amiable citizens, but Savannah does not know enough to compare them with their economic type. It ascribes all their shortcomings to negro blood. As a matter of fact they are a direct creation of modern industrial conditions which require an irregular supply of unskilled labor. This constitutes always and everywhere a difficult and dangerous class.

3. *The Negro's Excessive Immorality*

The facts concerning negro crime are various and perplexing. However, the more general statistics are clear enough. His prison population is two and one-half times his proportion to the general population of the nation.

In a typical Southern city, like Savannah, with a little larger negro population than white, three negroes are arrested to one white man. Vice is essentially incapable of statistical measurement. In the most reputable of Southern circles one hears the confident charge that a pure negro woman does not exist. As measured by statistics of illegitimacy, the race's sad preeminence in unchastity is undeniable. Vice and crime are alike excessive. Yet one must not immediately give them racial explanation. Is it that the negro is bestial? One cannot so conclude until he has wrung from every other explanation its least significance.

Is there any reason why a man who dies twice as fast as normal men do — a man who is a poor worker — should also be a criminal? There are at least some reasons; one is that virtue has a physical basis. He who is weak against disease is apt to be weak against temptation.

Virtue has a Physical Basis

It is well recognized that city conditions exact a moral penalty of the poor man, who is forced to herd with the bad man. Social stratification uniformly segregates the unfortunate and the evil from the good. Geographically poverty and crime are neighbors; physically they are in immediate contact, and their victims cannot help it. In many a Southern city the negro's best institutions are crowded into the same areas with the white's worst; the school is located in the same block with the brothel.

The Compulsory Herding of the Unfortunate with the Debased

Suppose one's mother locks one up in the house when she goes off to work in the morning; or suppose she leaves one to get his own breakfast and then to go to school, if he pleases and if there is a school (half of the 8000 negro school children of Savannah have neither seat, book, nor teacher, and cannot go to school if they would); or suppose one of tender years takes the only opportunity of breadwinning open to a negro boy, a menial position in a hotel, store, or office, where he sees men in their coarser, away-from-home moods; or suppose that the park is forbidden

Crime due to Neglect of Childhood

to the child at play and he is driven into the alley; what result should be expected? This is the average lot of the negro child's life. We know that to neglect his white brother is a sure means of making a criminal of him, but of the negro we think, as did the Tennessee "mammy" in a recent book by a Southern author, "Hit don't hurt niggers none to tote things too heavy for 'um." So America seems to think. It then wonders that the negro child becomes a delinquent, whom our medieval law mistakenly classes as a criminal. The explanation is clear; it is not racial, but social.

Suppose the lot of the white girl were that of the negro girl. In the first place, curiously, the race has an abnormal proportion of women. There is an especial oversupply of them in the cities, and their economic opportunities are extremely narrow. Domestic service is almost their only means of breadwinning; consequently economically, as well as socially, negro women are cheap. Social custom in the South is that a house servant shall not sleep under the same roof with her mistress. She is provided for in servants' quarters in the backyard — often over a stable. There live men and women servants without social or moral supervision. It is their parlor as well as their bedroom. What company they have they must have there. The superintendent of schools in one of the chief Southern cities, a Northern man, has told me about the tragical and unsuccessful struggle made by himself and his wife to keep their own premises from being a place of debauchery. Yet does any one suppose that the consequences would be different with any group of young people under like circumstances, especially under a common social sentiment that a woman's virtue is worthless? They would

[The Lot of the Negro Girl]

go wrong were they our own sons and daughters. Yet the negro girl is a breadwinner five times as frequently as the white girl, and these are the typical circumstances under which she must make her struggle both for self-support and for character.

The instability of the negro family, too, its excessive marital infidelity and frequent divorce, are due to specific social causes. A considerable proportion of the race is, in economic status, below the "line of family continuity," as the economist calls it. Why do better class families persist? Because of the superior virtue of their members? Only partly. The deeper explanation is that they have become established in a domestic scheme in which the prolongation of infancy compels family solidarity. Children do not become financially independent until full grown; the wife and daughters have no preparation for breadwinning; they are permanent dependents. The component parts of such a family must stick together in order to survive. Reduce its income by one-half or three-quarters and note what happens. The children are forced into breadwinning at a tender age, and income-bringing employment becomes the permanent and expected lot of mother and daughters. There can be but little home life. Day by day each member goes to his own appointed task; each as an independent worker is self-sufficient. The group has no outward compression to reenforce its inner cohesion. It is economically unstable. Consequently it frequently falls apart. All homes on this level, of whatever race, show the same weakness. The negro is no sinner above all the Galileans.

<small>The Instability of the Negro Family</small>

Savannah complains of its five to eight thousand negro "vagrants," whom we identified above as merely irregular workers, drawn together by the industrial demands of a great seaport, and showing all the marks of a well-known social type. Savannah charges them to the negro as a race. What her industry creates, her law in turn brands as criminal. To be an irregular worker — to have no permanent home or job — to have been brought down this morning from Atlanta in response to the call of a captain of industry, — to do necessary labor on terms not of your own choosing — is to be at outs with the law. Chiefly on account of this class the arrests of negroes in Savannah are nearly three times as frequent as those of whites, but two-thirds of these negro arrests are either for vagrancy, drunkenness, or disorderly conduct. All these go down in the statistical tables of the census against the race; but when the census bulletin turns to interpret its own statistics, it says explicitly that such minor offenses should not be called crimes at all. Two-thirds of the excessive negro criminality of Savannah is simply criminality by definition. The social inconvenience of Savannah on account of her negroes is due almost wholly to arbitrary, abnormal city conditions, such as crowding and the denial of parks to them, to the demands of industry for irregular workmen, and to a misunderstanding of the nature of crime. It is no just measurement of the negro as a social menace.

Creation of Criminals by Industry

Of the unequal administration of criminal law between the races, which all competent observers note, the Southern press itself sometimes testifies in moments of disgusted candor. Witness the following from the Nashville *American* of March 12, 1908:

Criminality by Administration

NEGROES AND FEE GRABBERS

Is the repeated arrest of negroes congregated around barrooms and other resorts by county officers in the interest of morality, or merely a well-defined scheme to secure fees? It strikes us many of these so-called raids are without warrant, and made for no other purpose than to line the pockets of the raiders. Worthless, idle negroes engaged in offenses against the state should be arrested, of course, but practically few arrests are made in the interest of law and order.

The fee grabber, as a matter of fact, is no better than the negro who has to pay the fee. One is as immoral as the other.

It is also said there are justices of the peace who have more interest in the fees they may secure from the arrested than in promoting law and morals.

The *American* has no patience with lawbreakers, white or black, nor has it any with the fee grabbers. It also feels that many negroes are arrested where white men equally guilty are never bothered. The fee grabbers should treat all alike, and not do a lot of raiding merely for the money there is in it.

As pastor in a border city, I had six years in which to study the relation between the city administration and the vicious element of negroes. The police studied to a nicety how much money a negro washerwoman could make, and then proceeded to arrest her husband, brother, father, son, or the man she lived with, as the case might be, just as often as she could pay their fines. Of course the men were drunken, boisterous, disorderly, but the vicious whites were not arrested in any such systematic way, and the policy pursued with the vicious negro in no sense had as its motive the protection of the community. Under the fee system the policeman who made the arrest, the police judge, his clerk, the jailer, and every other official connected with the case, got a "rake-off." It was legal grafting. The negro washerwoman washed for the city officials; they took her money under the guise of enforcement of the law. It was as regular as wash-day, as legal as the statute-book, and as damnable as any highway robbery.

William McArthur has been for many years the janitor of a white church in a former slave state. He owns a farm and city house; has a bank account, and could loan money more easily than most of the church-members he serves. His reputation for character is as good as any of theirs.

The Negro's Reaction against Racial Injustice

When, therefore, a disreputable white woman attempted to blackmail him by threatening to charge him with assault on a child, he naturally went to the church officers for advice. They believed in him as they did in each other, but put him on a midnight train for California. To his Northern pastor it was incredible that a man of his reputation should have to flee like a thief. The answer was: "This community is likely to lynch first and investigate afterwards." So McArthur went — he could afford to, — saying with pathetic humor, "I always wanted to travel West anyhow." After six months he felt safe to come back and take up his work. Not long after the community did lynch three negroes on an Easter morning. The grand jury, investigating afterward, found that two of them were certainly innocent. Only bayonets saved the negro quarter from burning. Then McArthur came to his pastor to know where under the stars and stripes a self-respecting and respected black man could buy his own vine and fig-tree, and go and sit down under them in the ordinary security of Christian civilization.

Now McArthur's character is fixed so that adversity, while it seams his brow and weights his steps, does not make a social rebel of him; but his boy, when I last saw him, was behind the bars.

Now, I charge that America did not give McArthur's boy a square deal. Of course he is a responsible soul, with heart, will, and conscience enough to make some impression on his own moral destiny. Let him bear his full share of the blame; but let us weigh this: he had felt the helplessness of the property-owning negro before the blackmailer; had seen his father a fugitive at midnight, his life hanging upon an idle word; had heard just men confess their inability to protect one in whom they had all confidence; had vainly longed for a fatherland which could guarantee somewhere a peaceful death to one who had lived in honor; had smelled the burning flesh of innocent men of his own race. Besides all this his own weakness had been trafficked in by a venal police power. Such things are not calculated to make a young negro into a model citizen. You tell me that after all the cord and the torch are rare, that statistically one is more likely to die from falling off a step-ladder at home than a negro is to be lynched. I reply that when one has once come under the shadow of such a tragedy he can never forget it. It stamps his imagination for all time and sears his soul against the social order in which it is tolerated.

How, then, shall the racial element in the negro's recorded criminality be measured? Manifestly by first subtracting that which is not racial; namely, that which is clearly due to his social handicap, proved physical weakness, neglected

How Much is Left for Racial Explanation?

child life, and the like; the criminality which is due to his moral handicap, including the physical and spiritual attacks by society on the virtue of the negro woman; the criminality which industry creates; the criminality which is such by definition only, and that which results from the unjust administration of the law against an unpopular race. When this is done there are not many facts left demanding a racial explanation. Such an explanation is not needed. To say that the negro is after all bestial by nature is gratuitous. Other factors fully account for his moral deficiency when allowed their legitimate significance.

In the destiny of the American negro one of the most crucial elements is the deep-seated determination of the American people to give a racial explanation to his deficiencies and to act accordingly. Our thought about our black fellow American is one of the cruelest of his environing facts. It can and does hold the balance of power for millions of lives and characters. The outcome hinges largely on the alternative of national justice or injustice.

Destiny of the American Negro

Already the hand writes plainly, "Thou art weighed in the balances, and art found wanting"; *but of whom primarily?* Of a nation which through blind misunderstanding does not correct the socially remediable causes of destruction in one of its weaker groups. Then, of some part of the negro population. No one can anticipate the salvation of the whole race. It is all too patent that part of it is failing daily, going to jail, losing its job, dying!

But this indicates no race tendency. The solidarity of the negro race in social destiny is neither a necessity nor a fact. Already a minority of its members are com-

pletely Americanized; they have arrived. The sifting of
the race will proceed still further, lifting some into the
emerged and conquering group and discovering to others
their "own place"; not as negroes, but as individual,
family, or group failures. Lying statistics, however,
arithmetically accurate, confuse the nation's mind by uniting in tables what are sundered in life, namely, the as-
cending and descending colored groups. At the worst
they do not apply to a large and increasing type within
the race. In the face of the facts it is sheer presumption
to prophesy the extinction of the American negro. Not
only is the chief tendency of our civilization toward the
checking of the struggle for survival as it exists on a
brute plane (if it were not so the majority of the white
race were also doomed), but the modern world ever discovers ways of utilizing a larger and larger proportion
of human material.[1] We do not follow out the law of the
destruction of the unfit to its bitter end. We do find place
for more and more people of very ordinary competency.
Besides, even with the severest sifting, some negroes would
undoubtedly survive.

What then shall be the relative proportion of the two
groups — the successes and the failures? If some are
beyond our help, others are above our harm; but for the
central mass, the five-sixths withheld as yet from their
sterner trial, the die is not cast. We shall hold their
hand as they cast it, either to help or to hinder. At the
core of the negro problem thus lies the problem of the
Anglo-Saxon; a difficulty not of the blood of Africa, but
of the spirit of America. "Lord, are there few that be
saved?" That depends upon whether those who are able

[1] See the acute application of this argument by Murphy, Basis of
Ascendency, pp. 64 ff.

to enter in by the strait gate shall widen it a little as they go through for the sake of their brothers. Let the nation do justice to the negro in those matters in which his deficiencies are remediable and then turn over to God and posterity their share of the business.

VII. TYPICAL MISSIONARY ACTIVITIES

I. SPIRIT AND POLICY

The Work of the American Missionary Association, Typical yet Unique

"THE first," said the late Dr. A. D. Mayo, "and still the most notable of the several great missionary associations for the training of the negro race in the Southern states, through schools of every grade and the ordinary methods of mission work employed by the Evangelical Protestant churches in the Northern United States, was the American Missionary Association." Its missionary activities are typical of those followed by several of the great Christian bodies of the North — Methodist Episcopal, Presbyterian, Protestant Episcopal, Baptist, and Society of Friends; but in spirit and policy its work has been unique.

Dr. Mayo continues: "Of all the mission educational enterprises of the Northern Protestant evangelical churches, the American Missionary Association seems to have borne in mind most completely the idea of working in connection with the Southern states and people in the upbuilding of the common school for the colored race. It has, more than others, discouraged the mischievous habit of engrafting the old-time parochial school on the churches that have been developed by its missionary activity. In three of these states — Virginia, Mississippi, and Georgia — at different times its larger schools have been subsidized by the state in the interest of their normal and industrial departments. It has not shown the usual desire to retain its original authority or to utilize its bounty to acquire the perpetual educational control of its schools. Four of the most important schools of the higher order with which it has been connected and which have been liberally aided by it are now entirely separated from it — Howard, Washington, D. C.; Hampton, Virginia; Berea, Kentucky; and Atlanta University, Georgia. The explanation of this may be found in the fact, already stated, that although the American Missionary Association first united with several of the evangelical Protestant churches in its work among the colored people, each of these associations in turn has preferred to separate itself from others and organize on a more decided and exclusive denominational basis, looking to the church it represents for its support and guided by the sectarian policy thereof." [1] This is to say that the Association has been a true nationalizing agency. Its work has been done, not as an adjunct to a movement of denominational extension, but in wholehearted devotion to the educational and civic uplift of the needy groups who constitute a national problem.

In policy it shows, on the other hand, a sharp contrast to the splendid group of larger schools which it has graduated into independence. It has always stood for diffusion rather than for concentration of opportunity. From the standpoint of financial support this has required courage. Experienced money-raisers testify that they can more easily secure funds for one or two big schools than for many smaller ones. Such is the tendency of present-day philanthropy. It likes great show and to settle upon large institutions: to the school that hath shall be given. The American is peculiarly under the spell of bigness. A single one of

Educational Diffusion vs. Concentration

[1] Report of Commissioner of Education, 1902, vol. i, p. 292.

TYPICAL MISSIONARY ACTIVITIES

the larger institutions of the Association might well absorb its entire current income. Such an institution would then be able to dominate the imagination of the public along with the one or two which now monopolize it.

In spite of all this the policy of diffusion is the deliberate choice. The most distinctive American school is **Need of Local Institutions of Adequate Standard** the small college, in intimate relations with its community and with a constituency chiefly local. As a type it is more widely useful than a great university ever can be. Not only is the education of the smaller school apt to be sounder and its administration invariably more economic — but it remains closer to the people. Distance itself is a selective agency. Those who go from remote states even to the great trade-schools, do not represent the average of their people. Every section, and especially the South with its backward population, needs more than anything else *local* institutions of adequate standard. Nothing can take their place.

II. STRATEGIC LOCATION

A certain prophetic foresight seems to have governed the establishment of the institutions of the Association. **Location in Line of Chief Movements of Population** The general tendencies of negro population within the last fifteen years — massing that population in the cities, North and South, and in a well-marked Black Belt stretching across the Central South from Virginia to Texas — has only emphasized its wisdom. They affect unfavorably a few small schools in the border states, but every considerable institution is either in a region overwhelmingly black, to which negro population is increasingly migrating, or in a city, with its daily enlarging need of ministry to a population undergoing an acute social transition. This may be established in detail by an examination of institutions state by state. On the whole, then, the course of events has fallen in with the foresight of the Association to put the great bulk of its work exactly where it ought to be. Such eliminations of unprofitable work as were necessary have already taken place and at little sacrifice of resources. This is in striking contrast to the case of numerous other agencies. The negro sects have too often lacked the instinct of statesmanship and failed to locate their schools with reference to the tendency of population. For sentimental reasons Berea College is now attempting the doubtful experiment of establishing a colored adjunct in a border state with a small and rapidly waning negro population. No agency has so little to correct in its strategy of education as the American Missionary Association.

III. CLASSIFICATION OF INSTITUTIONS

The diffusion of opportunity necessitates a wide variety of institutions falling under several well-marked types. An All-sided Work The work of the Association is truly all-sided, and the much debated issue of higher *vs.* industrial training is meaningless as applied to it. Its schools have not been founded on theory, but to meet specific concrete needs. They range from a three or four months' school with one teacher and twenty pupils, housed in a windowless log cabin, to the great institutions which, in promise, and even in present realization, do not disgrace the name university.

TYPICAL MISSIONARY ACTIVITIES

A. *Ungraded Schools*

Negro communities which are not furnished with even the rudiments of education are numbered by tens of thousands. What passes for a school lacks everything of educational value. The term is too brief; the teacher too ignorant, often immoral and totally unsupervised. One of these teachers taught in an entirely different district from that to which he was appointed, and explained that it was all the same so long as he was at work somewhere. The pay is often so little as to attract only the laziest and least successful; the housing conditions are unspeakably bad. A Talladega graduate taught an entire school year in a slab schoolhouse with solid blinds which were nailed shut, the authorities refusing to have them opened. In a score or more such communities the Association is touching the problem of educational uplift in its lowliest aspect. It sends an educated teacher — possibly a pastor or a pastor's wife — to supplement the public school with an additional two or four months' session, or adds a subsidy to the public funds so that a normal graduate can afford the place. Its loaves and fishes are not miraculously multiplied — and what are these among so many? The appeal of hundreds of similar places must annually be denied because it is more strategic to supply fewer communities more adequately. The policy of diffusion is already stretched to its utmost limit. Rudimentary education is essentially the business of the state, and to it the state stands committed. But the Association does all its work under a vivid sense of the need of these scattered communities, and of nothing is it prouder than of this feeblest aspect of its work.

[Sidenotes: Defects of Negro Rural Public Schools; Supplementary Work of the Association]

CHRISTIAN RECONSTRUCTION IN THE SOUTH

On what basis are these few ungraded schools selected and located? Almost invariably because a graduate of a more adequate school has gone to teach in a needy community and has been able to raise its people to help themselves — the Association merely coming in to supplement local initiative. Here is a concrete case. In southwestern Georgia, near to the Florida line and fourteen miles from a railroad, is a negro community called Beachtown. Few white natives live within a radius of ten miles, but much of the magnificent pine land has been bought up by Northern millionaires for winter homes and game preserves. The rest is mainly occupied and owned by negroes. A little group of crossroad stores constitutes the geographical hub of the community. Its energy and enterprise largely center around a remarkable trio of mulatto half-brothers whose fathers were leading white citizens of the old régime. They own the store which was the center of the old-time life, from the block in front of which hundreds of negroes were sold as slaves. One of them was once a student in Atlanta University. Yet the richest man in the community is an illiterate black negro who slaved his large family unsparingly until he now owns some hundreds of acres, but has lately come around to appreciate education for his younger children.

A Typical Case: Beachtown

Indeed it was the sight of their children growing up with so few privileges that roused these men to revolt from the dominance of an illiterate, grossly sectarian, and evil ministry, and to seek worthy leadership and adequate school facilities. So they sent for a Yale-trained preacher from the county-seat, and appealed to the Association which had been the help of their people so many times of old. They

How the Community Helped Itself

TYPICAL MISSIONARY ACTIVITIES

were told to furnish the building and a teacher would be sent. They managed to erect a rough structure on a foundation of posts, and partly to side and ceil it. Its windows were low and narrow, giving very poor light. There was no flue, and it was seated with almost impossible home-made desks — but it measured their ability to help themselves. A teacher was sent for. She had gone from her country home to Allen Normal School and later to Fisk University, but she had not been educated out of sympathy with her own region and her own people. Now she came back to them. She was janitor, Sunday-school superintendent, and moral leader of the community, as well as teacher. She fought bravely against overwork and ill-health. Into her rented house she gathered half a dozen girls from " further back " — girls whose communities had no school at all. Her pupils came to be too many. Then the community built a little addition to the schoolhouse — I found it in use without door or sash or interior siding. Again the Association came to the rescue with a promise to pay a second teacher's salary if the people would complete the building.[1] Thus our formula of Christian philanthropy is applied: an unprivileged community struggling for opportunity is made the neighbor of the more favored parts of the country through a nationalizing agency. The most impressive point to the story is the struggle of that community to help itself. There are thousands of other communities equally worthy waiting the outreaching of some helping hand.

Applying the Formula of Christian Philanthropy

[1] Still later the Slater Board added a third salary for an industrial teacher.

B. *Graded Elementary Schools*

Next in order comes a group of well-conducted graded elementary schools with good buildings and an average of five teachers each. They are located in the country or on the outskirts of small towns. Some have boarding departments accommodating from twenty to fifty students coming from a somewhat wide area. Others are purely local in influence. Each one, besides the immediate service to its community, has a worthy record of preparing and sending out pupils for more advanced training.

Trinity School, at Athens, Alabama, belongs to the first generation of American Missionary Association institu-
A Historic School tions founded during the Civil War. It began its work behind the bayonets of Federal troops for the refugees who flocked from up and down the Tennessee valley. One describes its early work as follows:

> A gaunt old house with wide-open cracks, through which pea-shooters and pop-guns were often introduced to the great discomfort both of teachers and pupils. In this building Miss Wells and two other women taught day and night school for a long time. Cannot you picture that night school; that frail, alert little woman surrounded by a sea of black faces, the man in the linen ulster, the seven boys who had one pair of presentable trousers between them, and so came to school turn and turn about, the old aunties in homespun, the girls in missus' cast-off finery? Learning to read was a task then, I can tell you, with any odd leaf for a book and a candle end between two for a light. But they came, day in, night out, and many of them learned to read " de bressed Book," and received enough to be willing to go

TYPICAL MISSIONARY ACTIVITIES

through fire and water, if only their children could get all which could be given them.

Athens now is a prosperous county-seat. Its people are building modern houses. The artisans are skilled negroes. It is pushing macadamized roads out into the country in all directions. It has some pretensions as an educational center, boasting of its girls', its boys', and its negro " colleges." But its white children, even, have never had a *free* public school; little chance, then, for its black children. Through all these years it is Trinity which has made them what they are. Practically the whole negro population can read and write. It has a number of prosperous business men, and has developed a pride in and sense of responsibility for its school which the Association has had abundant opportunity to prove. A year or two ago the old school building burned. When the fire broke out a small colored girl was buying a pair of doll's shoes in a near-by store. Catching up her nickel and crying, " I doan' want no doll shoes," she rushed out and gave the first money toward the rebuilding of the school, to which the negro community contributed in all considerably over $1000. The old location was abandoned, and the school rebuilt on the site and within the earthworks of an old Federal fort, which once defended and still commands the town. In a single year more than thirty negro homes were built around the school, many of them being neat and comfortable cottages. The white community showed its recognition of the work by a vote of $100 from the city council as well as by offerings in the churches. Now a commodious brick building stands within the fringe of trees which marks the outline of the old fortress; there Trinity still holds the fort.

<small>Holding the Fort</small>

The greatest need of the negro is frequently not found in the Black Belt where he outnumbers the white population and by sheer force of numbers demands recognition and a share in the educational provision of the state. It is often found among the sparser population of the Piedmont region, especially where the burden of the illiterate whites is great, as in the mill towns; or in decaying communities. Such a one is Hillsboro, one of the ancient capitals of North Carolina. It has a few hundred humble negro citizens who share the fortunes of a once aristocratic but now crumbling town. King George III gave the clock in the court-house, and Lord Cornwallis laid the rough pavement in front of the Inn. These are the last public improvements that Hillsboro has had. One of the very few Southerners I ever met who did not brag of his section was a man who was attempting to start a mill in the face of Hillsboro conservatism.

Where Negroes are Few

On the outskirts of the village stands a neat two-room schoolhouse with tower and bell. It is well equipped within with blackboards and maps and other school facilities. In it the Association has carried on for a hundred negro children of Hillsboro a better school than its white children have had for many, many years. The two teachers live snugly in an ancient brick house which is the headquarters of the higher life of the negro community. Their missionary work is of the old-fashioned but never-worn-out personal sort. They go out into the homes and share the joy and sorrow, the sickness and health of the people. They teach the mothers and gather in the young people. They have a little night class for young men ambitious for more education. They put moral character and Northern energy into the negro churches. There is nothing better

TYPICAL MISSIONARY ACTIVITIES

than work of this character done simply but effectively in the places of actual need. The South as represented in Hillsboro cannot begin to meet the problem of its poor white population. Here at least is missionary ground.

But after all the most frequent spots of need and helplessness are in the Black Belts. Such a one I found in Cotton Valley, in the same county with Tuskegee in central Alabama. I had been to Tuskegee the previous day and had driven from the junction to the Institute over a hard, sandy road on which the wheels made scarcely a mark. Cotton Valley was only ten miles distant, yet the four-mile journey from the railroad to the school was over unspeakable roads with mud to the hubs. At Tuskegee I saw the greatest single institution developed by negro energy; from the school at Cotton Valley I could not see a single farm owned by a negro. Hardly one of the fathers of the some two hundred and fifty pupils was known to have title to enough ground in which to bury him.[1] The explanation of the sharp contrast lies in the difference between sand and mud. Mr. Washington was able to acquire a great domain for his school because the land was originally of little agricultural value. The negroes of Cotton Valley have been unable to break away from the tenant system because their famous cotton crops have made the price of land impossibly high. Frequently the richer the soil the more tenacious the owner, the more grasping the money-lender; consequently the poorer the negro. The school has discovered striking exceptions, but I never saw more serf-like human beings

Where Negroes are Many

---

[1] Since this statement was written five families have begun to purchase little farms. This was made possible by the subdivision of small plantations. It was undertaken as a direct result of the leadership of the school, whose teacher made the business arrangements.

than the stolid groups of tenants gathered at the railway station and the rude country store.

The country store merits a second look, for it is the hub of the whole scheme of existence in which the negro finds himself, as Mr. Baker graphically explains:

> Many negro families possess practically nothing of their own, save their ragged clothing, and a few dollars' worth of household furniture, cooking utensils, and a gun. The landlord must therefore supply them not only with enough to live on while they are making their crop, but with the entire farming outfit. Let us say that a negro comes in November to rent a one-mule farm from the landlord for the coming year.
> "What have you got?" asks the landlord.
> "Not'ing, boss," he is quite likely to say.
> The "boss" furnishes him with a cabin to live in — which goes with the land rented — a mule, a plow, possibly a one-horse wagon, and a few tools. He is often given a few dollars in cash near Christmas time which (ordinarily) he immediately spends — wastes. He is then allowed to draw upon the plantation supply store a regular amount of corn to feed his mule, and meat, bread, and tobacco, and some clothing for his family. The cost of the entire outfit and supplies for a year is in the neighborhood of $300, upon which the tenant pays interest at from 10 to 30 per cent, from the time of signing the contract in November, although most of the supplies are not taken out until the next summer. Besides this interest the planter also makes a large profit on all the groceries and other necessaries furnished by his supply store. Having made his contract the negro goes to work with his whole family and keeps at it until the next fall when the cotton is all picked and ginned.

TRANSPORTATION, LIBERTY CO., GA.

HOMES IN THE LAND OF MUD-DAUB

TYPICAL MISSIONARY ACTIVITIES

Then he comes in for his "settlement" — a great time of the year.[1]

Now the actual goodness or badness of any human institution depends upon the character of the men who operate it. But some institutions give greater opportunity for good or evil, and the tenant system of the South under which the ignorant and friendless negro is practically and legally at the mercy of the white landlord, certainly gives the maximum opportunity for evil. Wherever I have inquired in twelve states, I have been frankly told that a considerable number of planters and money-sharks live by "skinning the nigger." I witnessed the signing of a belated contract between Jim Freeman and his landlord. Jim's worldly wealth consisted in "one blind mule named Nell," a few rude tools (the Department of Agriculture estimates the negro tenant's farm implements as worth $7.50 on the average), and a huddle of household goods which lay on the depot platform in the February rain. His human resources were five cotton hands, himself, a wife, a half-grown son, and two small daughters. It was plainly to his immediate advantage to get even a leaky cabin as a refuge from the rain, and a peck of meal for his children's supper, but I wish I had been certain that his accounts would be honestly kept by the merchant, his cotton honestly weighed, and his share at the end of the year proportioned to his toil; for however inefficient a man, it is always pertinent to ask whether he gets a just equivalent for what he actually does.

From its beginning, twenty years ago, the school at Cotton Valley has been in charge of a remarkable series of colored women as principals and teachers. They have had

[1] Baker, Following the Color-Line, pp. 74–75.

CHRISTIAN RECONSTRUCTION IN THE SOUTH

the genius for making much of little, a native faculty for business and an instinct for neatness and order. One sees this in the clean, well-kept look of the place, with its trim buildings, its newly swept yard and whitewashed fences. The nails still hold in the rude beams of the old, one-room cabin where the first teacher hung a curtain partitioning off her sleeping corner from the family with nine boys, thereby bringing the first dawn of a better womanhood to Cotton Valley. Efficiency and earnestness made a good school even when it was lodged in a little cluster of now disused cabins. I found a good school when the five teachers had but three class rooms between them and had to keep double recitations in process. Only just now has the Association been able to add two rooms to the building, and still the pupils average nearly fifty to a room. February being the birth month of certain great Americans, the teacher had the school review what it had learned on the subject. All remembered that Lincoln was born on the 12th. "Now, children, what happened on the 22d?" Inspired by the presence of company, Johnnie spoke up loud and clear, "He done riz on the 22d." Tuition is ten cents a month in the upper grades and Amelia's mother sent but five. Teacher said, "Tell your mother she must send five cents more tuition." Next morning the mother appeared demanding explanation. "Teacher, I doan' un'erstan' 'bout this yere ishun. I dun sen' one ishun; now you wan' *two* ishun."

A Humble History

The teacher's home near by the school is the pride of the Valley as its only two-story building, but its occupants find it a snug fit. Only by evolutions of military precision is the household able to gather round the dining-room table, and once placed one cannot move until all the rest do. There is a built-in sideboard,

Making Much out of Little

TYPICAL MISSIONARY ACTIVITIES

the work of a lady teacher whose father was an old-time mechanic. She also laid the front walk out of fragments of brick. In one of the dark and sagging old cabins she is pluckily trying to teach girls to make their own clothes. This touches the final need of Cotton Valley, — a small building and equipment for the teaching of industries — cooking and sewing for girls, simple farm mechanics for boys, and elementary agriculture for both. Then this fairly typical country graded school will have comprehended its ideal.

C. *Secondary Schools in Cities*

This comprises another distinct group of institutions. Their nomenclature is somewhat disguising. They are generally called normal schools or institutes. The plain word for them is that all are more or less satisfactory city high schools, doing solid work with somewhat limited curricula.

The boundary between elementary and secondary education is conventional, but is commonly located after the seventh or eighth school year. A fourth of the so-called white high schools of the South count the seventh year as belonging to secondary rank. Thus, not infrequently, the negro high school supported by the Association is found to be higher in grade and superior in equipment to the corresponding white school of its city. In fact, the work of several of them is as advanced and as worthy as that of many " colleges " in this section.

Almost all this group of schools have retained a part at least of the elementary course. This is necessitated by the

<small>Turning Elementary Education over to the South</small> generally poor preparation for secondary work furnished by the inefficient and crude negro public schools, which frequently do not include even a full elementary course. The

flourishing city of Macon, Georgia, for example, carries its negro children only through the sixth year. This compels the Ballard Normal School to furnish two seventh and two eighth grades in order to supply the hordes of applicants. Sometimes the elementary grades are perpetuated as a model school for the training of practise teachers. The general tendency, however, is to be aggressively insistent that the prosperous and growing cities of the South shall furnish the elementary education for all their children to which they are theoretically committed. Consequently, the lower grades are now being progressively abandoned in six of the leading schools of the Association. Such movements are frequently resisted by negro communities which prefer the sympathizing and generally superior instruction of the mission school to the lax officialism and neglect of the public authorities. They plead for the continuance of primary instruction on the ground that otherwise their children will get poor teaching in unsanitary buildings,— often on immoral streets. Yet experience has shown that this very attitude of distrust and disregard for the public schools on the part of the negro is frequently the excuse of the white authorities for not improving them. Negro public opinion has weight, and when it persistently demands its educational rights and recognizes the obligation to cooperate with public authority it often meets surprisingly cordial response in the ready betterment of elementary educational facilities.

But with the higher schools the case is quite different. The idea that it is the duty of the state to furnish free secondary schooling for anybody is imperfectly rooted in the South. The more conservative cities have but recently opened public high schools even for whites. There is not only no sense of obli-

Lack of Public High Schools

TYPICAL MISSIONARY ACTIVITIES

gation to do a like thing for negro youth, but on the whole a general agreement that all the negro is entitled to is five, six, or at best eight years of elementary training. This attitude of mind forgets that every citizen of a democratic state has a righteous claim to all the opportunity publicly provided for any. It also forgets the rapidly increasing differentiation of negro society and the diffusion of its members through all the occupations and callings of our modern civilization. In every Southern city there is a considerable negro minority which has fairly earned the right to high-school training for its children — by dignity of character, personal culture, wealth, and social attainment. The South — with some exception in the border states — disdains their aspirations and there are no signs that its attitude will speedily change. Except for the inadequate and grudging support of a few public institutions for the training of negro teachers, the whole field of secondary education is left to philanthropy and the negro's private efforts.

Take Savannah, for example, a typical Southern city, with a population of 33,000 whites and 39,000 negroes. Its negro school population is 8023 and its enrolment 2591 (or less than one-third); if every existing school, public and private, were crowded to the doors, fully one-half of Savannah's negro children would have neither book, desk, nor teacher. This in itself justifies Beach Institute. The situation loudly demands the help of the mission school, at least in its elementary grades. But what of the high school? Does the negro community need or merit it?

I went with the principal to find out what the constituency would contribute to add an eleventh grade and departments of manual training and domestic science to its work. First we called on the typical Southern gentleman — socially classified as negro — who holds the best federal office in Georgia — Colonel Deveaux, Collector of the Port. Before I knew the South, I supposed the appointment of negroes to such positions was mere politics; I now see that it is the appropriate recognition of the substantial achievement of the race and its considerable part in the development of its section. Savannah growls that the President sets a negro over its commerce, but it has itself set a colored doctor over a more important matter — the health of a whole district of its people. We visited him in his office and heard about the awful but slowly decreasing negro death-rate and the struggle of sanitary science with ignorance and vice for the life of children.

The chief negro commercial enterprises of Savannah are in the neighborhood of the Union Depot. Here we visited the bank, the newspaper offices, stores. The bank is a comparatively young institution for which the color-line is directly responsible. Jim Crow methods arrived slowly in this conservative city. When, however, it came to pass that a negro with money to deposit found that he had to go to a separate teller's window he decided to bank with his own race. In connection with the bank is a flourishing building and loan association which has enabled a hundred patrons to pay out on their homes and will help hundreds more. I found the newspaper — an influential race organ throughout the state — just moving into larger quarters, from a building where it had been continuously published for more than twenty-five years. Skilled negro mechanics were installing the improved presses. (There are seven negro trade-unions — the bricklayers, carpenters, coopers, building laborers, lathers, pattern-turners, besides colored members in other unions.) They can buy

TYPICAL MISSIONARY ACTIVITIES

their groceries at a negro store which for equipment and stock ranks with the better establishments of the city. Across the street from the bank, I was shown a row of houses acquired by a colored postal clerk through shrewd real estate investment. Every tourist makes an extensive acquaintance with the hackmen of Savannah. I found that many of them make a very good living showing the sights of one of the South's most attractive cities and that the negro boycott of the street cars — after their "Jim Crowing" two years ago — helped many of these Jehu's over into the ranks of the comfortable and property-owning. I visited two of the four negro public schools, and later met a group of the colored leaders of the city — many of them graduates of Beach — and most of them members of the two churches, Episcopal and Congregational, which have attracted the more intelligent classes. In each of these churches the service is habitually as decorous and restrained as in the middle-class white churches of the North. Their ministers are scholarly men of Northern theological education, respected throughout the city for character and trusted as conservative race leaders. Other denominations are much stronger, some of their churches dating back over a century; and several have pastors of distinct power in the pulpit. Recently an interdenominational Men's Sunday Club has been organized to minister to the social needs of the race on a somewhat broader basis than that of ordinary Y. M. C. A. work. A group of well-educated and successful physicians has been active with the pastors and educators of this movement. I met also a highly respected negro lawyer and got glimpses of more than one home of taste, culture, and all the true graces of life.

Now the facts are that if white Savannah should suffer

the fate of Sennacherib's army some night, black Savannah would wake up to carry on the entire business of modern city civilization with scarcely a jar. Yet the Savannah negro is comparatively backward in developing separate institutions. The relations of the races have been relatively

INSTITUTIONS HAVING AN ENROLMENT OF MORE THAN SIXTY IN SECONDARY GRADES	INSTRUCTORS IN SECONDARY GRADES EXCLUSIVELY	DEPARTMENT INSTRUCTORS GIVING PARTIAL TIME	ENROLMENT ABOVE EIGHTH GRADE	GRADUATES, 1908	VOLUMES IN LIBRARY	VALUE OF BUILDINGS AND EQUIPMENT
Ballard, Macon, Ga.	5	3	174	20	3000	$40,000
Avery, Charleston, S. C.	5	2	174	27	800	20,000
Le Moyne, Memphis, Tenn.	6	4	164	21	3500	60,000
Tillotson, Austin, Texas	4	5	102	3	2000	52,000
Straight, New Orleans, La.	5	7	65	13	2000	150,000
Beach, Savannah, Ga.	3	4	63	20	200	10,000

kindly; consequently the negro has not been forced upon his own resources as in dozens of more strenuous communities. But this is clear: there is a negro group there which has every right to a high school for its children that any American group has. They are not going into kitchens and the fields for the same reason that the white children of white " upper classes " are not; their economic status does not require it nor should it lead any one to expect it. I personally believe that it is not well for the nation to give any portion of its youth a merely academic and socially

TYPICAL MISSIONARY ACTIVITIES

ornamental education; consequently I am proud that the Beach Aid Association, organized by representatives of the groups I have just described, has made possible the addition of manual training and domestic science to the curriculum of the school. The equipment for these departments was secured partly by direct appropriations from negro trade-union treasuries.

The foregoing table indicates the scope and development of some of the larger city schools of the Association.

From such fully manned and equipped institutions, schools of this group grade down to those with twenty or thirty pupils, two teachers and only two years of secondary work. The teachers, however, are almost invariably college or normal school graduates, and the work, up to the measure of its facilities, acceptably fulfils standard requirements.

Ministering as they chiefly do to that part of the negro population which has arrived at a large measure of participation in American civilization, the educational problems of these schools are not peculiarly racial but are those common to the high-school situation throughout the nation.

Problems of City Secondary Schools not Racial

Beyond question they are serious enough; but they are being worked out along the most hopeful lines of modern progress, including enriched courses of study, increasing provision for specialization, laboratory methods in science, and the inclusion of commercial studies, together with generous provision for instruction in household and manual training. In many respects they are rapidly becoming model high schools.

D. *Rural Secondary Schools*

The most striking contrast between this group of schools and the one last considered is that between the boarding and

The Advantage of the Rural School the day school. A few of the city schools have boarding departments but these are proportionately small and invariably dominated by the ideals and relations of the day school. The institution gets its tone and character from the five or six hours of schoolroom discipline. The rural secondary schools on the contrary are permanent communities, often remote from towns. Within them all the activities of life go on, and the work of education is a matter of twenty-four hours in a day and seven days in a week. Consequently their opportunity both for educational impress and for the forming of character is infinitely greater. Their human material is less select, coming as it does directly from the woods and fields, and their scholastic results are hampered by the poverty of the students, most of whom are engaged in the struggle for a livelihood practically throughout their school years, and are consequently distracted in mind and irregular in attendance. Their secondary departments are all small and do not so generally reach standard results. Nevertheless their advanced work is genuine and its ideals give character to this whole type of institution.

It is characteristic of these schools not only to be located in the country but largely to get their support from the land. **The Most Economical and Effective Schools in America** They are typically farm schools in which a large majority of pupils support themselves in part or in whole by productive labor in connection with the institution. This necessitates farm-buildings, animals, and implements, the raising of produce for the feeding of the school, a wide range of practical activities involving business and administrative ability, and much industrial and domestic training, each theoretical stage of which finds an immediate practical application in the day's work. The narrow gap between what the pupil can earn for himself and the cost of his rigidly economical schooling is bridged by scholarship funds distributed in small amounts to a large number of pupils. This union of productive labor and education within the strong discipline and personal influences of a moderately sized institution, constitutes probably the most economical and effective type of education in America. Gradually the more promising group of these institutions are being developed into distinctly agricultural high schools, their aim being to add the education of insight for the few to the education of good habits for the many and to be centers of leadership and inspiration along all lines of rural betterment. For the training of farmers especially the opportunity of these schools is unrivaled. The prosperity of the South depends upon a great extension of diversified agriculture and a diffusion of the leaven of improved farm methods from many centers.

Unrivaled Opportunity of the Small Agricultural High Schools

The boy who leaves his community to attend a far-distant school all too frequently never returns. These modest rural high schools give him a rarely practical farm training without divorcing him from his native soil, and at a minimum of expense. I am positively convinced that in all lines of industrial training except specialized trades courses, the work of these smaller schools, which bring opportunity home to the masses, is more efficient, more in line with a sound social policy and more serviceable to the negro race than that of the great mass schools which so dominate the public imagination. The practical operations of a large group of such institutions — the building and repairing of their plants, the development and management of their farms, the running of their engines, the shoeing of their mules, the sharpening of their tools — train more practical mechanics than Hampton and Tuskegee have ever done. An acre which must supply to-morrow's pork and greens has more educational virtue in it than a play garden and a show farm. How little need of indirect educational devices when the situation itself constitutes an almost ideal opportunity for vitally practical training!

A typical school of this group is Dorchester Academy, located among the swamps of Liberty County, Georgia, about thirty miles south of Savannah. This county was originally settled by Massachusetts Puritans who established there one of the most famous and efficient communities in Georgia. Their great plantations were formerly chiefly given to the culture of rice. Now the region is almost wholly in the hands of negroes who are for the most part property owners. Out of this new material on old Congregational foundations the rebuilding of the commonwealth is going on.

A Typical School: Dorchester Academy

Every family in the present Congregational church owns its property and their case is general throughout the region. The holdings vary from five to three hundred acres, averaging perhaps fifteen. The rice industry was in economic collapse long before Sherman came that way and burned the plantation houses. Thus it happened that after the war the practically abandoned lands were easily acquired by the negroes. They are worth now from $5 to $10 per acre. Rice, cane, and corn are raised, but merely for home consumption and to be bartered by basketfuls for clothing and luxuries (tobacco, snuff, and canned goods) at the village store. Except for a few shapeless marsh cattle driven to the Savannah market

Old Medway Church   Threshing Implements of African Pattern

THE ENVIRONMENT OF DORCHESTER ACADEMY

TYPICAL MISSIONARY ACTIVITIES

and some scattering bales of cotton, the country sends nothing out into the world. The trucking industry has just begun, but with reasonable development it might make the region rich. From November to March the farmer expects to eke out a living by cutting wood for railroad ties, at which in good times he makes excellent wages. Crop mortgages are unknown and long-time credit is rare. Bills are paid monthly or oftener. Thus the Liberty County negro, however poor, is relatively independent with his little farm, his store of rice and grit and meat, his ox to drive and his supplementary cash wage; and his wife and daughter, though still to a considerable extent doing rough field labor, have more time for home-making than in the cotton-raising regions.

The poorer homes are sagging log huts, with mud-daubed chimneys, windowless and almost floorless. Sometimes they are without a table or chair, their only beds ragged blankets on the floor and their meals always eaten from the skillet; their children nameless savages, half-clothed and scarcely above jungle conditions. The best home, Isaac Morrison's, would be counted a comfortable ten-room farmhouse in New York or Illinois. Morrison has three hundred acres and above sixty head of cattle. These "rough it" for nine months in the year, and are fattened for three on wild hay and rice straw; they then bring about $15 per head in Savannah. He has his own cane-mill and reducing plant — a great iron kettle set in a mud furnace with mud chimney. He raises about fifteen acres of rice and ten of cotton, yielding half a bale per acre in good years. He has three horses and is well supplied with razor-back hogs and poultry. His outbuildings are well constructed; he has pine-thatched shelters for his cattle. In his well-kept gardens are turnips, cabbages, and fruit. He has had fourteen children, two of whom are dead, three married, and four now teaching country schools. His prosperity is due to the fact that he worked them all desperately hard. Yet with the mission school at their door, they got something of an education. Now Isaac rents out much of his land and hires less prosperous neighbors to do his work.

These are the extremes. As I rode through the country in the springtime and noted the homes I saw not less than two-score newly built houses within a radius of a dozen miles. These invariably were of frame and clapboards instead of logs, and had brick chimneys. The tough clay which made this region so long the characteristic land of mud-daub is now being turned at a near-by plant into a fine quality of roofing tile, and one frequently sees the anomaly of houses worth scarcely a hundred dollars with roofs which would grace a million dollar cathedral.

It is interesting to find under such an up-to-date roof domestic utensils of purely African pattern. Rice is threshed in a wooden mortar reminiscent of the jungle and winnowed by being thrown in the air and caught in broad " fanners " or baskets of rice straw.

In the outlying coast communities, where the influence of the mission schools has not been present, primitive traits tend to appear, especially in social and religious life. The coast swamp negro has many local dialects in which corrupted African words are alleged to survive. Sectarian church organizations are said to be declining in favor of the local lodges or burial and relief societies. This is undoubtedly a reversion from a higher to a more primitive type of social organization. The country is dotted over with the halls of such societies, whose thatched feasting

TYPICAL MISSIONARY ACTIVITIES

sheds attest the essentially sensuous character of primitive religions, out of which the negro is struggling. I recall a weird night meeting in such a hall; a gigantic lodge-leader, plainly a witch-doctor in thin disguise, standing before an enormous fireplace, whose lurid flames made mysterious shadows creep up and down the unhewn rafters of the cavernous room; a half hundred worshipers crouching in semi-darkness relieved only by the flashing of fanatical eyes; the alternate wildness and plaintive passion of prayer and song, till the mood of spiritual burden passed and the meeting resolved into a rhythmic dance of relief and joy, from which fleshly impulses were not entirely absent.

A few years ago, indeed, not far from here, a horrible revival of phallic worship broke out and was with difficulty suppressed by the authorities. It all bore the Christian name, and the scientific no less than the sympathetic observer would concede its profound religiousness and potential social power. We were all digged from this same pit and under the cruder emotions our boasted veneer of civilization dissolves into the primitive. If the Georgia coast negro puts rice into the grave for ghosts to eat, we put flowers there — for ghosts to smell! Each of us has forgotten why our ancestors taught us these ways. The negro is only a little nearer the savage. Yet when, as in the black counties and under the increasing tendency of race segregation, American civilization has deserted him, his gains hang in a trembling balance. We need all the resources of civilization to keep us up to our standard of life. He needs them to keep him up to and raise him above his.

The Dorchester Academy has about forty acres of land, some two hundred and fifty pupils, a dozen teachers, and a very good equipment of buildings. There is an excellent eight-room schoolhouse, a large girls' dormitory, and a church ministered to by a colored pastor. It has a boys' dormitory, a two-story woodworking shop, a small blacksmith shop, a bricklaying shed, a modest printing-office, a gasoline engine and wood-saw, and a well-equipped laundry, besides a barn with stock and farm implements, and a magnificent flowing well, furnishing ample water supply. There are special teachers for agriculture, farm mechanics, domestic science, sewing, and dressmaking. Only twenty-three pupils are in the secondary grades, but the work which they do is sufficient and worthy. This description, with greater or less variation, would fit Gloucester School, Cappahosic, Virginia; Lincoln Academy, Kings Mountain, North Carolina; Brewer Normal School, Greenwood, South Carolina; Fessenden Academy, Fessenden, Florida; and Lincoln Normal, Marion, Alabama. The presence of schools of this type is significantly lacking in the states of Mississippi, Arkansas, and Louisiana. Yet of the fifty-five counties in America with a negro population of over 75 per cent, thirty-four are in these very states. This is the most notable gap in the Association's system of schools, and the lack of other opportunities for the overwhelming black masses of the lower Mississippi valley make it the more unfortunate. If I had $150,000 for negro education, I would first of all found an agricultural high school in one of the blackest counties in each of these three states.

Primary Grade, Andersonville, Ga.

Graduating Class, Straight University, New Orleans

VIII. TYPICAL MISSIONARY ACTIVITIES (*continued*)

CLASSIFICATION OF INSTITUTIONS

E. *Girls' Seminaries*

THIS is an interesting and significant variation from the prevailing types of schools. The American Missionary Association has few such institutions, but it has been a favorite type with several of the Northern denominations.

The considerations which have led to the establishment of girls' seminaries are chiefly three. They are, in the *Why Special Schools for Negro Girls* first place, in line with the Southern educational tradition which the more select groups of negroes inherit. Coeducation in the South was a Northern innovation, which on the whole has justified itself as the prevailing policy of the negro school; but the more careful parents, especially those having some social pretensions, frequently demanded separate schools for the training of their daughters. Beyond this there is very real and urgent motive in the moral peril of cultured negro girls at the hands, primarily, of white men, but also from men of their own race. The more refined and ladylike the girl, the more constant and insidious is the attack. No social tradition protects her virtue; no social obloquy punishes its despoiler. This is the chief tragedy of the race situation. Now, however great the peril, it must be met on the whole by the strengthening of character — not by isolation and the erection of arbitrary safeguards. Yet there are numerous specific cases where considerations of moral safety make the policy of separate schools for girls wise. The strangest aspect of the situation is that not infrequently these schools are chiefly filled by the daughters of white men. The banker, the postmaster, and the leading merchant frequently show both a sense of responsibility and parental regard for the children of their illegitimate black families. Almost any one of our institutions could tell a series of curious and thrilling tales on this point. Conscience frequently tries to square itself by giving the daughter a protection which the mother did not have. Finally, girls' schools have been found to furnish the most simple and natural conditions for the training of home-makers. Not excessive laboratory methods remote from the actual conditions of housekeeping, but the daily round of duties in a family of moderate size gives the most practical training in the domestic arts. The Association has always given such training a large place in the education of the negro girl.

Its ulterior object has not been that which chiefly commends domestic training to the unthinking, the prepara-

Training the Mothers of the Race

tion, namely, of household servants. It is the negro home which has been primarily in view — the preparation of the girl for wifehood and motherhood. The deepest need of the race has been here, a need compared with which the preparation of cooks and domestics is insignificant. The moral peril of domestic service compared with that of other callings open to women is a commonplace of sociological knowledge, and is made tenfold more deadly by the prevailing attitude of the South toward the negro women, which we have just discussed. The hesitancy of some of our schools to send out carefully trained girls to almost certain insult and danger will at least be understood. At the same time

TYPICAL MISSIONARY ACTIVITIES

it is recognized that a poor race must learn to endure the moral risks involved in making a living, and it has been inculcated both by precept and example that efficient domestic service is honorable. The girls' schools have sent out a due proportion of competent servants and consequently have been especially favored by Southern communities.

Each of these considerations was consciously present in the establishment of Allen Normal School at Thomasville, Georgia. Shamed by the incendiary destruction of the Association's school in a neighboring town, a group of the leading citizens of Thomasville invited it to their community. They gave it both welcome and substantial financial support. Accordingly, in the founding of the school, the prevailing Southern idea of separate education for girls was followed. The institution was deliberately located apart from the negro quarters where a little school had previously been maintained, and sought privacy on a considerable tract of land in the outskirts of the city. Around it there developed a distinctly residential district for negroes, a region of neatly painted cottages, of well-kept fences, and flower gardens. The whole result was just such a select school as one might wish for his own daughter. Besides these provisions for protection and intensive Christian education, facilities were definitely planned for training in the household arts. Full realization of the ideal, however, was long delayed for lack of means. Besides the dormitory building there was but a two-room schoolhouse, housing four grades. The rest of the work of the school had to go on in the dormitory. This meant the invasion of children, noise, dust, and germs. The upper classes had to recite in teachers' bedrooms. The much

A Typical School: Allen Normal

desired systematic training, both in practise teaching and in household science was well-nigh impossible. But now, at length, a new schoolhouse has just been erected, and teachers are under appointment not only for sewing and domestic science instruction, but also for practical gardening and fruit growing. Thus a fine, wholesome, well-ordered institution is at length able to realize its ideal.

There would be many more such institutions but for the fact that they are disproportionately expensive. It costs more relatively to run a small school than a large one. The ideal of intensive culture in a closely associated Christian household does not permit of an institution of economical size. The Association is committed to the policy of the diffusion of opportunity, hence cannot emphasize the more expensive types of schools. Yet no one can learn the life of a seminary for negro girls without profoundly wishing that its type might increase. Nowhere does gracious and effective womanhood have more immediate and potent influence over earnest and receptive youth, and the results show in the aspirations and successful struggle of many a negro girl, — one of those future mothers of the race who are the source of all purity and all defilement.

Why not more of this Type?

F. *Colleges and Universities*

The negro higher institution is chiefly something else. With the possible exception of Howard University at Washington (a school subsidized by the Federal government), there is no one of them which has not the bulk of its resources, the majority of its teaching force, and the larger proportion of its plant engaged in work which does not

The Negro "College" chiefly Non-collegiate

TYPICAL MISSIONARY ACTIVITIES

go beyond secondary grade. The following table states the case for representative institutions in 1908:

NAME	ENROLMENT	COLLEGE STUDENTS
Fisk	571	124
Talladega	631	29
Atlanta	339	51
Tougaloo	500	6
Howard	1000	75 / 190[1]

This showing is wholly creditable to them, for it proves that, whatever their intentions, in actual practise they have served conditions rather than theories. They have turned their faces "home to the instant need of things," and have undertaken the work most fundamental for the race. If, however, undeceived by names and titles, one studies this group of institutions in its concrete variety, he will discover it to be a unique and vital part of American education.

The older of the negro colleges, established soon after the war, were invariably the offspring of Northern philan-

Ideal and   thropy under Christian impulse, and are still

History   chiefly supported and controlled by boards of trust representing the great denominations. From the very beginning these Boards have frequently included representative white Southerners and sometimes associated them with negroes as fellow trustees. Some of this group

[1] In teachers' professional course of collegiate rank.

have come to be independent of the agencies which founded them and others are on the way toward it. Later, the rising tide of negro race-consciousness brought into being other institutions ambitious to attain college rank. As a group they have been narrowly sectarian, miserably equipped, and of low educational standard, yet some of them have made real progress and are yet to be counted among the genuinely higher institutions. They have shared the ideals, at least, of the older group.

Starting with the purpose of demonstrating to the world the intellectual capacity of the negro race, the higher institutions have all found their chief motive in the conviction that the strategy of race development demands the preparation of disciplined leaders. To this end most of them originally had to begin with the primary school; yet the end was never forgotten, and by virtue of it — in spite of their continued occupation with elementary and secondary education — they are not unworthy to be reckoned as colleges in the making.

In external equipment the better negro colleges equal many well-known and representative Western institutions.

Equipment Fisk, for example, has a $100,000 dormitory sung into existence by the world-tours of her famous Jubilee singers. A visit to the American Missionary Association colleges would discover a notable group of chapel buildings, architecturally impressive and equipped with all the accessories of dignified religious services, including excellent pipe-organs, the one at Talladega being the gift of alumni. I recall a good many classrooms better lighted and furnished than some in which I have sat at old Harvard. Mr. Carnegie's inclusive beneficence has given numerous artistic and modern libraries to negro institutions. Facilities for adequate science work have been

SWAYNE HALL, TALLADEGA COLLEGE   CHASE HALL, FISK UNIVERSITY

JUBILEE HALL, FISK UNIVERSITY   DeFOREST CHAPEL, TALLADEGA COLLEGE

STRIEBY HALL, TOUGALOO UNIVERSITY   BEARD HALL, TOUGALOO UNIVERSITY

TYPICAL MISSIONARY ACTIVITIES

somewhat lacking, but in its new Chase Hall, Fisk has a science building which for architecture and equipment would be envied by the average college. One of the characteristic buildings of Northern institutions is notably lacking, namely, the gymnasium. But in lieu of that the negro college is likely to have industrial shops and farmlands, which some will think a profitable exchange. Atlanta University has a splendid model school building — the gift of George Foster Peabody — and other schools have less pretentious special quarters for the training of teachers. Talladega College, located in the country, has a plant worth $250,000, while that of Fisk, by reason of its greater urban values, is estimated at some half a million.

In the forty years and more of their history no negro college has been able to acquire even a fraction of the Endowment and Support necessary endowment for its support. Every one must annually beg the greater portion of its running expenses. In other words, the utmost that Northern philanthropy has done has not been sufficient to put a single school upon its feet. Talladega leads with an endowment of some $160,000, Atlanta reports $72,000, and Fisk about $70,000. The preoccupation of philanthropy in recent years with industrial education has made the financial problem of the college well-nigh desperate. Tuitions are but one-third or one-half those charged by the more modest Northern schools. The Missionary Board remains the chief source of supply.

The older and better known negro colleges, especially those controlled from the North, draw students from very Constituency wide areas. A surprising number of Northern negroes prefer the fellowship of their own race to the educational privileges of the famous institutions open to them at their own doors. The systematic provision of opportunities for students to support themselves, in part by manual labor, and the development of student aid funds have made it possible for these schools to be attended by young people from all social classes. At the same time, the opportunities of higher education are in their very nature selective, and the negro college student, like the white, is doubtless above the average of his people in natural capacity. Probably there is a disproportionate number of mulattoes among them. The colleges, though young, tend to develop distinctive characteristics, as do all vital institutions. The familiar visitor soon learns to sense the institutional tone and atmosphere. Sometimes it tends toward social exclusiveness and educational display; sometimes toward solid results. But probably from no group of American colleges are the regrettable features so largely absent.

Christian education as interpreted by the able and devoted men and women who set the standard and gave the tone to the better negro colleges, meant thoroughgoing and effective moral control. Discipline is therefore a sterner reality in these schools than in the average American college. The going and coming of students is under strict limitations. The oversight of girls is especially conscientious and watchful. Because the negro as a race is unused to the strain of prolonged intellectual labor and also because many students are so poor as to be underfed, the care of health becomes a peculiarly insistent problem, and instruction in personal hygiene a fundamental part of college education. From the earliest times it has been a tradition that every student should give at least an hour of manual labor in addition to all other payments toward the cost of his education. This takes the form of dining-room and dormitory work

Discipline

TYPICAL MISSIONARY ACTIVITIES

for girls and industrial and agricultural work for boys, while a few of both sexes are employed in clerical capacities. The strict regimentation of negro college life impresses every observer. Yet its grounds are only partly racial. It is chiefly not because the students are negroes but because they are mostly in elementary and secondary grades. I question whether the negro student of collegiate development requires especial severity of discipline.

College life from the student standpoint has many features in common with those of typical institutions. We
Student Life have noted the unique insistence on manual labor. Naturally the constituency of the negro college is poorer than that of the average American school. This means a larger proportion of students who are working their way. There is probably, therefore, less surplus energy to be worked off by student devices. Social functions, however, are frequent and varied. A careful and rational control of the relations of the sexes is always maintained. While coeducation is the rule a few of the higher institutions have departed from it. Athletics are moderately developed and the "big" football game between negro universities has most of the marks of similar occasions in the North. The culture agencies of college life are frequently superior. Lectures and literary societies flourish. Musical organizations have a unique place and get magnificent results from the negro's rare gifts in this direction. "If you were a negro," wrote an enthusiastic visitor, "your college songs would be written by a real poet, their music composed by a genius and sung by a highly trained student body whose rendering would do credit to the Handel and Haydn Club." The student press has an extensive development made possible by the frequent presence of printing as part of the industrial curriculum.

One familiar phase of white student life is almost totally absent in the negro colleges, namely, the playing of lawless and destructive pranks. Perhaps it would be equally so from the Northern college if the student knew that his exploits would be rewarded with lynching rather than laughter.

The educational standards of the negro colleges are high rather than broad. Most of them have narrow and traditional curricula, and probably not one absolutely reaches the standard of either the Northern or Southern college associations as to entrance requirements, teaching force exclusively given to college instruction, or developed course of study. This is simply the story of the American college in its beginning in all sections. The negro institutions have had a rare measure of that splendid personality and teaching ability which supplies a genuinely higher education in schools of small resources. Much of the work attempted has been of superior quality. Colleges no better developed have educated the majority of eminent Americans. I happen to have gone immediately from a chair of psychology in a reputable Western college to the inspection of negro college work. I found standard texts in use. I heard classes and sometimes set examination questions. The results were up to the average of student attainment as I know it in the white schools, and in individual cases were truly remarkable. Graduates of these colleges have now for many years gone in considerable numbers to the great Northern universities for advanced work. The representative Fisk and Talladega graduate can make the junior year in Yale or the senior year in representative colleges of the Middle States. The notable careers of exceptional negroes in some of the most famous seats of American

Educational Standard and Achievement

TYPICAL MISSIONARY ACTIVITIES

learning are a splendid revelation of the capacity of picked men of that race in competition with picked men of ours. Nor is it always the extraordinary negro who comes North. Oberlin has seen a full seventh of her students black. The average negro is an average student in the lines of his reasonable preparation. For the more accurate scientific work and for technical courses his schools have not hitherto been able to fit him.

The checking of Northern beneficence toward the negro college is resulting in their rigorous sifting. The future will show its results in two directions: first, in the acceptance of the secondary rôle by many ambitious schools which it is neither strategic nor economical to develop as colleges. Precisely this thing is taking place among the white schools of the South, and is being practised by the American Missionary Association toward its higher institutions. Second, in the achievement of real university standards and breadth along distinct lines by a small group of the best schools. The faith of their founders providentially wrote charters calling for many-sided institutions. The needs of the race have required broad foundations, and splendid superstructures will yet be built. Fisk, Atlanta, Talladega, Tougaloo and others will be able to raise their many departments of specialized instruction to the highest grade and will thus justify the name university.

Future of the Negro College

G. *Specialized Instruction*

Specialization in the negro college has not been able to wait upon theoretically complete preparation in its students. The manifold practical needs of the race have been too urgent. They have compelled the use of imperfectly trained leaders. Technical and professional courses, therefore, have been generally parallel to or assimilated with secondary and college studies.

Theological. — Some of the most splendid and consecrated personalities ever engaged in negro education — including a heroic group of Southern men — have given themselves to the task of training ministers; and with notable results. Probably a greater proportion of negroes of first-class ability have gone into the ministry during the last generation than of whites. I can recall recitations of negro classes in systematic theology and in modern social problems which compared favorably with those of Northern seminaries. A large proportion of the students, however, are mature men — working pastors who recognize their own deficiencies and are seeking to remedy them. Their efforts by no means merit contempt. A goodly proportion of students are training for missionary service in Africa, for the redeeming of the mother continent is a growing aspiration of the American negro and is one of his unique spiritual assets. Instruction is directly adapted to racial needs. Teaching of Hebrew and Greek is the exception. The core of theological training consists in study of the English Bible and practical methods of religious work. The exceptional student who needs more can generally be helped on to a Northern divinity school. The theological departments of the American Missionary Association have always been recognized as entirely non-sectarian; and however intense the denominational feeling of the negro churches, they have recognized the superior training of the Association's schools, and have been willing to trust their religious breadth. For example, take the history of the Talladega Theological Seminary: It has graduated and sent into the ministry sixty-five men. Of this number one-fourth have served or are serving other than Congregational peoples; five as pastors of Baptist churches, two as presidents of Baptist colleges, six in the Methodist communion — one being dean of a theological seminary, and another trustee of a college, while three became Presbyterian pastors. Sixteen students were enrolled in the Seminary during the year just closed. Of this number one-fourth were pastors of local Methodist and Baptist churches, fitting themselves for better service in their congregations. And none are more emphatic in their commendation of the work of the Seminary than these men. Indeed many representative men of these dominant negro churches have had their training in it.

Pedagogical. — The majority of secondary institutions for negroes offer their graduates special work in preparation for teachers' examinations. Only a few of the better schools, however, have made a real beginning in the direction of advanced professional courses. The presence of elementary schools in most of them affords opportunity for active apprenticeship. The plan most in vogue is to follow a three years' general secondary course with two years of intensive study of teaching methods and school administration, including a large amount of practise teaching. Howard University has a still more elaborate and extensive course.

Domestic Science Training. — Beyond the required daily household service from all women students in connection with school dormitories and boarding departments, there has recently been an extensive introduction of facilities for a more scientific study of home-making in all its aspects. Many domestic science laboratories have been furnished. Model homes, for which completely equipped buildings have been provided, are a distinctive feature of this training in several of the American Missionary Association schools. In them senior girls in all courses are given a finishing-off in housework and management just before their final going out into active life. Under careful supervision they keep house for themselves for a series of weeks, each doing in turn the whole round of necessary work from scrubbing and laundering to planning for and presiding as hostess at a course dinner.

Nursing. — In connection with the larger schools daily health inspections by regular officers and school hospitals for the care of the sick have been provided. The practical work of these has been expanded into a number of incipient professional courses for nurses. This profession furnishes one of the best opportunities to the negro self-supporting woman, the trained colored nurse having almost an unlimited field among the white people of the South. The best of these courses are approximating their standards to those of similar ones in the North, and extensive hospital practise is in some cases possible. Talladega College has been able to unite with the community in the establishment of a hospital receiving both students and out-patients, an ample building for which is in process of erection.

Trades Instruction. — Missionary schools in the main have sharply differentiated themselves from those giving trades-instruction. They have insisted upon the necessity of general intelligence to make special skill practically effective, and have devised their industrial work as a part of general education rather than as trades-apprenticeship, with immediate view to a livelihood. Many of the trades have indeed been in actual operation in connection with the building up and care of the plants of the larger institutions and hundreds of students have thereby been enabled to work their way through school. A few missionary

COTTON PICKING ON SCHOOL FARM
Brewer Normal School, Greenwood, S. C.

FOOTBALL TEAM
Burrell Normal Institute, Florence, Ala.

schools which have large industrial equipment, like Tougaloo University and the J. K. Brick School, North Carolina, have allowed a small number of pupils annually to take a minimum of academic work and to specialize through a series of years in a trade, receiving a diploma when it has been satisfactorily mastered. Courses in dressmaking, millinery, cooking, blacksmithing, carpentry, brickmasonry, and stationary engineering have thus been provided. In almost every school the various lines of repair are assigned to students who are working for their education and who in time become practically expert along various lines. In the forty or fifty such institutions of the American Missionary Association hundreds of students are thus receiving actual training in the trades. Thus a system of apprenticeship has grown up, antedating and still rivaling the work of Hampton and Tuskegee.

Agricultural. — The Federal government will not draw the color-line in education. The Southern states, therefore, in order to receive national appropriations for white agricultural colleges, have had to establish parallel institutions for negroes. Aiming as these do at agricultural training without thought for general culture, their constituencies have naturally been very crude; their equipments have been meager as well and the grade of work correspondingly low. Yet if the destiny of the negro is to be worked out close to the soil, there is critical need of a trained rural leadership, such as the state schools do not give. The following from the Tougaloo University catalogue indicates the range of such practical training in a well-equipped school:

> The attention paid to agriculture has been increased. Practical farm operations have been steadily carried on. The plantation now produces nearly all

the meat, milk, and vegetables for the boarding department, which averages over two hundred, besides what is shipped to market. Eighty to a hundred cattle, seventy to eighty sheep, about the same number of swine, are yearly raised, the animals all being of good breeds. About a thousand bushels of sweet potatoes, the same of corn, one hundred tons of hay, cane enough for many barrels of molasses, made on the place in the open kettle fashion, cotton enough to show what can be done by intensive methods in producing two or more bales to the acre, are yearly raised. Several acres of strawberries, two hundred apple and two thousand peach trees provide fruit for table use, preserving, and shipping. Students do the work and the practical experience is of the highest value. Besides this field work there is school-room work in agriculture, by a special instructor, in the last grammar and first normal classes, and to special students in the higher grades. Lectures are also given regularly to all the grades.

The central idea is that of uniting culture and high ideals of life with special skill for the betterment of rural conditions. Fisk has been a pioneer in the introduction of agricultural courses of college rank into its curriculum and Talladega is following with the appointment of a professor of scientific agriculture.

Productive Scholarship.—A small but creditable amount of original work of genuine scientific merit has been done in a few institutions — notably in negro history and sociology at Atlanta University under Dr. DuBois, and in negro music at Fisk; while a large and distinguished group of negro professors has contributed to the scholarly as well as to the popular discussion of the race problem in many aspects.

TYPICAL MISSIONARY ACTIVITIES

IV. THE OUTREACH OF THE MISSION SCHOOLS

No mission school is merely a school; all are definitely intended centers of uplifting influence upon their communities. The policy of the diffusion of the educational opportunity means also the multiplication of such centers of moral life. The American Missionary Association schools constitute social settlements for some sixty negro communities. No concentration of equipment and endowment upon great mass schools can match this wealth of social ministration.

In its least developed form, the mission school has a definitely parochial idea; that is to say, it has felt bound to try to improve its environment. The monthly report of each teacher has for forty years asked, "How many calls have you made on pupils?" "What community enterprises have you participated in?" Classroom relations have been regarded merely as the beginning of missionary service. Thus one of the most exploited ideas of a sociologizing age, "the school a social center," is an original and long-practised principle of the negro schools. The relations between them and the home have been most intimate. At their beginning, especially, many adults were enrolled as primary pupils and the grown-up negro has not felt aloof from the school as the average citizen does. His habit of clinging to his white folks has made the ties more binding. Thus mothers' meetings, sewing classes, talks on sanitation and care of children, besides manifold religious activities are among the earliest commonplaces of missionary method; and, however innocent of all pretensions, they have been carried on with sure common sense and an instinct for practical

Parochial Responsibility and Work

results which have been an immeasurable tonic to the negro race.

In an earlier chapter was noted one of the two vast movements of negro population, namely, that from country to city. The city negro is a new thing under the sun. Africa had no cities, nor had the old South. Such aggregation of population as it had, lacked completely the characteristics of modern urban life. Five-sixths of this population is still rural, more people being gathered in the cities of Massachusetts alone than in the whole South. Yet nowhere is the movement cityward more rapid or the social changes involved therein more critical; and especially for the negro. All this means that the missionary institutions must adapt new methods to meet the demands of the changing situation.

The Adaptation of the Mission School to Urban Problems

Some of them have attacked the problems of recreation and amusement. The playground is recognized by modern education as one of the most fundamental aspects of the school. President Roosevelt told the recent Mothers' Congress, " A school without a playground is no school," and Dr. Woods Hutchinson said to the National Playground Association, " If you must omit either the schoolhouse or the playground, omit the schoolhouse." Now no one realized forty years ago how marvelous the growth of Southern cities would be. The Association had no money to buy much ground and now that real estate is high and the vacant lots are built upon, our pupils are forced to play in the alleys and streets; and the case is desperate. Almost without exception our city schools are calling for play-places.

Recreation and Amusement

Why do not the children play in the parks? Does any one think that they are equally available for negro and

TYPICAL MISSIONARY ACTIVITIES

Southern Parks closed to the Negro — white; that the negro boy can play in the streets as the white boy can; that a group of colored young people can frequent a park for pleasure, or a gang of negro workmen rest there in the shade; that a black mother can take her child to a park for respite from the August heat? I do not know of a city in the South where this would be allowed. As cities have grown, have robbed childhood of its play space, and shut man out of immediate contact with nature, there has been practically no provision made for the negro of the substitutes which the city must furnish or else turn innocent and righteous instincts into vicious and criminal channels. Memphis has a negro reputed to be a millionaire, but he cannot use as a citizen a park which his taxes help to sustain. It has a beautiful tract of some two hundred acres of unimproved park, well out on the edge of the city, but we could not get permission to use it for an afternoon picnic for our Le Moyne school, even under most careful supervision. I have repeatedly urged city teachers to pay more attention to nature study. "Tell us where we will be allowed to take the children," they have invariably responded.

Athletics have never held a very important place in the missionary scheme of education. Recently, however, some of our younger university men in principalships have begun to develop interest in scholastic games, arguing that city conditions make them necessary, and that their interest tends to hold boys in the school to the completion of their courses.

Athletics

The negro's pitiable lack of wholesome entertainment has also appealed to the schools. True, in large cities they are coming to have race theaters, the influence of which is by no means altogether ill. Yet

Entertainments

no one can follow the year's entertainment course at such a school as Avery Institute, Charleston, or Straight University, New Orleans, or Le Moyne Institute, Memphis, without realizing the superiority both of their musical and dramatic occasions.

Every student of sociology is familiar with populations which have plenty yet starve from general underfeeding.

Health The negro does not always have enough of any sort of food and a study of his dietaries proves that he rarely has enough of the right kind. Much of the irritability and criminal tendency of city populations is directly traceable to this fact. Several of our schools, therefore, have attacked the problem of the noon lunch. If you are a negro, you know, your mother is out at work and cannot get dinner for you; she went early and had not time to put up your lunch in the morning; so you have been in the habit of going to the grocery-store or to a cheap restaurant, where you have paid more than you ought for things that are not good for you. Some of our principals have realized this and have tried to meet the situation. Generally the work is planned and sometimes it is done by the department of Domestic Science. A wholesome soup or stew is sold for five cents, and perhaps an appetizing dessert such as black children like. They sit down at decent tables and learn some of the proprieties of life while eating proper food under school supervision. So the noon hour passes without the demoralization of children running the streets, and the school shows its adaptability to the new demand of the city.

Few of our city schoolhouses close their doors when the children go home at dusk. Not only are there night schools for backward adults, for mechanics and seamstresses, or for teachers preparing for examinations, but frequently

College Choir, Fisk University

College Y. M. C. A., Fisk University

TYPICAL MISSIONARY ACTIVITIES

community libraries and reading-rooms are provided. The most extensive enterprise of this sort is the Crossett Library in connection with the Le Moyne Institute, Memphis, Tennessee. This is the branch public library for colored people supported by public funds and supervised by the regular library commission. In many other ways Le Moyne, though a missionary institution, has grown to hold a place in popular esteem as a semi-public enterprise. The colored teacher's examinations are usually held there, and for forty years it has been the recognized fitting school for the teachers of Memphis and the whole surrounding region.

Educational Extension Work

Beyond all such enterprises conducted by the schools they have a large place as civic centers for manifold community activities. Almost all non-sectarian and non-political gatherings for race betterment meet in their auditoriums. Sometimes a glee club or orchestra or labor-union or any other of the dozen organizations is housed there. In a number of interesting cases the promising interracial conferences which took place throughout the South following the Atlanta riot found their natural meeting place on the neutral ground of the mission school platform. In brief, they tend to centralize the higher life of the whole negro community about them.

The Mission Schools as Civic Centers

With equal definiteness the rural schools have reached out and met the larger problems of their constituents. Their most effective method has been fair and helpful dealings with their own tenants, for the Association is an agricultural landlord in eight or ten states as well as a producer on at least two-score farms.

Such rural work is carried on most extensively by the Joseph K. Brick School at Enfield, North Carolina. On

The Rural Social Settlement

its educational side this institution is a secondary school like those described in a previous section, but its equipment is immensely superior, consisting of half a dozen brick school and dormitory buildings, with shops, stock, and machinery all on a magnificent domain of 1129 acres of level bottom land. No other negro farm school has so much fertile soil and few have so good a plant.

There are seven families on the estate besides two grown sons living at home who rent land independently, fifteen acres each. The farms average thirty to forty-five acres to a family, or about ten acres per working member, and are rented generally for a specified number of pounds of lint cotton. No mortgage is given and instead of the endless verbiage of Southern crop lien contracts, there is a simple agreement of twelve lines requiring that no part of the crop be removed until the rent is paid, and plainly stipulating the amount of rent in cash or produce and the repairs or other betterments to be allowed the tenants. The most significant clause is as follows: "I also agree that there shall be no use of intoxicating liquor except for medical purposes, prescribed by a physician, in the house in which I reside, or upon the lands which I rent, and no violation of morality injurious to the farm, and no conduct which is not in harmony with the teaching of the school." Naturally this acts as a selective influence and with the fair treatment and excellent school privileges secures a superior class of tenants. Six of the seven families have been on the place from six to ten years each. Each is furnished with a clean, well whitewashed, four-room cabin which, compared with the average farm habitation, is clearly entitled to be called a model tenement. The Brick School tenants (though by no means

The Brick School Tenants

TYPICAL MISSIONARY ACTIVITIES

equally reliable and free from vice) are without exception deacons in Baptist churches. At present they furnish an aggregate of twenty children to the school.

Number 1, for example, has been but two years on the place. He drinks and has no credit, consequently is not allowed to go in debt at the store. He could only pay half of his rent in 1907. He has no stock save a mortgaged horse, and his expenditures are disproportionate to the size of his family. His is decidedly the poorest record. Yet the school does not despair of him. It has taken poor material and made men of it.

Number 2 has been on the school-farm eight years. There are three working members in his family. He paid his rent in full and had $200 cash surplus in 1907. His advances at the store average $350 per year. Though somewhat in debt he owns a horse, a buggy, a mule and wagon, a cow, and some poultry. His agricultural habits and methods leave much to be desired, for his grown son, a graduate of the school, raises four times as much cotton on fifteen acres as his father does on thirty and borrows money at the bank at 6 per cent, while the father still pays from 12 per cent to 20 per cent to the merchants.

Number 3, a widow with two sons of laboring age, had $250 surplus last year and is probably out of debt. She owns a horse, cow, buggy, wagon, and poultry and lives industriously and comfortably on thirty acres of land.

Number 4 has a working family of six. He drinks and only just about came out even last year. He is perhaps $200 in debt now, but has more stock than most of his neighbors; namely, two horses, three cows, hogs and poultry, besides a buggy and wagon. He has been nine years on the place.

Number 5 has a family of seven working members. He

was $10 short on his rent last year, but this was due to serious sickness. He is probably not in debt. He has fewer possessions than the average man, but lives with corresponding economy.

Number 6 has been eight years with the school and is easily the star tenant. Last year it took only half of his cotton to pay his rent. He is out of debt and has extra credit. He owns three horses, three head of cattle, hogs, and thirty chickens which yielded him two hundred dozen eggs last year. His son is studying architecture at Cornell University.

Number 7 is a tenant of ten years' standing who has educated his children and now has a crop of grandchildren in the school. There are now six working hands. He had fourteen hundred pounds of cotton after paying last year's rent and is even at the store. He has no vices and though he lives closely, his large family of the third generation keeps him poor. He has a horse, three cattle, hogs, poultry, and a buggy. An unmarried son who rents independently owns a three-hundred-dollar horse.

It is interesting to note how these more than average tenants used their surplus last year. Number 2 bought a mule and buggy. Number 3 traded for a better horse and got a new buggy and furniture. He had also to pay a large doctor's bill. The model tenant, Number 7, made a small payment on the eighty-acre farm but could not resist the temptation to buy an extra horse and new buggy. Perhaps the conditions of tenancy here are too ideal to excite ambition for landownership. Nevertheless the lesson has not remained unlearned, as an individual case testifies.

When the school began, twelve years ago, Mr. Hilliard Phillips lived about twelve miles away on a farm rented on the "mortgage system," and lived otherwise as the mass of negroes are living in rural districts. He had the usual number of poor dogs and ignorant children. He worked hard and spent much for tobacco, snuff, and dram. He did not see how he could spare the money to send even one child to school. I reasoned with him that if he would quit his habits we would take his girl in school for what his tobacco, snuff, and dram cost him, amounting to four dollars a month. We allowed the girl to work out the other four. She came to school that one year, where she learned to cook all the necessary foods for the home family. She attended school five or six years in all. She is now one of the best teachers in the county. She is a fine seamstress and a good housekeeper. Mr. Phillips has bought and paid for one hundred and three acres of land near our school. He has built a four-roomed cottage on it for himself, and two other cottages adjoining his for his two married sons. He mortgages nothing, but pays cash for what he wants, and can get money from the bank. He raises his own feed and table vegetables. He has the best house and the best farm of his community, cleaner premises and cleaner crops. Whatever he is to-day he attributes to the influence of the school. I might name any number of old and young men who live on their own places as the result of this school. Families which once lived in filth and crime now live in clean quarters and in healthful conditions. Better schoolhouses, better churches, better homes, good gardens, and clean community life. Good pictures have taken the place of whisky and tobacco advertisements. Sunday-schools, literary societies, farmers' meetings, and reading circles have supplanted Sunday baseball, chicken fights, and neighborhood dances. In nearly all the homes there are Bibles, in about all are Christian papers, in very many of them are found the Woman's Home Journal and The Woman's Companion.

I had the privilege of attending the Annual Farmers' Day at Brick School one Washington's birthday. The gathering was mostly of tenants and neighbors, parents of pupils, with some well-wishers from the village and from greater distances. There were morning and evening sessions with a barbecue and picnic between. There were four invited speakers, two white men, an expert from the State Agricultural department and a visiting minister, and two negroes, a professor and a lawyer. The expert preached the gospel of diversified farming, of green-manuring and deep plowing. He explained the bacteriology of the soil and praised the peanut as an article of diet. He especially advised attention to forage crops and the development of stock-raising in the South. The professor spoke of the negro's superior advantages in the country; warned against the evils of city life, and exhorted parents to make the rural home more attractive. The lawyer dealt with the crop mortgage system. Mortgages, he said, were not an evil but an advantage to the borrower and lender. They were intended to be kept and should therefore be understood. The negro should know both his obligations and his rights and insist on the latter. He must have education enough to figure his own bills and decline to pay illegal rates of interest on advances. The minister talked about the farmer's life from the side of expenditures, health, and amusement. Education and character, he said, are more important than lands and goods and no people ought to be satisfied with mere material prosperity. Each speaker was repeatedly interrupted with eager and intelligent questions. An open

A "Farmers' Day" Gathering

TYPICAL MISSIONARY ACTIVITIES

parliament followed at which successful farmers told their vicissitudes and triumphs. All questions showed the genuine and practical influence of previous farmers' conferences and for the first time the old plantation owner, who had had some of these men and many of their fathers as his slaves, came to compare his farming experience with theirs as freedmen. These are typical examples of the influence proceeding from every mission school, constituting a vast outreach for the well-being of the most representative negro — the farmer.

Every practical effort for the freedman from the beginning has had to face the staggering fact of his poverty.
Philanthropy Not only is the whole fabric of missionary education a philanthropy which has cost millions — but the annual conduct of every school involves innumerable individual cases of the assistance or relief of the poor. Its methods range from the sale of old clothing from barrels from the North (a ministry not to be despised since it annually involves goods worth tens of thousands of dollars in the aggregate) to far-reaching land-acquirement schemes, combining philanthropy and five per cent.

The policy of the Association has been to confine its activities primarily to school and church work. Incidentally, however, it has founded, fostered, or sympathized with almost every form of organized charitable service. Its institutions have never been called homes or orphanages, but have annually performed the functions of both. Every school grants free tuition in special cases and carries a minority of free pupils from year to year — some of them from infancy to independence. I happened to be at our Marion, Alabama, school one day, when the principal received an early morning gift of three homeless children; a man brought them in a mule-cart, said they were for the school and departed. This is no rare experience. Many teachers have undertaken the rearing of abandoned children — sometimes legally adopting them. Probably the Girls' Industrial School at Moorhead, Mississippi, is carrying this phase of service further than any other school at present. Its recent new dining-hall has a large ward on the second floor as a dormitory for small girls. Here some forty are cared for by a motherly colored woman. By no means all of its pupils belong to the needy class but some are orphans, others motherless, and more fatherless. They are sent from as far as California, to share with children from along the bayous of the delta, children from the sawmill quarters, illegitimate children of Greenwood or Indianola merchants and children of prosperous, aspiring Tougaloo graduates, " the pure atmosphere of a happy, Christian home. The law of kindness and obedience is the natural law in this, to them, charmed spot. Orderly habits, pure language, the daily devotion, grace at each meal, the study of the Bible, the weekly prayer-meeting, the large, enthusiastic Sunday-school, the gospel service of song have an indescribable power." Thus, as always, the outreach of the mission school is also an upreach which tries to teach the little child why the cup of cold water is given him and in what Name, that he, himself, may become a giver as well as a receiver.

IX. PROBLEMS AND PROGRAMS OF NEGRO EDUCATION

PROBABLY more Americans hold cherished opinions upon negro education than upon the education of their own children. The average parent is blissfully unconscious that the whole educational field bristles with interrogation points, yet he is very likely a partisan on race training. Ask the principal of a New England academy or Middle West high school whether his institution is solving the social problem in its own community. He will look blank and reply that it never professed anything of the sort, and he is too busy teaching school to think about it. Then he will turn and express grave doubt whether negro education is solving the race problem. Only in this case is the nation conscious of the close relation between schooling and statesmanship. Thus it does negro education the honor of applying to it more than ordinarily exacting standards.

<small>Wide-spread Partisanship on Negro Education</small>

And this is well for negro education, which already need not be ashamed of any competitive showing. In working out through conflict its own program it has done some pioneer thinking for the whole nation. Both the experimental and the logical foundations of the most significant of present educational movements — that of incorporating industrial education into our common school system — go back to Hampton. Armstrong is positively the

<small>Its Pioneer Service to Education at Large</small>

nation's most original educational genius. Popular ability to appreciate current discussions of educational statesmanship is the product of debates about how to train colored youths.

It is well, too, that much be required of the school; then perhaps much will be given to it. Only by ceasing to be mere school-teaching and undertaking definitely to meet social aims, can education get proper regard from popular judgment. Let other schools meet the same test. Judge them by their success in solving their peculiar social problems; then frankly admit that it is the business of negro education to be the most influential single factor in assimilating to our national civilization the largest and most deficient group of incomplete Americans. This is why it is important and why its claim upon patriotic philanthropy is so good. Philanthropy does well to insist upon a sound social policy in its administration, and the South is perfectly justified in insisting that the Northern benefactor think of the deep effect of his gifts upon the entire and complicated problem of its dual civilization. That the school wields immense power over national destiny; that "through education society can formulate its own purposes, can organize its own means and resources, and thus shape itself with definiteness and economy in the direction in which it wishes to move";[1] and that the test of social efficiency must be met, we wish both to admit and to insist.

The Propriety of Severe Tests

The practical task then is to work through the manifold problems of negro education to a program which meets this test.

[1] Dewey, "My Pedagogical Creed," p. 17.

NEGRO EDUCATION

I. HIGHER *vs.* INDUSTRIAL EDUCATION

<small>Higher Education an Attempt to Meet the White Man's Test</small>

The earlier negro schools founded by Northern philanthropy were intended less to teach the negro than to teach the nation. Their attempts were to help him meet the white man's — especially the Southern white man's — test. This test was not utilitarian but ideal. It was reported that John C. Calhoun had said, "Show me a negro who knows Greek syntax, and I will then believe that he is a human being who should be treated as a man."[1] At any rate the argument for slavery had finally rested upon the alleged natural inferiority of the colored race; consequently the first task of freedom was naturally to prove the capacity of the race. The early-founded universities were thus a testimony to that capacity, a demonstration in the persons of a selected few of what the negro mind could do. As such they admirably succeeded. Hundreds of negroes during the reconstruction period learned to read Greek as part of the higher education of the age. Both instinct and theory maintained that such would constitute the natural leaders of their people in its new era. Further than that this higher education was not designed to adjust the race to the immediate practical demands of its life. There was no fundamentally thought-out program for leadership to follow; no clear recognition of stages of necessary development. Was this failure an essential error, or was it part of a deeper wisdom? We shall return to this question a little later.

In view of its theoretical impulse the ideals of higher

---

[1] See Crummell, "The Attitude of the American Mind toward the Negro Intellect," Occasional Papers of the American Negro Academy, No. 3, p. 11.

education for the negro were simply and easily formulated. The motives underlying "industrial education" on the other hand are more obscure, having emerged from a more complicated course of evolution. It was originated by Armstrong at Hampton; urged as a social policy and inadequately practised by the South; developed and used by Booker T. Washington for the upbuilding of Tuskegee; and given a theoretical basis by Northern scholarship. Each of these four interesting phases may be briefly traced.

Four Phases of Industrial Education — Armstrong

It is a sorry caricature of the original impulse of Hampton to define it in the terms of a pedagogical ideal. It was rather a man incarnate — Armstrong himself, multiplied and in action. Born on missionary soil, he inherited the devotion and profited by the experience of noble efforts for the uplift of a backward people. At Hampton, first under the Freedman's Bureau, a little later with the commission and support of the American Missionary Association, he had to face the problem of masses of ignorant negroes, deficient in the very rudiments of civilization. His practical solution was to put them at manual work in connection with elementary schooling. This was the manifest, immediate solution and indeed the ordinary one in all the mission schools. For whatever his theories, the man at the front is always an opportunist — or else he does not stay long. But Hampton so bore the stamp of Armstrong's personal genius, and that genius was so splendidly independent and pervasive, that its ideas and general methods became a shibboleth. He was wholesomely disgusted with the veneering process which conventional missions had frequently employed upon undeveloped peoples. His sincerity and sense of instant need united to demand that negro education should rest upon solid foundations; yet he never urged the Hampton policy as exclusively right, nor doubted that the higher institutions were also necessary. It was a matter of emphasis. He was not devising a panacea; the Hampton way was simply his way. And industrialism is altogether too lean a name for his way. The personal and ideal incentives which he put into manual work were the secret of its chief virtues. Industrial education has never been in other hands what it was in his. No other has been able to mix its elements with such consummate art, or so to inform them with the Christian spirit. His instrument has mastered lesser men. He alone could bend his own bow.

Worlds away both in motive and method was industrial education for negroes as it came to be the sectional program of the South. Its coming was on this wise:

In spite of the tremendous social and political upheavals of Reconstruction, habit, that great balance-wheel of our humanity, held the men of that generation largely to the substance of the older order. There were new external relations, but those whose life and thought were hardened before the war remained inwardly much the same after the war. It was only with the dying off of that generation and the wearing away by time of habitual race relations, that the South began to realize how profound was the revolution that had befallen it. The North does not realize it to this day. Many of the most deeply disturbing results of emancipation were not manifest during Reconstruction, and this explains why the second generation of Southerners is frequently more bitter over it than was the first.

The South's Delayed Demand for Industrial Education

The change which most impressed the South was what it took to be the deterioration of negro labor. Slavery-trained craftsmen grew fewer and fewer, and there were none to take their place; while the will to work under white direction seemed steadily to wane. Thus arose a demand for institutions which should teach the freedman to do the things for which he had been trained on the plantations — to become a skilled workman in the simpler manual industries. The negro's education was to be vocational, with no expectation that he would want to change his vocation. Education was not conceived as a key for wider opportunity, but a tool for the negro's use in his present status. This was a splendid ideal in that it was a frank attempt to adjust men to some of the actual possibilities of life, but deficient in that it limited those opportunities by a narrow expectation. To the South the negro was naturally inferior, and it had not faith to approach his educational problem with those incentives which were the soul of Armstrong's method. Industrial education by no means meant the same thing to him and to the South; yet because they favored common external forms of schooling they had the immense practical advantage of being able to work together. From the standpoint of national peace and good will this must be counted an immeasurable gain. Virginia subsidized Hampton as Alabama later did Tuskegee. Dr. Lyman Abbott has recently observed that the most significant thing about them is that they are state-supported institutions.

The third great factor in working out the ideal of negro industrial education has been the personality of that greatest Southerner of his generation, Booker T. Washington. Inspired by his teacher Armstrong, and by his own experience as a Hampton instructor, he undertook the foundation of a similar institution at Tuskegee for the service of his race. In the

Washington at Tuskegee

fashioning of pleas for money for this institution, and in its defense, largely against negro critics, he has formulated his educational philosophy and bolstered it with mildly theoretical arguments.

He early saw that the external features of Armstrong's gospel — plenty of manual work for negroes — might win the favor of the South. Convinced that the friendliness of his white neighbor is practically more important to the negro than any immediate exercise of political power, he has been content to gain that favor by holding controverted issues largely in abeyance and by emphasizing what the South likes. For this "quiescence, if not acquiescence" in the South's race policy he has been attacked with incredible bitterness by the more militant party within his own race; but he has steadily and wisely, perhaps desperately, held to his own clue to the difficulty, namely, *that the negro as a producer is indispensable to the South.* He may so maintain and strengthen his economic hold that political and social privileges also must be granted to him in the long run.

Mr. Washington and his Temperamental Aversion to Trouble

The negro in the South has it within his power, if he properly utilizes the forces at hand, to make of himself such a valuable factor in the life of the South that he will not have to seek privileges: they will be freely conferred upon him. To bring this about the negro must begin at the bottom and lay a sure foundation, and not be lured by any temptation into trying to rise on a false foundation. While the negro is laying this foundation he will need help, sympathy, and simple justice.[1]

On one hand this is making a virtue of necessity, but it

[1] "The Future of the American Negro," pp. 220–221.

probably also reflects Mr. Washington's mind. Undoubtedly the material prosperity of his race is his most spontaneous interest. Only by taking thought does he appreciate the significance of spiritual affairs. His secondary emphasis upon them is a sincere thought, but an afterthought. He leads his race after the pattern of his own heart. Every oratorical period is ended with a plea for character and service; but these things are not original passions with him as with Armstrong. One does not doubt the worthiness of it, but one feels the transition from immediate to remote enthusiasm. Mr. Washington's earlier attacks upon mere bookishness in negro education were never as necessary as he thought, either to put his own people right or to attract Northern philanthropy into profitable channels. They served, however, to point out the needs of Tuskegee. The institution, however, certainly did not lack positive grounds of appeal. Its marvelous success is the most impressive single evidence of negro energy and practical ability. By reason of this great achievement, and of his persistent and peace-loving optimism, Mr. Washington has become the official ambassador of his race in its group-relations to the nation. Particularly he has given the doctrine of industrial education for the negro national standing.

The extraordinary appeal of his ideas to the North is due partly to Mr. Washington's rare eloquence and tact in their persistent presentation; partly to an increasing desire in the North to accept what is also acceptable to the South; but partly also to the circumstance that these ideas fall in with prevalent theoretical tendencies. The social theorizing of to-day is largely dominated by the idea of the primacy of economic progress

The Primacy of Economic Progress Accepted by the North

in human development. Men must first acquire, then use wealth. The effective exercise of the higher capacities of a people is conditioned upon their possession of a material surplus, which permits complete nutrition, efficient labor, a normal play of incentive, and finally the turning of interest to ideal pursuits. If there is any racial justification for Greek it can only appear after victories have been won through industrial education. This is the negro's first need. Influential Northern journals, like *The Outlook*, have figured largely in popularizing this view.[1]

In practical outcome neither the higher nor the industrial idea has had any sufficiently wide application to negro education. The typical agency, whether public or private, has been and is an elementary school in which the rudiments of learning are bookishly taught. Many more dollars have been spent on such institutions than on all others combined. The most important exceptions to this rule, numerically speaking, are not schools supported by the South, nor yet Hampton nor Tuskegee, but the large missionary boarding-schools which have had to maintain themselves and their students largely by productive work. The chief administrators of these schools have done essentially what Armstrong did, though less consciously, systematically, aggressively. They have been opportunists who, in setting out to train leaders, have found it necessary first to educate masses of raw material from which to choose leaders. Whatever the theories of men in Northern offices, the men at the front have become fundamentally interested in this more extensive task. How broadly they have met it appears in detail in other chapters.

Higher and Industrial Education alike more Talked about than Practised

[1] For a typical utterance, see Hyde, A National Platform on the Race Question, *The Outlook*, May 21, 1904, p. 169.

CHRISTIAN RECONSTRUCTION IN THE SOUTH

Higher education, then, has been more talked about than practised. There is not actually a surplus of negroes who can read Greek. With the exception of the ministry, statistics show that all professions are numerically undermanned by negroes. A trained colored physician, just out of school, has an immeasurably larger opportunity to start out with a good practise than an equally trained white man. Negro teachers are proportionately only one-half as numerous as white; and if quality and character count in the ministry there is no calling more in need of highly trained men. Out of the ten million negroes in the nation there are to-day less than seventy thousand in all schools higher than elementary — academic, industrial, commercial, and professional, North, South, East, and West.

Nor, on the other hand, has industrial education begun to be adequately furnished. As practised in its chiefly exploited centers it has had limited scope and confessedly has come far short of the ideals of its leaders. Only about one-third of the present enrolment of Hampton (1300) is actually receiving industrial training either in agriculture or trades. Less than fifty per cent of its graduates and less than twelve per cent of Tuskegee's have followed the industries in after life.

In an address on the trade-school ideal, Major Moton, commandant at Hampton, said:

> Hampton does not by any means approximate its ideal in trade-school work, for it is necessary now — and probably will be for a long time to come — to teach a large number of undergraduate pupils, who learn their trades while they are taking the academic course, but post-graduate work is without question

the ideal toward which trade-school work should be tending.[1]

He added that for its first thirty years of existence, Hampton did not teach the trades in any adequate sense. Most of the purely state-supported agricultural and industrial schools for colored citizens are feeble indeed. North Carolina and Mississippi have creditable institutions; a larger number of states scarcely do more than transmit Federal funds, leaving their negro institutions largely to shift for themselves. Probably there are a dozen missionary institutions which have incidentally done more in actual industrial training than has any state institution in the South.

To-day's need, therefore, is for many more schools of more sorts than the original contestants over negro education dreamed. This need has become undeniable by reason of the actual social and economic differentiation of the negro population.

Need of more Schools of all Sorts

While the white men were debating what kind of an education was best for him, the negro has been quietly engaging in all the activities of life, until no one who studies his census record or learns his varied functions in any representative city can doubt that he needs an all-sided training *to fit him for his actual opportunities.*

The question of the relative emphasis upon different forms and types of training is now being settled for any given locality or calling by an objective scientific measurement of the extent of negro opportunity in it. As a practical issue between educators the old controversy is virtually dead. Of Mr. Washington's own development Prof. Kelly Miller justly writes:

Practical Agreement of Former Partisans

[1] "The Negro Artisan," Atlanta University Publications, No. 7, p. 65.

He began his career with a narrow educational bias and a one-sided championship of industrial training as an offset to the claims of literary culture which had hitherto absorbed the substance of Northern philanthropy. But he has grown so far in grasp and in breadth of view that he now advocates all modes of education in their proper place and proportion.[1]

The champions of higher education, on the other hand, are now consciously and confessedly emphasizing what they incidentally tolerated all along. Within the last two years the American Missionary Association has added more than thirty industrial teachers and equipments to its educational forces, while its higher institutions are engaged in putting an educational top upon the lower forms of practical training by beginnings in advanced technical courses.

From the vantage-ground of the present era of good feeling, it will seem rash and almost impious to turn back to ask which emphasis of the past was right. Indeed it would not be worth while to do so except for the fact that the essential issues may again become crucial in the future. Indeed they are even now becoming so in the movement for "vocational education for the masses." Was the early insistence on higher education and the delay of industrialism wise or wasteful? Was it true statesmanship or a sentimental blunder? I confess that I think it justified itself both psychologically, as fixing the negro's favorable status in the mind of Christendom, and practically, as the most effective strategy of race development. It sifted out a group of leaders. These gains infinitely outweigh any loss from the postponement of industrial training.

Which was Right?

[1] "Race Adjustment," p. 25.

NEGRO EDUCATION

The parallel between negro and woman — although at first thought unflattering to woman — is extremely and **Negro and** suggestively close. Both are struggling out **Woman** of a status of legal and social inferiority; both suffer transitional handicaps, such as inferior wages for equal work; both have made their most striking initial gains not at all by evolution from below. The higher education of women was in no sense an attempt to adjust them to the practical demand of their lives, but rather to extend the boundaries within which practical demands might grow. Why did woman want to go to college? Not better to fit herself either for home making or for economic competition, but to prove that her higher capacities were equal to man's. She succeeded; and no extension of woman's activity as an economic producer has had half the potency for fixing her modern status, both in her own mind and in the mind of the age, as the fact that Dorothy Klumpke has discovered stars, that Madame Curie tamed radium, and Mary Calkins elaborated a psychological theory.

Similarly, in the light of the proved capacities of his select men, civilization simply cannot regard the negro **It is Good** as it otherwise would. Every race is judged **Strategy to** by its best as well as by its worst. It is good **Exhibit the** strategy to exhibit the best first. The insti-**Best First** tutions of higher education set the standards of the emerged group — the negro's finest and racially most significant flower. Its achievements have been the ideal capital of the struggling masses. From the schools founded by missionary zeal, race leaders came to the kingdom for just such a time of early trial and development. Mr. Washington is wrong in thinking that the negro who most impresses the South is the thrifty, property accumulating negro. The dominant South bitterly and increas-

[277]

ingly confesses that the ominous man from its standpoint—the negro whom it thinks about and fears — is the educated negro. Its social policy forces every other issue to be subordinated to the issue of negro capacity on the higher levels. The higher education is still the white man's test. Mr. Washington is wrong also in arguing, "During the first fifty or hundred years of the life of any people are not the economic occupations always given the greater attention?"[1] This might be true of a people undergoing an independent evolution, but not of one whose chief problem is that of its adjustment to an enveloping civilization, — one both highly complex and progressive. Under the negro's circumstances in America the first problem was to fix his ideal status. Whatever their incidental blunders it is the imperishable glory of the Fifteenth Amendment and the missionary universities to have done this.

II. THE GENERAL EDUCATIONAL PARALLEL

For the more minute guidance of an educational policy for negroes the general educational situation is to-day suggestive as never before. Now, for the first time, the American school faces directly and at large the problem of special training for different social classes in a democracy. With the immigration of millions of new and incomplete Americans, with their stratification into social classes, their self-discovery, group organization, and various demands, vocational education for the masses becomes a central issue. For Massachusetts, as much as for Mississippi, special types of industrial schools are being talked about. The large experience of the educator of

American Experience with Industrial Education not Theoretically Significant

---

[1] "Future of the American Negro," p. 228.

negroes with the problem enables him to give certain advice and warning to the nation at large.

At first thought the very idea of class education seems repugnant to democratic ideas. No one was bold enough to propose such an idea until it had been discovered that whether we like it or not we had it already in our supposed uniform schools. In less than half of its range does our boasted public school system meet any general popular demand; less than fifty per cent of entering pupils complete the sixth grade, and only three out of a hundred finish the high school. With the changed character of our population the upper grades have become merely schools of the more well-to-do classes. In atmosphere and general social tradition the average city high school is one of the most distinctly marked of American class institutions.

Can a Democracy Tolerate Class Schools?

Furthermore, the great falling out of pupils at the sixth grade is not chiefly due to economic necessity. Why do parents allow their children to stop here who can well enough afford to continue them for the seventh and eighth elementary years? Frankly, because they see nothing profitable in those grades in the present schools. Pupils stop, not for lack of means, but for lack of interest. The discovery of this fact by the Massachusetts Commission is epoch-making for American education. *Schools which more than half our people do not want, nor use, are class schools*, become such by failure to respond to the widening needs of the varied groups of our population. The policy of uniformity has broken down. The only solution, and the one adopted by all progressive European nations, is the establishment of more class schools — enough to go around. Munich, for example, has forty kinds of indus-

Yes, if it Provides Enough Class Schools to go Around

trial continuation schools. The practical problem is how to secure an educational policy in America which shall offer a similar variety of opportunity, and still be faithful to the ideals of democracy.

The moment of this attempted readjustment through the multiplication of class schools is fraught with grave dangers to our dearest convictions. In the letting go of old forms of democracy, ostensibly in order to get a better hold on its essentials, some part of our faith in its spirit may easily be lost. Back of this cry for vocational education is an economic demand which lacks much of being pure patriotism or philanthropy. The master classes, North and South alike, want to train workers for a particular industrial status. They are concerned about the creation of productive agents who can compete with other sections or with Germany at a profit to themselves. They do not think of fitting human beings for the enlightened satisfactions of expanding lives. The simple-minded educator is deceived by the glitter of " increased national efficiency " and caught by the promise of more money for schools. There is great need to sound in America the noble word of the English Consultative Committee, that *no education is truly vocational which does not prepare for life as well as for livelihood.* However much the schools may create special skill, only justice to the worker can furnish motive for efficiency.

<small>The Danger of the Attempt</small>

Thus, though all must bow in the temple of industrial training, we need not worship the commercial Rimmon. In the South, Mr. Washington wisely uses and cooperates with sectional sentiment, but without accepting it as final. In the North educational policy must shrewdly fall in with economic demand, while avoiding its narrow-

<small>Industrial Education must be Safeguarded and then Practised</small>

Domestic Science Laboratory, Talladega College

Blacksmith Shop, Tougaloo University

ness and lack of heart. Democratic education in America will undoubtedly be secured in the future through a multiplication of special schools so as to match the needs of all social classes. This should be cordially admitted for the negro. His friends should welcome all existing interest in his industrial education while profoundly distrusting much of its motive — both Northern and Southern.

III. EXPERT INTERPRETATIONS OF THE LESSONS OF EXPERIENCE

Apart from its epoch-making but untheoretical experiments with the training of the negro, America has practically no experience in industrial education, either sufficiently old or extensive to be enlightening. England and the Continent are more fruitful, and the lessons of their policies are recently made available through current educational discussions, notably by the Report of the Massachusetts Commission on Industrial and Technical Education.

English and Continental Experience

All experience unites to commend Browning's counsel,

> "Oh, if we draw a circle premature,
> Heedless of far gain,
> Greedy for quick returns of profit, sure,
> Bad is our bargain!"

Thus the application of the vocational idea to the elementary school consists simply in keeping its general spirit in touch with the practicalities of the child's life. The illustrations and activities of the school day should relate to the life of his parents and community and his own probable future. Problems in arithmetic, for example, should be such as a child will be likely to meet as one of the world's workers. He should

The Elementary School

have nature study, gardening, manual training; but upon all this educational authorities insist, on strictly pedagogical grounds, without any hint of vocational motive. In short *the vocational method as such does not apply to the elementary school.* All experts agree that no sort of specific trades instruction should begin before the child is twelve.

For the youth who is between the ages of twelve and fifteen it is agreed that industrial education should be distinctly vocational, but not technical. This distinction means that the schools should impart general rather than specialized industrial skill, and at the same time maintain in full measure the other elements of education — cultural, humanistic, and manual. The Report of the English Consultative Committee on Higher Elementary Schools (1906) is especially adverse to specialization within these years. Employers, it says, are unanimously against it on practical grounds. Even commercial technique (stenography and typewriting), which requires slight manual effort, cannot wisely be undertaken yet. Skill must come first in processes involving only the simple, coarser, and more massive muscular coordinations. There should be special pre-occupational schools for those classes of pupils who are later to learn trades, teaching them fundamental industrial processes; but technical trade-methods are neither psychologically nor practically as yet justified.

<small>The Lower Secondary School</small>

In virtual agreement the Massachusetts Commission's Report declares that, while short-cut trade-courses for younger pupils at first increase their productive wage-earning power, yet the " child commencing at sixteen overtakes his brother beginning at fourteen in two years."

More particularly it specifies:

That the responsibility of the child is not developed is declared to be the weakness of such schools. The employer has discovered by bitter experience that the fourteen to sixteen-year-old child is physically undeveloped, and irresponsible for any sort of work except the actually unskilled.

The development of policy in the industrial world and the experience of educators shows that the productive power of the child before fourteen is negative, and that it has not the power to handle anything but the simplest processes in the simplest and smallest way; that from fourteen to sixteen he is of productive power only for the large processes of manufacture, or for errand work; but that the child in those years, by teaching, may gain the principles of industrial work, which may be put into practise after sixteen; that, therefore, the training before fourteen should be in the simpler practical lines only; that between fourteen and sixteen it should combine the practical training in specific industries with academic work, as applied to the industrial problems, to develop intelligence and responsibility.

Higher Secondary Schools — After sixteen the pupil may wisely enter upon different trades education, but even then the acquirement of genuine industrial efficiency is no slight task. Modern, and especially American, industry is so excessively specialized that men do not live by trades but by branches of trades. " If they are manufacturing shoes of the heaviest kind in one district and of the lightest kind in another, the teaching must be adapted to each place separately." The expert further continues thus:

> We do not say to the artisan students, You shall be acquainted practically with the whole trade; but we say, There are some things in the shoe-trade that,

if you claim to be an intelligent worker and desire to advance, you should be acquainted with. We have put those subjects in a general section. At the same time we say there are also some subjects in which you will no doubt wish to qualify as a practical man and get your living by it. We allow you to select any one of these special subjects.

Thus even the trade-school has its general and its special courses, and even when they are finished the trade is not acquired. No mere school training is sufficient for that. Sir William Mathers, who headed a committee of the British Parliament to investigate industrial education throughout the civilized world, brought his wisdom to the Massachusetts inquiry. His last words were these:

> Please take notice of what I said about the avoidance of teaching a trade to the extent of causing a lad to say, after leaving the industrial school, " I am a printer," " I am a cotton-spinner," " I am a mechanic or a carpenter." In the first place, it is detrimental to the lad's own interests. He becomes somewhat conceited before he has got through the proper training by actual practise. It tends to deterioration of skill and intelligence in trades, which can only be fully acquired through work done on a commercial scale. It will tend to discredit industrial education.[1]

Similarly, in the light of the best American experience, Mr. Charles F. Warner of the Springfield (Mass.) Technical High School says:

> Whatever method of teaching trades in schools may be adopted, provision should be made for continuing

[1] Report of the Commission on Industrial and Technical Education, p. 164.

the training by at least one year of work under actual shop or factory conditions; and no certificate of proficiency should be granted until this requirement has been satisfactorily met.[1]

Application of these Lessons to Negro Education   The application of these lessons to the education of the negro must of course allow for his peculiar social and industrial situation in the South. He lives in an industrially backward section, one given largely to agricultural pursuits. His lot is by no means that of the Northern urban populations. Nature is inexorable; she may be hurt but not hurried; the psychological objection to premature specialization is as great for him as for any other race. But social policy must have regard to the peculiar environment in which he must work his way. Much might have been said yesterday showing that the experience of the older civilizations does not apply to his case.

But the South is not standing still. Already its industry and agriculture respond to, where they do not lead, modern progress. The peculiar and critical mission of industrial education is to the exceptional man exactly as is that of the colleges. Its unique justification is that it serves the negro in a crisis. He is as yet economically indispensable to the South, but his opportunities, especially in skilled labor, are menaced. The race needs industrial leaders to lead their people into efficiency. Without this they will certainly fail in competitions now impending. Just so far as the South becomes modernized, the negro is thrust into the world's struggle. The

[1] Report of the Commission on Industrial and Technical Education, p. 190.

preparation of his people to meet this struggle is Mr. Washington's central idea, which he has by no means as yet satisfied at Tuskegee. He says:

> Just now the need is not so much for the common carpenters, brick-masons, farmers, and laundry-women as for industrial leaders, who, in addition to their practical knowledge can draw plans, make estimates, take contracts; those who understand the latest methods of truck-gardening and the science underlying practical agriculture; those who understand machinery to the extent that they can operate steam and electric laundries, so that our women can hold on to the laundry work in the South, that is so fast drifting into the hands of others in the large cities and towns.[1]

This tallies exactly with the doctrines of the Massachusetts Commission: "Our technical colleges have produced superintendents — captains of industry; there are plenty of helpers and lumpers and young labor among the rank and file of the army, but there are no expert journeymen, second-hands, foremen."[2]

The demand, then, is for highly skilled men. No second-rate industrial education fits the negro's case. It must give him genuine efficiency in accordance with the rapidly advancing standards of his economic life.

This principle immediately rules out much that the South understands and means by industrial education for the negro; such crude proposals, for example, as the following from Governor Hoke Smith of Georgia:

Inadequacy of the South's Version

[1] Washington, "The Future of the American Negro," p. 81.
[2] P. 90.

TEACH NEGROES TO WORK

There is one suggestion which I desire to make, which I have made before, and which I wish again to make with reference to the negro schools in rural sections.

Education to be useful must have in view definitely the future of the child and the condition of the child. I believe that the negro school, to be of any benefit to the negroes, ought to teach them how to work. I commend to the county boards of Georgia the propriety of requiring that a considerable portion of the time at the negro schools be given to actual labor. The land immediately by the schoolhouse could, in most instances, be utilized for the labor, which should constitute a large part of the training which the young negroes receive in the rural schools.

The negro should be taught how to put the land in proper condition, how to protect it from washing, how to cultivate it so deep that moisture can come to the roots of the plants from below, and should be made to do the work during the school hours. Instruction of this kind can be given with practically little expense and the time taken away from book study will be worth more to the negroes than the time given to book studies.[1]

This means that the negro child shall be taught the habit of industry — which is well; but it assumes that his life will continue to be narrow in ambition and outlook. In opposition to such a policy the best interests of true industrial efficiency, as well as all larger human standards, demand that the negro child in the common school be instructed as any other child is, in the rudiments of human

[1] Report of an Address at Summerville, Ga., September 14, 1907.

knowledge. Manual and agricultural practise should not be absent. All instruction, indeed, should be based on activity, but for psychological, not racial, reasons. No one can be taught to work well by being worked too young. The elementary schools should be vocational in atmosphere, but not technical in method. And Governor Smith does well to conclude, " I do not pretend to have worked out the problem in detail."

In negro city high schools, in which pupils of a given grade do not vary greatly in age from those of similar white schools, there are the same objections — both educational and industrial — to premature specialization, as European and Northern experience has discovered. Actual trades technique should not be begun before the last years of the high school. Yet the South, while it professes to want the negro to be well trained as a worker, flies in the face of all educational counsels in not generally admitting his right to a sufficient preliminary schooling. In general it provides him no high school at all.

Better Negroes need such Schools as do Corresponding Whites

In the rural secondary schools for negroes the physical and psychological objections to specialization are largely overcome by the greater age of the pupils. These pupils are frequently old enough in years to begin the acquirement of their trades at once. This they have all along been doing at Hampton and Tuskegee. Nature permits it, but the social and economic wisdom of such a policy is open to question on three grounds.

The Case of Rural Secondary Schools

First: Modern industrial efficiency demands an ever broader general intelligence in the worker. England has found it necessary to give its Reform School boys culture studies to make good their trades skill. Germany has outdistanced the world commercially and industrially by giving the maximum of general education along with high technical training. In adjusting himself to his changing social conditions, the negro has as often failed through lack of intelligence and integrity in social relations as through deficiency in special skill. Entangled as his practical problem is by the complicating color-line, he needs an education which develops the broader economic virtues, involving both knowledge and character. To take the simplest case, no matter how good a workman he is, unless he can "figure" he is sure to be beaten out of his earnings; unless he has decided moral and social resources he will be debarred from the trade union.

The Negro fails from Lack of Intelligence oftener than from Lack of Skill

Second: Remember that the supreme function of industrial education just now is to train negroes who can lead their race through an industrial crisis. This involves something more than skill, and this "something more" existing schools largely fail to give. The American Missionary Association employs annually more than fifty industrial teachers, more than half of whom are negroes. It has found difficulty in using the average graduate of Hampton and Tuskegee in such capacities. This is not strange in the light of the report of 1907 by Principal Frissell of the former institution:

Industrial Schools fail to Train Proper Industrial Leaders

> Nearly seventy-five per cent of the boys are in the night school, giving their days to the trades or agriculture. Many of them leave the school after having learned their trades, although they have only completed a year and a half of the four years' academic course. Last May, sixty-three boys were candi-

dates for trade certificates; of these only three were candidates for the academic diploma; nineteen returned to go on with their studies, and forty-one did not return. It is most desirable that a larger number of trades students should complete the full academic course and graduate with the school's diploma. The academic superintendent feels that while the trade-school boys receive too little academic training, the day school boys receive too little industrial training. Progress has been made in combining academic and industrial training but the problem is not yet solved to the satisfaction of the school authorities.

Educationally interpreted, the facts thus confessed mean that forty-one students with trades certificates, but without an ordinary common school education, went out from Hampton in 1906. If the nineteen who returned could have finished their academic course there, they would still scarcely have begun standard secondary work. Such results are not meeting the ideals of industrial education as recognized by the best educational authorities.

Might Hampton and Tuskegee not supply successful craftsmen though not good teachers? Yes, but not efficient industrial leaders. The inability to organize and communicate their special skill, and weakness in the management of men, condemn them as race-saviors in an age of industrial revolution, of a "new agriculture," of an ever-deepening envolvement of economic in social and racial problems. They have been educated under arbitrary conditions — far from home problems — and are at a loss to apply their educational achievements to the small resources and limited opportunity of the average negro community. This is the common difficulty of all school-trained skill, which pupils of all races have to overcome.

But in the case of the negro industrial-school graduate the defect is deeper. He has generally not acquired the inner means of making practical readjustments. He has — to borrow Dean Russell's distinction — the "education of habit," but not the "education of insight."

But what the average Southerner — and probably the average Northerner — means by industrial education is the education of habit, such teaching as enables a man to work by rule and rote; to work as profitably as possible under fixed social limitations; in brief, to perpetuate the rule of some class and trade-tradition of a departed or departing age. This does not at all meet Mr. Washington's sense of his people's needs, and is what Hampton is confessedly trying to get away from. It is not a criticism, then, of the best ideals of these greater negro industrial schools, but only of their average present achievement, to record that the Association has usually found its effective industrial teachers and organizers in the more thoroughly educated graduates of its own schools. These have frequently been deficient in technique, but such deficiencies have been more than made up by their broader theoretical background, and by the more practical character of their apprenticeships in the daily work and actual building up of institutions. Such experience has developed adaptability and resourcefulness. The industrial schools themselves have always found their best teachers among college and university graduates. Without such neither Hampton nor Tuskegee could run for a day. A Fisk collegiate graduate is now at the head of the J. K. Brick Industrial School, at Enfield, North Carolina. He has managed some highly difficult feats of rural engineering on the school's eleven-hundred-acre domains and has set up engines in its shops which are the wonder of the white neighborhood. They ask, " Where did you learn it? " He replies, " Oh, studying Greek at Fisk."

Finally, mere industrial education fails most significantly because it cannot supply *motive* to industry. It is vain to teach better methods of production to those who can already produce more than they know how to want or to use. The psychological problem of inefficiency is really more serious than the economic problem. At this point particularly the negro fails. He is often content to live for five days on the earnings of two. He must be led to want more before he can be made to work more. The problem of consumption is prior to that of production, as hunger is prior to hunting. Even for, perhaps especially for, the poor man, an awakening imagination is the root-cure of practical ills. Armstrong supplied this dynamic by the infection of his own religious and moral genius. Every teacher must supply it somehow. It is the final justification of the cultural and ideal elements in education that they create incentives; they give a scope to life which necessitates the efficient making of a livelihood for its fulfilment.

No " blind alleys," then, are wanted in negro education. No amount of increased production through industrial efficiency could repay the loss to society if the schools should hold to lower levels men whom nature had destined for leaders. Georgia, in instituting the nation's most extensive experiment in agricultural secondary education, was wisely alive to such a danger with respect to a part of its citizens.

We were, therefore, to arrange for technical agricultural and industrial schools of secondary grade which would provide technical occupational training for the eighty-five per cent of the young farmers who would attend no higher school, and, at the same time, give a good education for citizenship; open at the top, so that the other fifteen per cent, who through ambition and fitness should desire to pursue their studies in college, might do so, on equal terms with pupils from other schools. The law forbids the restriction of the farmer's boy and girl to the three R's and manual labor; it forbids the shutting of the door of opportunity to those as the means of keeping them on the farm; but required a high school course equal to that offered in technical schools for other occupations and preparation for higher college training.[1]

The report significantly adds:

We want no "blind alleys" nor inferior training for the white youth of our state.

Shall we understand by implication that an inferior training is good enough for the negro youth? No one will admit it who sees the race's need for competent leadership of its own, or feels its right to lay the higher products of its genius in the lap of a common civilization.

All this argues that, for the negro as well as for the white, specialized industrial education should be based upon and postponed until after a thorough general education is acquired. This general education should include the manual arts, as justified alike by pedagogical theory and vocational purpose, but should not enter upon technical trade-training. For the actually needy classes, earlier specialization is justified as a social makeshift, for the same reason that the Manhattan Trades School is justified

Conclusion as to Negro Industrial Education

---

[1] Report of J. S. Stewart, p. 3.

in New York City. Even Professor Kelly Miller, author of a "Brief for the Higher Education of the Negro," advises special schools for domestic service in Southern cities. But nature imposes physical and spiritual penalties upon short-cut methods. They cannot solve the negro's main economic problems, nor satisfy the ideals of industrial education, let alone those of human progress. For a very few, in its postgraduate course, Hampton is doing what ought to be done, and probably as well as it has ever been done anywhere. For example, she has graduated seventeen students from her advanced agricultural course, which approximates the ideal of a secondary industrial school. Most of Hampton's trades courses, however, represent, I believe, specialization without sufficient general education, as do Tuskegee's. These schools are willing to give the negro a type of schooling which Georgia is unwilling to give to even the humblest of its white children.

On the contrary, the accepted ideals and standards of industrial education, as they have been worked out in the general educational field, agree in demanding thorough general preparation for technical training. The trouble with the negro trade-schools is that, under their practical and sectional limitations of the past, they have not even been practising good industrialism. Yet a large part of the nation has mistaken or approved their makeshifts as a permanent policy toward a handicapped race.

Now when the ideal of this chapter is popularized and its standard practised, when it is made the basis of appeal for money and money is spent on it when received, the old contention of the partisans of higher education will in all its substantial elements have been adopted. Except in temporary, social-emergency schools, *industrial*

<small>Substantial Admission of Ideals of Higher Education</small>

education will be an advanced form of popular schooling. In policy and purpose it will complement rather than conflict with general education. No sting of racial implication will remain in it. Democratic opportunty will be allowed by groups of coordinate institutions, not sacrificed by inferior schools for the poor. The technical and agricultural college, neither of which yet exists for negroes, will take its place beside the college of liberal arts, as independent institutions or as a department of the great negro university of the future.

IV. PRINCIPLES OF DEMOCRATIC EDUCATION

In the light of these leisurely approaches, first historical, then educational, a group of principles emerges. They are controlling for negro education only because true for all. They may here be enumerated and briefly characterized.

1. Of course, democracy must be true to its genius. It must conceive education as a means of equalizing opportunity, of assimilating incomplete Americans to the best national type, and endowing them with their full social heredity as sons of this crowning age. No expression of this principle could be nobler than the recent declaration of the Southern Educational Association (1907):

A Policy of Education for a Democracy

> (1) All children, regardless of race, creed, sex, or the social station or economic condition of their parents, have equal right to, and should have equal opportunity for, such education as will develop to the fullest possible degree all that is best in their individual natures, and fit them for the duties of life and

citizenship in the age and community in which they live.

(2) To secure this right and provide this opportunity to all children is the first and highest duty of the modern democratic state, and the highest economic wisdom of an industrial age and community. Without universal education of the best and highest type there can be no real democracy, either political or social; nor can agriculture, manufactures, or commerce ever attain their highest development.

(3) Education in all grades and in all legitimate directions, being for the public good, the public should bear the burden of it. The most just taxes levied by the State, or within the authority of the State or of any smaller political division, are those levied for the support of education. No expenditures can possibly produce greater returns and none should be more liberal.[1]

2. Education as a social policy must follow probabilities while keeping an open door to possibilities. It must therefore be adapted to the special needs as well as to the general needs of the people. A wise democracy will not offer its masses merely the schools of the professional or leisure classes, but will multiply class schools until there are enough to go around, and thus one to fit each American group.

3. As an invitation to the fairer possibilities — because the best wealth of a nation is always its poor boys — all these diverse groups of schools will be "open at the top." The State, as destiny, must never forbid the university to any child because he is poor or black.

4. A just educational policy toward any group which has recently suffered, or is suffering from social repres-

[1] Quoted by Baker, "Following the Color-Line," pp. 284–285.

sion, must seek to find adjustment, not to its present fragmentary and distorted manifestations of natural capacities and traits, but to its future completely emancipated mind and genius. The immediate task of education with respect to such a group must be to rouse and discover that suppressed capacity. I am afraid that the justest and most generous thought of the South does not give this consideration due weight as regards the negro. The ninth resolution of the Southern Educational Association on negro education was as follows:

> On account of economic and psychological differences in the two races, we believe that there should be a difference in courses of study and methods of teaching, and that there should be such an adjustment of school curricula as shall meet the evident needs of negro youth.[1]

This needs examination and elucidation. In the first place, millions of white Americans, and in the South, have an economic status exactly parallel to that of the negro. His psychological traits are largely the result of that status and are shared by the corresponding white groups. In the second place, the differences in courses of study and methods of teaching might easily be — in the South would inevitably be — such as tend to fix the belated group in its present distorted and limited mental expression.

The woman-parallel is again in point. The deepest difficulty in applying the ideal of vocational education relates to her. What is woman? At any rate not a completed being. President Stanley Hall, the psychologist, ventures an "Outline of a higher education for girls based on their nature and needs, and not on convention or the demand

---

[1] Quoted by Baker, "Following the Color-Line," p. 286.

of feminists." Her scientific training, for example, should omit the theoretical rigidity and advanced technique of the man's and should lay stress on the moral and esthetic aspects of nature, " the poetic and mythic factors, and some glimpses of the history of science."[1] And all along the line her education should suit her psychical peculiarities. But immediately comes the anthropologist, Professor Thomas, to exploit the " adventitious character of woman," asserting that in many of her seemingly most distinctive traits she is not a natural but a social product. Her characteristic mentality is only her inner response to her social status. Like the negro she gains her ends by deceit and lies, because those are the natural — and legitimate? — resources of unprivileged classes. She is an instinctive clinger, as is the negro, but this reflects her long-time economic dependence. Even her alleged incapacity in the most rigid scientific fields, Professor Thomas argues at length,[2] is a cultural rather than a natural lack. In short, the mind of woman is the result of centuries of social pressure. Man's thought of her and her consequent thought of herself have restricted and artificialized her instinctive character, but have not maimed her mind beyond repair through freedom and opportunity. Professor Thomas' point is clinched by a conclusion from a highly scientific study *by a woman* of the psychological differences of the sexes.[3] A program for the education of woman cannot therefore be made until the true woman is recovered, and President Hall speaks too soon. The evident first business of a scheme of feminine education is to find the true woman.

[1] *Cf.* "Adolescence," vol. ii., ch. xvii.
[2] "Sex and Society," pp. 30–61.
[3] *Ibid*, p. 257.

THEOLOGICAL GRADUATES, TALLADEGA COLLEGE

TRAINED NURSES, TALLADEGA COLLEGE

In his chapter on "The Mind of Woman and the Lower Races," Professor Thomas directly touches on the present application of the argument to the negro. The general conclusion is, "Differences of sex will, I think, hold also for differences of race."

Well, then, a program of negro education must wait upon the recovery of the true negro, upon the unloosing of his repressed capacities, the unbinding of his normal self. *First find your man.* This should be the immediate business of education; for lack of it any policy toward him is sure to blunder. "What a thing is when its becoming is completed, that we call the nature of a thing," said Aristotle. Because strong sentiment in the nation persistently urges a type of training which would fix the negro in his incompleteness, let the educator, patriot, anthropologist each beware. This is the crux of the problem.

5. When this central issue is secure it freely follows that the immediate economic and practical needs of any historically peculiar or socially handicapped group of Americans, such as the juvenile delinquent, the Indian, the immigrant's child, the unskilled worker, may dictate a temporary policy of special training for them. The actual employment of such a policy can be justified only by a detailed sociological study of their actual situation. But such a study reveals that the negro's case is not parallel to these cited. His life is infinitely broader than that of any social group. His millions contain groups of all degrees of development. *The only analogy for him is the analogy of white population in its entirety.* He needs not one but all kinds of American education for the diverse grades and classes of his people.

6. The profoundest educational right of any people

is the right to have its inner resources of character utilized for its own uplift. For the teacher of negroes there should be no commentary here like his own heart.

What keeps the exceptional and gifted man at his task, — a task so appealing yet disheartening as that of the education of negroes under American conditions? What is the secret of victory and patience for Strieby or Curry, Armstrong or Cravath? Nothing short of some personal version of that experience to which Matthew Arnold testifies in his "East London."

> "I met a preacher there I knew, and said —
> 'Ill and o'erworked, how fare you in this scene?'
> 'Bravely!' said he; 'for I of late have been
> Much cheered with thoughts of Christ, the living bread.'
>
> O human soul! as long as thou canst so
> Set up a mark of everlasting light,
> Above the howling senses' ebb and flow,
>
> To cheer thee, and to right thee if thou roam —
> Not with lost toil thou laborest through the night!
> Thou mak'st the heaven thou hop'st indeed thy home."

In other words, the deepest need of any man is the need to have the inner resources of his own character released to energize his service. Equally the deepest need — yes, right — of any race is to have its inner resources utilized for its own redemption. It is the only way.

As to the negro, this is denied. He is contrasted, to his great discredit, with the Indian. The Indian thwarted all attempts to enslave him by dying. When he could no longer be free he ceased to live. The negro, on the contrary, thrived in servitude, thus showing, it is alleged, his essentially servile nature and adaptability to external compulsion.

But there is more than one way to resist oppression,

as a glance into any schoolroom shows. Here and there one finds the child rebel, the Indian fiercely resisting by overt acts all encroachments upon his personality. The more usual type of uncontrolled pupil is the mind-wandering, docile child, who conforms outwardly and inwardly follows his own devices. The proud teacher, deceived by appearances, may exclaim, " See my well-behaved and studious thirty," when, all told, she has hardly the equivalent of one child at work. Nine-tenths and more of each, though physically present, is spiritually absent — on the ball-ground or some other juvenile Island of the Blessed. Limbs and lips are at school but hearts are far afield.

Woman, in the main, has followed the negro's rather than the Indian's method of resisting oppression. There have been a few feminine revolutionists and radical innovators; most of the sex have seemed to yield — and contrived to manage. Woman has ruled by indirection, but she has ruled.

Now the lazy, adaptive negro has adjusted himself to necessity exactly as our wives and children chiefly do. He has given the minimum of work and obedience necessary to save his skin, and has stubbornly maintained the freedom and integrity of his own inner life. In labor power one Northern worker was worth a half dozen of slave-time plantation hands or house servants. I know nothing more creditable to the negro's humanity than this. He has never worked well under compulsion, and, before God, I hope and believe he never will. Only the full opportunity of American manhood will prove sufficient to summon the whole negro to life's task.

Subject groups, whether children, women, or dependent races, while they cannot be controlled unless their own souls are enlisted in the task, may be and have been warped and distorted by external pressure. It can hinder but cannot help. It never succeeds. The modern school confesses that when it fails to awaken the child's own interest its failure is absolute. Some are bold to believe that the world-wanderings of the "new woman" will lead her back to many of her old tasks, but if so it must be because her heart comes around to them again. Her return cannot be of compulsion. At all hazards she must follow the inner light.

The question of incentive is equally central for negro education. Vocational efficiency in the long run must be the same as social efficiency. Train, indeed, for the child's "actual condition in life," but be quite sure that condition is understood. We inhabit many-storied houses and our true calling is to occupy them throughout. The effort to make any man a good worker without making him a full man will fail; and could it succeed, it would but give us a blinded Samson grinding in the prison-house of spiritual bondage.

X. THE OLD MEN OF THE MOUNTAINS

FOR six years the fortunes of the author of this book were identified with a prosperous and progressive border city of thirty thousand people. It was located on two trunk lines of railway, giving unusually direct access to the four corners of the Union. It supported several worthy institutions of higher learning and was surrounded by a county of great agricultural productiveness; yet most of the tributary country within a radius of a hundred miles consisted of a rough, infertile land, inhabited by a decidedly rude and under-developed population, an offshoot of the larger Appalachian stock. No equal area east of the Great Plains had so small a railroad mileage. I have sometimes taken friends, representatives of completer civilizations, on hunting or fishing trips through this back country and have afterward been chagrined at the accounts of it they have written for Eastern papers — as though it represented my environment and opportunities. They described the picturesquely primitive as they saw it, but forgot to record the commonplace — that there were also electric lights, colleges, wealth, and an extremely self-conscious life which thought itself as good as any in America. Having thus suffered with their kind, from the confusion of the injudicious, I am the more anxious to speak of the people of the Southern Appalachians with discrimination, justice, and profound appreciation.

CHRISTIAN RECONSTRUCTION IN THE SOUTH

I. THE PROBLEM OF THE MOUNTAINS

The Southern Appalachian region is roughly six hundred miles long and two hundred miles broad. It includes two hundred and twenty-six counties in nine states as follows: Maryland 4, West Virginia 35, Virginia 42, eastern Kentucky 28, eastern Tennessee and the Cumberland Plateau in middle Tennessee 46, western North Carolina 24, northwestern South Carolina 4, northern Georgia 26, north-central Alabama 17. Their combined area is 101,880 square miles, or twice as large as the state of New York, and their gross population nearly four millions of people (1900).

Geographical: Southern Appalachians

Their average civilization is decidedly below that of the general standard of the nation, but the submerged minority, whose excessive backwardness greatly depresses the average, is but a fragment of the whole. Within this area live some of the most vigorous and progressive of Southerners. Not only is the great Appalachian Valley, running from Pennsylvania to Tennessee, one of the most ancient of national thoroughfares and a most poetical, productive, and beautiful region, but in the Appalachian province are located mighty industrial cities like Knoxville and Chattanooga, Tennessee; Bristol, Virginia; and Birmingham, Alabama; while just at its southern border lies Atlanta. There are famous health resorts like Asheville, North Carolina, with its magnificent Vanderbilt estates adjoining. Appalachian Tennessee even boasts of four ancient colleges, locally renowned and widely useful, three of them dating back to 1795. Much of the capital which has developed the industries of these

Unequal Development of their Civilization

cities and smaller centers is from the North and the mixture in them of Northern and Southern population and ideals against the mountain background creates one of the most interesting and stimulating of American environments. Yet even these progressive centers tell the tale of their human sources of supply. Knoxville has 71.81 illiterate white children of native parents per thousand, Chattanooga 39.3, Atlanta 34, against 8 per thousand in the most backward of the Northern cities, and then only in regions notoriously affected by Southern immigration.[1] Very unequally then, within this general area, have the mountains been a barrier to participation in the best of national life. We must find out to what degree and discover the particular local areas of backwardness.

Areas of Special Backwardness — A glimpse at the population maps in the volumes of the last census reveals the fact that the mountains are peopled to an average density about that of the agricultural states of the Mississippi Valley and of the rural South. The much exploited feud-counties of Kentucky, for example, have about the same population per square mile as Iowa. Only in West Virginia, in small areas including the great Smoky Mountain between North Carolina and Tennessee, and in parts of the Cumberland Plateau in middle Tennessee is the population notably slight; while, just between these two last-mentioned areas, the valley of the upper Tennessee and its tributaries has been since 1810 one of the most densely populated of American regions of equal area. Manifestly, then, isolation, as a ground of backwardness, is present in very unequal degrees. Other census maps show great unevenness in the distribution of improved land, of agricultural productiveness, and of

[1] Census Bulletin 26, p. 53.

transportation facilities, while the statistics of manufacturers show similar irregularities. Wherever there are people, farms, railroads, factories, there is likely to be education, an ordinary development of civilization, and a fair degree of progress; but where deficiencies in all or most of these things coincide in the same area — where there are few people, little productive land, no markets, no industrial development — one finds, in all of these nine Appalachian states, whole counties of extreme backwardness of life. Throughout all of this area there exists also a submerged class, the product of former isolation and lack of opportunity, in the midst of the generally hopeful population. Manifestly the true strategy of philanthropy is to find out these particular areas of need and to devise help for especially backward classes.

Attempts at Numerical Statements of Mountain Need The various attempts at a numerical estimate of these backward classes are more interesting than instructive. To tell the truth, nobody knows; the statistical means of finding out do not exist. The following quotation certainly implies a gross overstatement:

> Berea's work to-day has an absorbing interest to the scholar and the patriot. The institution has discovered three million British descendants who have been in a very real sense "lost" in the Southern mountains.

Naturally, it is possible to quibble over the meaning of being lost, but in no just sense does three-fourths of the Southern Appalachian population constitute a specially needy class or call for national philanthropy. On the other hand the following from an experienced educator in the mountains as surely understates the case:

THE OLD MEN OF THE MOUNTAINS

Of the four million inhabitants of the region perhaps only one-tenth are very backward. The rest compare favorably with the inhabitants of any other section.

The physiographer, Brigham, speaks of two millions of people of pure American stock waiting to be assimilated to modern conditions.[1] President Samuel T. Wilson of Maryville College, Tennessee, the chief Presbyterian authority in this field, writing from a vantage-point of lifelong intimacy and educational service for the mountain people, ventures to guess that there may be from a quarter to half a million of the lowest and really degenerate class.[2]

Compensations of Backwardness

President Wilson very properly defends his people against the charge of generally inferior character and intelligence, and insists that mountain backwardness has compensations in the greater ruggedness of body and mind preserved there, the resourceful strength and the absence of urban vices and follies, with their train of too strenuous nerves and tempers. No one who knows the mountaineer will fail to make these allowances, and every one who writes of him should insist that his readers make them also. Illiteracy by no means always indicates lack of mental alertness. I recall Uncle Jimmy Yeakley, who could neither read nor write, and did n't much need to. He could remember the exact terms of every transfer of land back to the beginning of records. As telephone-king of his region he had strung hundreds of miles of wire from tree to tree over which to talk with his neighbors; thus avoiding the necessity of writing. No one who had ever

[1] Brigham, "Geographical Influences in American History," p. 323.
[2] "The Southern Mountaineer," p. 38.

undertaken business dealings with him doubted Uncle Jimmy's mental capacity afterward.

How far is the backwardness of the mountains due to inferiority and how far merely to lack of opportunity? This is their deepest problem. To some extent undoubtedly the mountain environment has been selective, choosing for itself such types of mind and character as preferred and were fitted to its ruder life. To get the bearings of this problem we need to take a more accurate look at the physiographical peculiarities of the Appalachian area.

How far is Backwardness due to Inferiority?

The Great Appalachian Valley is recognized by geographers as the axis of that mountain system. For detailed descriptions of its internal relations the reader must consult special authorities;[1] but it is at least possible to note that all the true mountains — typified by the peaks of the Blue Ridge of North Carolina — lie to the south and east of this valley; while a larger mountainous area lying to the north and west of it — the so-called Alleghany and Cumberland "ranges" — is really only a prolonged plateau. Now, curiously, it is not in the true mountains with their higher peaks, their broader and deeper valleys, but on the scarred and broken top of this long-weathered plateau that by far the greater part of the needy mountain population lies. They crossed over and around the true mountains, passed the fertile and smiling valley, and paused in the rugged Cumberlands, almost in sight of the Blue Grass and rich Mississippi plains — like Moses just outside of the Promised Land.

Why did they not go on and complete the crossing, the most marvelous and epic movement of American history?

[1] Brigham, "Geographical Influences in American History," p. 81.

THE OLD MEN OF THE MOUNTAINS

Why did they stop in the mountains? Were they too weak to go on? Was it always the "tragedy of the broken axle"? Were they afraid? All of these. On the one hand, the mountain barrier caught and held such people as lacked physical resources to overcome them. On the other hand, to some extent at least, it sifted the westward emigrant, and kept the less energetic and resourceful for its own. And, indeed, the transition was not easy. It took daring to meet the strange conditions of the plains, to abandon the mountains for the prairies. The tradition of the author's family tells that when its forbears left the Tennessee mountains for a prairie state, they hunted out a spot in the bluffs of the Mississippi River and grubbed out a farm from the timber while thousands of clear acres were at hand for the asking. For the mountains were doubly indispensable to the imagination. They both overawed and won the hearts of their children.

The Mountain People cannot be Saved Wholesale

Thus, in its most backward areas, the mountain stock represents a part of the original colonial emigration whose hearts failed at the sight of the prairies; who loved hunting and fishing and the rude old ways. The conservative element and the incapable element mixed together, became further depressed by the poverty of their land, and were fixed in the mental traits of reckless but curiously unadventurous men. We can never disentangle the influences at work or give them numerical expression; but all educational effort in the mountains discovers plenty of natural capacity only awaiting opportunity, along with not a little hopeless stuff sifted out and left behind by the sturdier stream of American progress. Thus part of the mountain shiftlessness may be removed by the instruction of one generation in rural economy, part rests

CHRISTIAN RECONSTRUCTION IN THE SOUTH

back on the original shiftlessness which left its victims on the far side of the hills from civilization; part of its incapacity utterly disappears when the tools of progress are put into the hands of its youth, part persists in a deep-seated nervelessness and apathy before the more complex demands of modern life. No more than the negroes can the mountain people be saved wholesale. The offer of opportunity only compels them to register their inner differences and thus completes the ancient sifting.

In terms of general educational need the problem of the mountains has been most carefully measured by the Southern Educational Board.

Statistics of Educational Deficiencies

In that portion of West Virginia, Virginia, Kentucky, North Carolina, Tennessee, South Carolina,

	LITERATES	ILLITERATES	PER CENT ILLITERACY
West Virginia	202,459	24,229	10.68
Virginia	107,790	20,422	15.94
Kentucky	93,530	25,851	21.65
North Carolina	102,918	25,460	19.83
East Tennessee	134,138	30,127	18.34
South Carolina	42,577	6,572	13.37
Georgia	44,813	9,651	17.72
Totals	728,225	142,312	16.34

and Georgia, contained between the foothills of the Blue Ridge on the east and those of the Cumberland

Primitive Industry of the Mountains

Modern Industry of the New South

Mountains on the west, there were in 1900, in a total number of 870,537 male whites twenty-one years of age, over 142,312 or 16.34 per cent, who could not read and write. The table herewith gives the figures for the Appalachian section of each state.

Figures for illiteracy may not be very accurate, but where sixteen per cent of the white voters report themselves to the census as illiterate, it means that at least fifty per cent of the white population over ten years of age is wholly without letters.[1]

The case of a typical mountain county, Harlan, Kentucky, reveals both extreme educational poverty and rapid recent progress. This county has fifty-nine districts, none of which previous to 1904 had a graded school nor one with as much as a six months' term. Even according to Southern standards its teachers were miserably prepared. Half of its fifty-three schoolhouses were built of logs, and the total value of the fifty-three was less than ten thousand dollars. Not three-fourths of its school population was enrolled, and the average attendance was but forty per cent of the enumeration. Its only graded and reasonably efficient schools were two conducted by missionary societies, each of which had four or five teachers. It will be noted that the county did not lack for schoolhouses, such as they were. Indeed there were altogether too many. But measured by any reasonable standard its educational deficiencies were awful to contemplate. Its school period was far too short, its teachers wofully inferior, its facilities ridiculously inadequate; besides, half of its children were not using even such opportunities as were afforded. Probably more than fifty per cent of its white population was illit-

A Typical Kentucky County

---

[1] Quoted by Wilson, "The Southern Mountaineers," p. 69.

erate. That it might have been better is proved by the rapid progress since 1904. In a single year, under the inspiration of the general educational revival in the South, and with the aid of state funds, ten schools lengthened their terms to over six months, a considerable proportion of teachers acquired higher grade certificates, salaries were decidedly advanced, seven new schoolhouses were built, and the average attendance was raised to seventy-seven per cent of the enrolment. Though desperately poor, Harlan county chiefly needed and needs stimulus from without and a practical expression of its solidarity with the more favored regions of its state.

II. HOW THE MOUNTAIN MAN LIVES

It will help our understanding of the life of the mountains to study Harlan county further as one of its characteristic seats. Its many streams constitute the head-waters of the Cumberland river. Surrounding their valleys rises an almost unbroken circle of mountains cut only by distant gaps and otherwise crossed, if at all, by incredibly rough bridle-paths. Within this encircling barrier of lesser mountains lies the great Black Range. On either side are Piedmont valleys, themselves carved by streams into lesser valleys two thousand feet and more deep. The mountains have narrow, winding crests and steep sides, interrupted here and there where some ledge of more resistant rock has remained to uphold a bench or "cove" of gently sloping land just above it. Along the lower courses of the greater valleys are narrow strips of tillable bottom land which disappear higher up into broken gullies. Farming is crowded out of these too-narrow quar-

The Head-waters of the Cumberland, a Typical Region

THE OLD MEN OF THE MOUNTAINS

ters onto the lower slopes and even the high benches of the mountains.

My first incursion into this "Lonesome" country was on a magnificent morning in November. Before light I had left the regular railway on the Virginia side, had boarded a coal company's train for a dozen miles' ride over a rough spur of track, and had been met at the mines by the principal of the Black Mountain Academy. The mist was still in the valleys when we took the mail-carrier's trail leading over the very ridge of the Black Range. More than once we were forced to take to our feet and hands while the horses scrambled up the trail ahead of us. Two hours of breathless climbing brought us to the top, where, through magnificent portals of gray rock, we passed into Kentucky and began the descent, the path soon finding and following the windings of a mountain stream. Into this snug nook even winter had failed to penetrate. We rode under great chestnuts still in leaf and just dropping their nuts. The wealth of laurel and rhododendron foliage in the deeper ravines gave the landscape almost a look of spring, while all along the way the holly flamed under its burden of berries.

The ragged flanks of the mountain rising on either side of the trail nowhere afforded a level space as large as a city lot, yet we passed no fewer than a dozen cabins in half that number of miles. This is the mountain home. It clings to its steep slope; frequently it consists of but one room; usually it is built of logs and rough hand-split shingles, its chinks and chimney being daubed with mud. It is uniformly windowless, though perchance furnished with a solid shutter or two. Its surroundings are less slovenly but poorer than those of any negro settlement I have

The Mountain World

ever seen. Attached to each house is a half acre or less of sickly corn patch, clustered among the gaunt and protesting ruins of the forest. The Indian was cruel to trees as well as to man, and the mountaineer clears his field by the savage's wasteful method of girdling the standing timber, which remains until it rots and falls. All "carrying" is done with a sure-footed ox and sledge, for no wheeled vehicle could possibly be handled on these steep hillsides. Behind the cabin huddles a rough shelter of logs and pine boughs for the single work-beast. The only other stock, a scant dozen of razor-back pigs, sweeten but rarely fatten on beechnuts and the plump acorns of the chestnut-oak. This is mountain agriculture.

On the lower slopes we pass lumbering oxen, slowly dragging great tulip logs to the skidway, whence they go crashing down to the stream below to wait a "big tide," which will float them to the lumber mills on the lower river. This is mountain industry.

Suddenly the trail turned and showed a glimpse of a cluster of cabins below. "There," exclaimed the Principal, "is n't that a fine spot for a town?" I agreed that it was beautiful but ventured a suggestion that the space was too narrow to afford much room for growth. "Well," said he, "this is the largest level spot in the county." Such is the "pent-up Utica," the mountain town.

But it is not fair merely to cross over the mountain; one must also ride up the valley. This is the thoroughfare of the county, a way infrequently traversed by wheels. The horses splash through Poor Fork innumerable times, while pedestrians cross on logs or leap from stone to stone. Manifestly this bridgeless road might be cut into fifty sections by an hour's thunder-storm. After an ordinary summer freshet I have

A Ride up the Valley

THE OLD MEN OF THE MOUNTAINS

squatted on the river bank for half a day and watched the gathering knots of mountaineers waiting for the water to fall. A similar group gathered on the other side. They showed no evidence of haste, little speculation, and no inclination to take risks. We simply waited until the mail-carrier, whose pay was at stake, ventured to try the ford; then the rest followed after. Such contingencies are not conducive to school going, and "Reckon ye kin ford the branch to-day?" discourages much social intercourse. Many of the valley homes, however, are in striking contrast to those of the slopes and shoulders of the mountain. Here is compressed all that that mountain calls wealth. Where the bottom-land widens, agriculture may yield a fair subsistence or even a rude plenty. Two-story, solidly framed houses are not infrequent. In some of them I have seen and envied bits of colonial furniture or plate, reminiscent of tidewater Virginia. The spinning-wheel still hums and the loom clatters, keeping alive the fireside industries and preserving a tradition of beauty in weave and color. Farm touches farm for miles along the valley, and some traveler or other on his jogging mule is rarely out of sight. At intervals one passes a rude cabin country store — for the valley is Broadway as well as Fifth Avenue — or a grist-mill with great, picturesque water-wheel. The schoolhouse is not absent. Indeed, as we have noted, the county has fifty-three, most of which stand in the valley. The Principal reports that on his recent round of eighty miles to solicit students he passed seven. Four were built of logs and three of slabs; four had windows, two had shutters, and one had no light save from the open door. There were two stoves for the seven schools and two blackboards; while in two the only seats were rough planks laid across stones. We passed, however, one framed and neatly painted building revealing the uplifting influence of the academy, and of the general educational revival.

Down the valley, at the confluence of Poor Fork and two other streams, is the county seat, the mountaineer's metropolis. Its type is well depicted in Fox's "Trail of the Lonesome Pine." Its central features are a squat court-house of brick and a jail in which rough-hewn stones set a few inches apart in its frowning walls, like the embrasures of a fortress, serve in lieu of windows and bars. Perhaps two dozen frame buildings, with a single corner brick store, house the merchandise of the community. Blacksmith and harness shops are in evidence, for the hitching racks are lined with horses, and the streets (there are almost no sidewalks) are filled with booted men. There is a hotel, chiefly frequented by lawyers at court time or by an occasional drummer; a small sawmill; frame houses for the merchants and county officials, while the cabins of the poorer population crowd back into the gullies or hide on the mountainside. There is probably a doctor or two and several lawyers, but no regular dentist and no editor. President Frost of Berea used to tell of twenty contiguous mountain counties without a printing-press. Four or five church-houses may be found, in varying stages of dilapidation; but not one will have a pastor who gives his entire time to his congregation. The preacher is usually a farmer who preaches irregularly and makes his living by some other calling than the gospel. Services are held in each church " once't a month." The preaching is apt to be vociferous, intensely sectarian, but sometimes shrewdly pointed. As repository of doctrinal weapons the Bible is much on the lips of the people, and the backwoods

The County Seat; Contacts with the Larger World

county seat probably hears more religious "argifying," in a day than the whole of New York. A revival, like a hanging or an election, will fill the settlement with a motley, high-strung crowd, generally armed with carnal as well as spiritual weapons; or perhaps instead of the revivalist there is a politician organizing the more adventurous into a mountain army with which to descend to intimidate a legislature or slay a governor.

Twenty miles away, beyond the Gap, is the railroad. That and the river yonder are the infrequent avenues to the dimly-imagined larger world, the Blue Grass, the city, the college, and even the nation's capitol. But poverty and a strange inertia, half fear and half conceit — far more than mere physical remoteness — keep the mountain masses less responsive to the world's call than are the Slavic peasantry of eastern Europe.

III. MOUNTAIN LIFE REFLECTED IN THE MOUNTAINEER'S TRAITS

In economic development the life of the mountains represents an incomplete transition from the hunting and fishing to the agricultural stage. Partly from an unconquerable love of the wild and partly from the pressure of necessity, forest and stream are regularly searched for their store of food — wild turkey and occasional deer, fish, and honey, with a relish of nuts and berries. Often the call of the chase is louder than the more prosaic call of the corn-field, and lures the mountaineer to the neglect of his little farm. Even in the face of extreme need he remains a spasmodic and irregular worker, and when caught by the coal or lumber company his first industrial efforts are highly unsatisfactory. The

The Stamp of the Primitive

professional trapper is a familiar character, and his pelts form a habitual currency of mountain exchange. Isolation from the world means two things — first, a lack of industrial instruments and of resources for the easing of human misery, but also poverty of aspiration. Thus it happens that many children of the mountains look backward; not toward American civilization, but toward the life of the savage. Shut out from the characteristic currents of their age and standing on an inadequate basis of economic resources, they tend to be forced back upon the primitive, which in turn stamps itself upon their minds.

I recall one of my earliest visits to a mountain home in company with a man who had come to inspect it with reference to a real estate loan. Examination discovered eighty acres of limestone débris and a backwoodsman's cabin. The family consisted of middle-aged parents and four half-grown children. Absolutely their only implements of labor and livelihood were hoes, axes, and guns. Livestock was limited to a few fowl. There was no draft animal and on this farm not even pigs. Naturally the loan had to be refused; yet this man called himself a farmer, and with such slender resources was vainly trying to support himself from the soil.

Farming with Hoe, Axe and Gun

The distinctive social and institutional traits of the mountains show clear marks of their environmental origin. The clan loyalty of the feudist, for example, comes by historical descent from the Highland Scotch. It has survived also in the Southern Appalachian because it is the natural cooperative resource of poor and weak men who have been forced by a limited habitat to excessive intermarriage. They strive with instinctive ferocity to maintain the blood-bond. The

Environmental Origin of Social Traits

OLD WATER-MILL

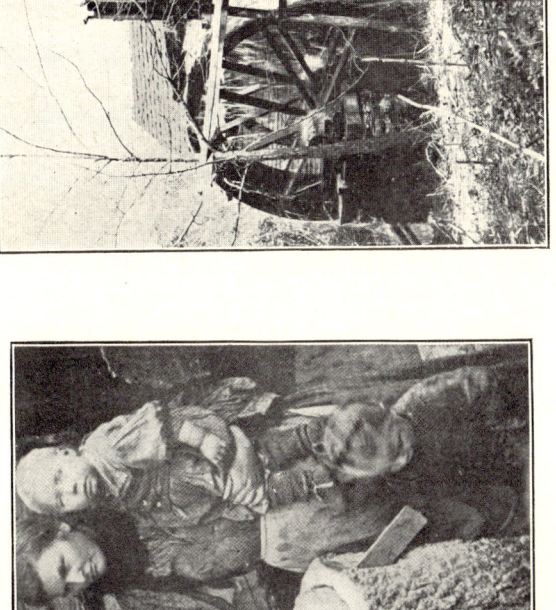

DOMESTIC GRINDING-MILL

SOUTHERN APPALACHIAN MOUNTAINS

author's mountaineer ancestors preserved their clan organization through successive migrations covering at least four states, the habit surviving long after the necessity had passed.

On the other hand, there is an almost total absence of those more complex human relations, to express and control which social institutions are developed. The breakfast-table of the "middle American" may hold food products from a dozen states and from lands beyond both oceans. These stand for ten thousand human ties, each of which has some systemized and interrelated social process to guide it. The mountaineer's table holds the scant product of his own acres, raised and prepared by the labor of his own hands. Hence there is little sense of the need of institutions beyond the blood-bond. The primitive barter of the country store, the irregular religious services of the settlement, the short term school, and periodic visits to the county seat are too far apart and too often interrupted to serve as centers for definite and dominating organization. Local institutions, therefore, do not rise to break the clan allegiance.

Lack of Social Institutions

In contrast with his feeble sense of the community, it is interesting to discover in the mountaineer a unique sense of the nation. That he is part of a larger life he has two impressive reminders — the revenue officer and the soldier. The one forces from the mountains tribute to a social order of which they are not conscious. Their manner of life does not depend upon a vast machinery of civilization which must be supported by taxes; consequently they are not convinced of the nation's right to impose such burdens upon them. But the soldier reminds them of a relation of which they are most conscious. The mountains know

The Unique Sense of the Nation

and are proud of their record in war. In the chapel of Berea College I saw a student body of over a thousand arise, almost as one man, to testify that they were children or grandchildren of Union soldiers of the Civil War. On winter evenings in the lonely cabins, the battles of the nation are mingled with the battles of Israel in fireside story, and tradition keeps the memory alive of how the mountain men bulwarked the nation against the Cherokees or followed Jackson to New Orleans. The call of war has always touched their natures and stirred their profound instinctive loyalty to an abandon of patriotic response to their country's need. In '61 they followed the nation against their own states. These war memories, moreover, are the clue to mountain politics. Not from any sense of present national issues, but because of that party's association in their minds with the cause of the Union are they so stubbornly Republican. The nation exists for them as a far-off, mighty tradition, an unknown but extremely genuine object of allegiance; but between the clan and the nation there is no intermediate institution which holds their hearts. Community life, the manifold relations of local citizenship, the complexity of civilized institutional activity—of these they are innocent.

In the characteristic traits of mountain family life, especially in those concerning the relations of man and woman, there is much that suggests the Indian. The man lives an essentially outdoor life, using the house rather as a place to eat and sleep than as a home. To the women is consigned not only the household drudgery, but often the cultivation of the soil, while the man leads the woodsman's life. This is universally the primitive division of labor. Like all similarly situated peoples, the mountaineer makes little outward show

Relations of Sexes

of affection. Not often does he frolic with his children, and even the mother holds her babe stolidly. At public gatherings, like church services, the sexes generally sit apart; while the assumption of masculine superiority is clearly written in the simple yet unyielding fabric of mountain convention. The callow youth and even the schoolboy assume this pose as their natural birthright. The girl on the contrary accepts, as does the woman of the Old World, the social estimate put upon her and would be horrified beyond measure at the independence which the modern young woman claims as her due. Even when one comes to know the mountain girl well as a student he is made to feel in a hundred ways an unfathomable reticence which is both a defense and a barrier. Frequently even considerable education fails to eradicate the old instinct, and the cultured and well-equipped girl returns to the cabin life as the fulfilment of her nature. All this necessarily affects marriage relations. The most subtle and exquisite interpreter of the mountains, herself born of them, puts it thus:

> A rift is set between the sexes at babyhood that widens with the passing of the years, a rift that is never closed even by the daily interdependence of a poor man's partnership with his wife. Rare is a separation of a married couple in the mountains; the bond of perfect sympathy is rarer. The difference is one of mental training and standpoint rather than the more serious one of unlike character, or marriage would be impossible. But difference there certainly is. Man and woman, although they be twenty years married — although in twenty years there has been not one hour in which one has not been immediately necessary to the welfare of the other — still must

needs regard each other wonderingly, with a prejudice that takes the form of a mild, half-amused contempt for one another's opinions and desires. The pathos of the situation is none the less terrible because unconscious. They are so silent. They know so pathetically little of each other's lives.[1]

I have seen just this trait characteristically illustrated in families which I have known intimately for a number of years.

An apparently contradictory but equally characteristic primitive trait — and one of the most interesting — is the unusual respect sometimes given to old women. One whose body and brain have run the harsh gauntlet of privation and labor may develop a lean and wiry endurance and a practical resourcefulness, which with age ripen into a unique social authority. The savage woman used frequently to achieve a similar position by reason of her dominant share in primitive culture. In a social group as dependent upon itself as are the mountaineers, the home industries in the hands of women produce most of the comforts of life and much of its wealth. I noted that Jackson's "old woman" was the real head of the house. I understood why, when I saw her heaps of homespun blankets (enough, she explained, for all her daughters' children; and they expect large families). She would not sell one at any price, though for a sufficiently large sum my companions secured enough jeans for a suit. In such characters we discover under mountain rudeness the same capable woman of whom the Hebrew Proverbs sing, examples of capacity left in the rough, as in a statue of Rodin's.

Social Authority of Old Women

[1] Miles, "Spirit of the Mountains," pp. 69, 70.

> "She riseth also while it is yet night,
>   And giveth meat to her household,
>   And their task to her maidens."
>
> "She girdeth her loins with strength,
>   And maketh strong her arms.
>   She perceiveth that her merchandise is profitable:
>   Her lamp giveth not out by night.
>   She layeth her hand to the distaff,
>   And her hands hold the spindle."
>
> "Her husband is known in the gates
>   When he sitteth among the elders of the land.
>   Strength and dignity are her clothing;
>   And she laugheth at the time to come.
>   She openeth her mouth with wisdom,
>   And the law of kindness is on her tongue,
>   She looketh well to the ways of the household,
>   And eateth not the bread of idleness."

Savage or civilized, highland or lowland, she is rare; but where she exists " her price is above rubies."

The religion of the mountaineer, too, feels the modifying touch of the wild. As a personal solace and an emotional energy and resource in the hour of crisis, it is a genuine and momentous thing. But, on the other hand, the mountain barrier has prevented the institutional development of the church. It has defeated the missionary in common with the other agents of civilization. Throughout the mountains there is a large lack of the most characteristic outward expressions of church life — buildings, regular services, a professional ministry, a systematic parish organization, manifold activities of present-day Christianity. Besides this, the mountains have produced a temperamental change in religion. The original Scotch-Irish stock went into the mountains Presbyterian. Their descendants are now most largely Baptist and Methodist. The breaking off of the Cumberland branch from the Presbyterian body marked

The Touch of the Wild upon Religion

a tendency toward the present characteristic type of religious life; more emotional, less staid and orderly than it originally was. It is with great difficulty that pupils in certain mission schools are induced to attend Episcopal services, and the admirable work of this church has had a difficult handicap in the distaste of the mountaineer for ecclesiastical form. The ill-balanced temper of the poorer population, reflecting their under-nourishment, craves religion, as it does whisky, as a stimulant. The " right hand of fellowship " concluding a mountain preaching may be as frankly primitive as the negro's most boisterous church service. Both are reversions to the religious spontaneity of the earlier ages.

Naturally, religion cannot become the reenforcement or guaranty of a social system which the mountaineer does not have or believe in. It does not tend, for example, greatly to back up the revenue laws. On the other hand, it does mightily reenforce clan loyalty. It is tribal rather than Christian (as indeed is much of the religion of more privileged people) and does not demand the exercise of Christian virtue toward those beyond the pale. It is intermingled with a larger number of particular superstitions than is that of the average American; for the mountaineer's thinking has not been persistently schooled away from the early race-imagination, which peopled the world with mysterious powers. And because the mountain environment is niggardly, the religious impressions drawn from it are fearsome rather than tender. Thus the mysterious " T'other mountain " does not yield the adventurer " glimpses which should make him less forlorn," but rather an ever-present sense of impending danger. Finally, the brooding temper of the mountain, wrought upon by the potent spells of forest and stream, fiercely fed by omen

THE OLD MEN OF THE MOUNTAINS

and arbitrary Scripture, shows itself in all manner of quaint and sometimes dark vagaries of theology and religious imagination. The mountains are prolific of seceding sects. Marauding faiths, like Mormonism, find apt pupils there, and contradictions of personal character occur like that of old Red Fox in " The Trail of the Lonesome Pine," mystic and assassin, preacher and traitor!

Enormous illiteracy and an almost total absence of books and of the habit of reading, such a phenomenon as that of twenty contiguous counties without a printing-press, naturally do not tend to those outward expressions of literary and esthetic interest to which completer civilizations are accustomed.

Rudimentary Literary and Esthetic Interests

Nevertheless the mountains have a traditional literature, an elaborate and highly artistic folk-lore, a simple yet genuine musical tradition — coming straight from the ballad makers of the Scotch border, as well as a conventional art, by no means despicable, in their old weaves and dye-colors, their basketry and furniture patterns. They use many archaic words and phrases, preserving a pure and ancient English speech from which we have departed. There is a curiously complex mingling in their folk-stories of myths from over seas with those of the Cherokee Indians. Another genuinely artistic creation is a rude minstrelsy — less primitive, original, and emotionally penetrating than the negro's, but equally characteristic of its people. No American group is more dependent on, responsive to, or critical toward, the spoken word, as many a Northern missionary has found to his sorrow. Oratory is still the chief art, and eloquence is vital rather than traditional. Thus the mountain fiddler, the looms, and dye kettle of the valley, the fireside storyteller, and itinerant preacher attest the life of the imagination; while the mountains themselves perpetuate the sense of awe and stir the quick love of beauty.

His fundamental lack of a sufficient basis of economic support needs to be insisted upon as the real explanation of the mountaineer's less amiable traits, both mental and moral. His deficiencies, like the negro's, are the legitimate results of his social station. His violence, for example, is primarily the fruit of under-feeding and poor housing. Ill-nourished nerves crave "moonshine," and in lives touched by the wildness of nature, deficiency in motor control expresses itself in sudden murder. The sensational exploiting of mountain communities by novel and newspaper, grievously misrepresents their average social condition. Yet they undoubtedly surpass the rest of the nation and even of their section in the reckless taking of human life. I am sure that the holiday season, in the immediate region of the mountain town where I recently spent six months, was a time of more killings than would occur in a rural county of the Middle West in ten years. It is probable that the habit of homicide was fixed in the mountains by the bushwhacking exploits of the Civil War — such as the fratricidal strife of "Rebel Jake" and "Union Jerry" in Fox's story. One who has spent his life among them tells me, "Before the war they used to fight with their fists." Thus from the great struggle in which the mountains bore so splendid a part, has come the custom of avenging wrongs with the bullet.

Less Amiable Qualities: Violence

Such an explanation seems not to fit such a mountaineer as the late Judge Hargis of Breathitt County, Kentucky, the reputed king of feudists and assassins. He was neither poor nor ignorant, and had had no little contact with public affairs in the larger world of men. The mystery is dissolved by the reflection that habit tends to live on after the original conditions which created it have disappeared. In each generation there are still enough mountaineers whose poverty keeps them wild to renew continually the springs of violence. The contact of the mountain masses with the higher stimulus of the larger world is still extremely limited. Lacking as they do the antidotes of a completer civilization, they are persistently inoculated by the more violent minority, and the homicidal habit is propagated by social tradition.

The mountaineer's most irritating fault is the fatalistic acceptance of unnecessary evils, especially apathy in the presence of misery. It also goes back to the economic deficit. These are the marks of men with whom life has so long been niggardly that they have ceased to hope. The hardness of the mountains soon wears out the most buoyant. One of my earlier pleasure trips into a typical region led me to Zach McDowell's. Zach's home was more spacious than most in the settlement and in it he entertained strangers for a price. My roommate for that night was a burly United States deputy marshal in search of timber thieves. During the evening a merry group of neighborhood young people had been singing around the " parlor " organ, and we had both commented upon the fresh and wholesome face and full voice of Zach's youngest daughter. Two years later I came that way again, and was horrified to find her a sunken-faced and back-bowed mother. Her husband was a mountaineer above the average. They had had only the common adversities of their people, but she had broken under them. This was my first introduction to a group phenomenon, the early fading of the mountain woman. For their chief tragedies are not the slaughter

Apathy in the Presence of Misery

of men but the sufferings of mothers and children. The struggle with the wild means not only racking labor, but frequent accidents, far from civilized help. It involves such risks, for example, as the jamming of the log raft so thrillingly described in Fox's "Little Shepherd of Kingdom Come." I think I never saw a school with so many maimed children as Black Mountain Academy. Childbirth without a physician; an unequal struggle for the poor necessities of life; a lack of the essential elements of civilized dietary; miserable cooking and resulting dyspepsia; the absence of dentist and oculist; the lack of social stimulus to make pride preserve what it can of the victim's wreck — all these conspire to depress the mountain woman's soul and to rob growing childhood of its strength. The result is paralysis of the will to strive, as exemplified in one of Mrs. Miles' mountain types:

> I have never seen anything greatly resembling Mary Burns. A certain maid, once of the village of Nazareth, may have had the same pure, modest sweetness, but her loveliness was of a type belonging to another race. For this Mary's hair was rich chestnut, and her eyes were blue — such a blue, softened by lashes of a length one notices on the lids of children. There was little light of intelligence in those eyes, but one felt that Mary's capacity for doglike devotion was unlimited. Excepting its innocence, the rich coloring of her face was its most striking feature. She had such a complexion as the first masters, knowing the effect of Southern sun, painted without stint of olive and golden velvet and perfect rose. Gentleness and simplicity are characteristic of the faces of mountain girls.
>
> There are those of a genuine exquisite modesty who have never in their lives slept in a room apart

from the men of their household. But this was a child's face, with a child's ignorance behind its lovely mask, a child's readiness to flash into smiles at the least provocation, a face that ought surely to have met only with tenderness everywhere.

And with all her beauty she had not even the mountain woman's poor best of cheap calico to wear! I tried to imagine her dressed in a white dimity, such as young girls wear in more favored regions, but even this seemed incongruous, although she could not have been more than seventeen years old. As we coiled and fastened her hair, I asked if she were going to the feet-washing, knowing how dear to the mountaineer heart is the privilege of attending every form of religious service.

"I reckon not," she answered, in her sweet, hushed, nun-like tones. "I ain't been to church sence my shoes wore out, sometime last March." So she had trodden the freezing mud of early April with bare feet! It would never have occurred to her to hide her poverty or her present physical distress; she hardly realized that in this respect she was ill used by her husband.

Superstition ascribes misery to mysterious sources and forbids rational remedies. To the cabin where a missionary was entertained came a mountain father at night-time carrying a child delirious with fever. He wanted to borrow an old shoe to get water out of a healing spring! The deep capacity of the Scotch stock for varied, tender brooding degenerates into mental vacuity. When the body rests there is little energy left for intellectual effort. When the body fails an almost unconquerable apathy sits and watches its decline.

The Tragedy of Sickness and Age

A new missionary teacher thus describes her first experience with sickness in the mountains:

We had heard that Sallie's mother was sick and consequently that Sallie could n't come back to school this year. So yesterday Miss B., the matron, with a group of schoolgirls, started to carry them some necessities, with a little jelly and fruit; and I went along. It was about three miles, and the path followed the Pacolet, at this point a mountain stream breaking into innumerable rapids and cascades. We found the cabin in a deep gully, surrounded by a clearing of about half an acre, thickly covered by gravel brought down by a recent freshet. A few stalks of sickly yellow corn still stood, and an old white pig, who came to meet us, was the only living possession of the family. Sallie's brother of twenty is a "farmer." In the winter he gathers chestnut bark for the Old Fort tannery. They have no other means of support.

The cabin seemed to have suffered from freshets, too, for the foundation had been washed away at one end and it lopped down into the damp earth. Inside, where the floor had come in contact with the ground, it had rotted away, leaving jagged holes either side the fireplace, which furnished the only heat for the two rooms. In one corner lay the sick mother on a disorderly bed, with horrible dirty coverings and no linen at all. She was all bloated with dropsy, but shrilled out many blessings on our heads for the presents. Sallie and two other older sisters were pictures of helpless inefficiency. It made me wild to see them sit and sit and do nothing. Miss B. impressed upon them repeatedly that they *must* put the fresh linen on their mother's bed and not eat the oranges themselves, but I am not sure what happened when we got away.

THE OLD MEN OF THE MOUNTAINS

When the body dies, isolation compels its consignment to the ground with the slightest delay, in the expectation that in six months or a year a funeral service will be held at the church-house. This custom of deferred burial rites is frequent even at the county seats and railroad towns. Thus a habit born of mountain necessity survives in populations now far beyond its compulsion. Similarly the general mental cast of the region is touched by the traits of the most backward. The constitutional nervelessness and apathy of the minority deeply influences the energies of the whole group.

On the other hand, where the struggle with nature has not too deeply depressed the body and mind, all of the splendid, homely virtues of the pioneer survive, and often take on rare attractiveness in the sons and daughters of the mountains. Their delayed development conserves much that this age lacks of unspoiled elemental manhood and simplicity of spirit — both profoundly urgent moral needs of to-day. Beneath a reckless individualism and ignorant conceit one discerns resources of sturdy independence. The mountaineer faces his hard circumstances with a heart at once undaunted and resigned. A saving sense of humor breaks every fall and turns defeat into more than half a victory. Having shrewdly fathomed human nature as it exists in his narrow range, he finds his judgments surprisingly just and accurate when opportunity comes to apply them to the larger world. He undertakes unwonted responsibility with a certain honorable largeness and perspective; thus showing that wisdom is born of insight rather than of the mere multiplication of experiences. Lincoln was such a man and had such wisdom. "He that is faithful in that which is least is faithful also in much." Training in the

[Marginal note: Mountain Virtues]

school of adversity often develops in the mountaineer a practical capacity for making small resources count which spells marvelous success when once the instruments of modern life are put in his hands. Recently I watched a mountain student's first inspection of the newly installed hot-air furnace in a mission school dormitory. The mountaineer, like the Indian, studiously refrains from confessing surprise at the unaccustomed; but this boy's curiosity and interest got the better of him. Soon he was freely speculating on the operation and success of the innovation; yet not for a moment did he admit to the world or to himself that he was not its potential master. He seemed to me typical of the mountaineer facing modern civilization. The mood of the forward-looking among them is the mood of conquest. Put it to the test by furnishing it an opportunity and it will justify itself as it has done ten thousand times.

The conflicting traits of their people, evil and good, I have watched in successive generations of students, each adding conclusiveness to the judgment that the problem of the mountain is twofold; partly that of a suppressed population possessing but not utilizing the normal capacities of Americans, and partly that of a remnant, sifted out in the westward march of civilization as deficient in energy and progressiveness. Education simply discovers these differences. We record this solemnly, as if the case of the mountaineer was unique. All peoples have these two classes and all education simply systemizes the processes which sift man.[1] Thus it frequently appears that the mountain boy has too much inborn inertia to respond

Good and Evil Traits of Mountain Students

---

[1] Thorndike, Educational Psychology, "The Influence of Selection," ch. ix.

The Mountain Weaver

The Cotton-Mill

to the steady discipline of study. His nature is not sufficiently elastic to adjust itself to school conditions. Such a one was "Big Scotch," who strayed from the hills, and was laid hold of and made "center" on a college football team. The gridiron gave ample scope for the primitive in him, and he quickly became an academic hero; but neither flattery nor abuse could keep him at his books, and only strenuous appeal to clan loyalty under the guise of college spirit held him through the season. At night, for utter homesickness, the big fellow would cry like a child; and when football was over for the year the call of the wild became irresistible. Back went "Big Scotch" to the cabin. Another year the college, in desperate need of him, tried by all manner of persuasion, including ample financial inducements, to dig him from his hills; but in vain. He remained a mountaineer, not of necessity, but through natural affinity for the life of the past.

On the other hand, I count it among my chief compensations to have known somewhat intimately a number of mountain students in an institution of higher learning. I have watched and in some measure shared in their transformation. They were raw material but most capable stuff. Gaunt and unawakened boys grew into alert, self-reliant, well-equipped modern men, invariably with a strong grain of idealism in their make-up, and able to stand the test before the kings of commerce and industry. There is only one finer thing than this, namely, that wonderful expansion of the mountain girl's nature under the new incentives of culture. Her earnest and capable womanhood is sure to be a center of wholesome home life as she goes back to her mountain community — generally first as a teacher in her own country school. Perhaps this back-

Judging the Mountains by their Possibilities

ground of experience helps me when I sit in some little cabin on the Upper Cumberland and see the parent incarnations of mountain simplicity. An old grandmother faces me. She sits tilted back against the wall, her rough-shod feet on the rungs of the hickory chair, and her knees mannishly apart. Her pipe is between her teeth and periodically she spits across the room into the fire; but her face reminds me of the Cumæan Sibyl, and an awe surrounds her, as if she were the Prophetess Deborah under the palm-tree in the hill-country of Ephraim.

With an unexplored wealth of such material to work upon, the assimilation of mountain life to the best American standard waits but two things — first, the development of the natural resources of its region by the larger instruments of civilization, capital, machinery, transportation; and second, the extension of educational institutions to furnish both technical skill and ideal guidance. These are both coming with almost alarming rapidity. Of men to respond there will be no lack. They are there waiting, offering a primitive American character, unspoiled and largely unused, plastic yet wholesomely resistant, to the touch of our full-fledged destinies as men of this crowning age.

The Mountain's Needs: Development of Resources; Guidance of Ideals

XI. THE PASSING OF THE MOUNTAINEER

PRESIDING over the future of the mountains are two ominous characters, the millionaire and the missionary. The passing of their characteristic life is predestined on the one hand by two facts — the very heart of its region holds the largest unworked coal fields in the United States, while its superb scenery and equable climate, both summer and winter, make it a national playground. On the other hand, neither the state nor the Christian conscience can longer endure the waste of mountain manhood for lack of opportunity.

There is thus a new chapter in the history of the Southern Appalachians.

I. THE EXPLOITATION OF THE MOUNTAINS BY INDUSTRY

The mountaineer is not so much to-day the man who has been left alone as he is the man whom we will not leave alone. For the wealth of mineral and of timber which these mountains hold, but especially for the wealth of labor power, industry is fast penetrating their most inaccessible nooks and corners. The industrial exploitation of the mountains is far advanced, and with it the passing of the mountaineer. We call this progress, forgetting

The Man Whom We will not Leave Alone

that to this belated man it brings a strain of body, mind, and heart which the best of us can scarcely bear, and for which he is one hundred and fifty years unprepared.

Consider first the effect of the cotton industry on the men, or rather on the women and children of the mountains. The chief Southern seats of this industry are the Carolinas. If you will study the location of the hundreds of mills which dot the uplands of these states, you will find that they are parallel to and frequently in sight of the mountains. Twenty years ago there was scarcely one of them; now this has become one of the great manufacturing centers of the nation. Whence came the men and women who labor in these mills? Most largely, naturally, from the upland farms of the immediate vicinity, but largely, and increasingly in recent years, from the fastnesses of the mountains. An intelligent mill owner has told me that the next census will show many mountain counties practically depopulated to swell the ranks of cotton-mill operatives.

The Cotton Industry

The unlovely life of the Southern cotton-mill town has been often exploited. It is a harsh measure of the poverty of the mountains, but in fact the mill town may constitute a decided advance in the conditions of life. First there is better housing, a steady cash wage, and a more varied diet of inexpensive food. The Scotchman rediscovers oatmeal, exchanges his corn bread for wheat, and makes the acquaintance of rice. There is a steady upward pressure of institutional and civic life. Schools are few and poor compared with those of more favored sections, and the mill child too often does not go; yet the opportunity is there, which public opinion, through child labor laws and educational improvement, is steadily extending. The imagination finds new food in the activities and impulses of town and city. Those who have ears to hear, hear.

In this crisis of transition, however, the economic and moral unpreparedness and even essential incapacity of part of the mountain population is also revealed. To them a cash wage means excess and drunkenness. They gorge themselves with newly discovered food. From being fixed by narrow isolation, they go to the other extreme and become industrial nomads. Such wandering families — for all ages and both sexes work — pass by hundreds from mill town to mill town, their scant possessions dragged about in sacks, or carried in their arms. The Southern mills have generally been short-handed in recent years, so that even the inefficient have been sure of a job. With mountain shrewdness, the father sets employer to bidding against employer for the labor of his wife and six, eight, or ten children — often no small labor force. To close a good bargain he will often throw in the labor of a child or two under the legal age. He himself does not work but is the walking delegate of his domestic trade-union. Naturally the down-draught of the city soon catches families of this type. They sink finally into a peculiarly inert and hopeless class of criminals and paupers. Thus the sifting proceeds.

But not only is the mill drawing the mountaineer out of his mountains; it is itself going up into the mountains to find him. I have recently traveled three branch lines which lead from the main line of a Southern railroad into the mountains, and have been amazed at the degree to which industry has followed the mountaineer into his own home. Here is a mill, fifty miles from a cotton field and eight

The Going of the Mill to the Mountain

miles from the end of a branch railroad. The cotton is shipped by rail and hauled by wagon over a rough mountain road; is manufactured, and the product hauled out again. What makes it possible thus to disregard all conveniences of transportation? First, the presence of good water-power, but chiefly the accessibility of cheap labor. Here is a population unused to industry; intensely individualistic; innocent of all knowledge of labor organization; which has handled very little cash, and is consequently willing to sell itself for an incredibly small sum in weekly wages. Adults receive perhaps $4 and children $2 per week. Their parents willingly swear that children are twelve, when they are only nine or ten, and "Everybody works but father" is not poetry here, but sober prose. There are coming to be many such mills among the mountains, as well as other industries. In the midst of the most picturesque stretch of mountain scenery in North Carolina the train suddenly stops over against a million dollar tannery, which is robbing the whole "land of the sky" of one of its most splendid trees, the chestnut-oak, that the nation may wear tan shoes.

Thus the old problems of the belated and ignorant highlander mingle with the new problems of child labor and of modern industry in general. But now, while we have gradually worked up to this industrial age through a century and a half, this man, our belated ancestor, our "contemporary grandfather," is hurled into the very midst of its strange perplexity and struggle without preparation. Take the single aspect of sanitation. I know a mill village in as beautiful a valley as the mountains possess. The employer has honestly tried to create wholesome industrial conditions, yet as time has passed the sources

The People a Century Unprepared for Industry

of water-supply have been contaminated by drainage until the whole smiling valley is sodden with hidden corruption, and women and children drop and die with typhoid as regularly as months come and go. The only possible remedy is a thorough job of sanitary engineering, so expensive that the resources of the mill corporation could not possibly justify it. Against this unwonted peril of sewage the mountaineer is helpless. His cabin has been cold, but well ventilated above, below, and on all four sides. Now he works in a steam-heated mill, and all the perils of the wilderness, the tomahawk of the savage, and the harsh struggle of the pioneer with the niggardly mountains, brought no such danger to life as is involved in bad air.

Farther west, in Tennessee and Kentucky, there are few cotton-mills, but industry has searched out the nooks and corners of the mountains for their coal and timber, and there also the old mountain life is fast passing.

Coal and Lumber

We went a three days' horseback ride from the railroad over the Black Mountain; down into the valley of Yoakum Creek; down that creek to its junction with Poor Fork of the Cumberland; up the fork; up Looney Creek, until we came at nightfall to the cabin of Old Man Jackson on the border of Letcher County. Old Man Jackson is a sort of nabob of the mountains, where the valley widens a little and furnishes the possibility of a bottom farm. He has a four-room cabin with three great stone chimneys, and there with his strong sons and daughters he dwells in self-sufficiency. His farm and pasture furnish food; his wool, clothing. The loom stands on the back porch, and the family, both men and women, are chiefly clad in homespun. We slept under many thicknesses of homespun blankets, in a room where rings of pumpkins were drying on spikes stuck between the stones of the great fireplace. The household is literally independent of

"*The butcher, the baker, the candlestick-maker,*"

for the only lights are the dipped candles and the flare of the open fire. If the mountains had suddenly risen and fenced the valley on either side, its life might have gone on indefinitely without ever missing the world, and I thought that of this spot at least I would be safe for fifty years in telling the old story of the mountaineer and his isolation. Yet, within three months, I read in a chance newspaper something like this: "The Blank & Blank Company of Indiana will spend a million dollars in Letcher County in the coming year. It will build thirty miles of railroad and open nineteen coke ovens." And why? Because the Lord sent a freshet which ran under Old Man Jackson's kitchen and laid bare a bed of coal. In the morning he could get up with his pick and get his fuel from underneath his house; and men heard about it. Therefore, where never in all the world had the shadow of one human habitation fallen upon another, a narrow valley will be crammed with crowded miners' huts. Those pure mountain streams will be fouled with the refuse of industry. Perchance a hundred negroes of the worst type — the irresponsible, unskilled labor class — will be thrust into the midst of a quiet mountain county which has scarcely seen a black face, and the worst possibilities of the race problem will be presented; and Old Man Jackson's sons, who have never been in bondage to any man, now for more money, indeed, than they have ever seen in their lives, will toil under ground.

The following press despatch indicates the industrial

and financial magnitude of this present partitioning of the mountains by the powers that be:

Bristol, Virginia, March 10, 1908. George L. Carter, President of the South & Western Railroad, has just closed a deal for an immense tract of coal and timber property in eastern Kentucky, including ninety-two per cent of the total acreage of ———— County and extending into other counties. The property was purchased in his own right, and some thirty thousand acres in fee simple. The consideration is not known. This purchase is a private investment of Mr. Carter, as the property will not be touched by the South and Western. It is believed that his ultimate object is to build another railroad through Kentucky.

<small>The Partitioning of the Mountains by Financial Powers</small>

The Martz Iron and Timber Corporation, of Kentucky, of which Mr. Carter is said to be the head, has just sold to J. H. Wallis & Co., Philadelphia Bankers, a tract of land in middle Tennessee and another in eastern Kentucky at $44,000. Attorney T. Irving Hart of Johnson City, in the employ of Mr. Carter, has just returned from Philadelphia, in connection with the deal.

South & Western Meeting

The annual meeting of the stockholders of the South & Western Railroad of Tennessee, will be held in the office of President Carter, at Johnson City, March 22, and will be attended by Thomas F. Ryan of New York, and probably Norman B. Ream of Chicago, Thomas Jefferson Coolidge of Boston, and other multi-millionaires interested in the project.

The company now has ample funds to complete the road, and it is believed that it will be ready for operation early next year. It is now about seventy per cent completed, and will require in the neighborhood of $10,000,000 before completed. The Clinchfield Coal Corporation, which is allied with the Ryan and Carter interests and owns 300,000 acres of coal land in southwest Virginia, is actively preparing to open the mines next year, and the $2,500,000 appropriated last year for this purpose is being expended. This is a $30,000,000 corporation, and is headed by George L. Carter, and for the development of which property the South & Western is being chiefly built.[1]

What will happen to the thousand families to whom this enormous project must mean sudden dislocation and a complete break with their whole scheme of life? The more fortunate will receive a few hundred dollars for their land or mineral rights. Utterly unaccustomed to a cash economy, they will not know how to use their sudden wealth, and will squander their lifetime's chance. It is exactly parallel to the case of the negro who buys a top buggy with the cotton surplus money he should pay on a farm. An agent, who has bought up such rights for years, tells me that rarely is the mountaineer wise enough to reestablish himself with the proceeds of his sale. Cut from his moorings he drifts; out of sight of his landmarks he is lost. There is no sadder human fate than these banishments decreed by progress.

This is the crisis of the mountaineer, the sudden presence of that sifting process in which the negro is caught in the city. It all means progress for those who can enter its gates of opportunity; the chance of an awakened mind, of a broader outlook; of wealth, with all its possibilities. But, oh, the

The Human Cost of Progress

---

[1] Knoxville Sentinel, March 10, 1908.

tragedy of it for those not able to meet this sudden stress, and its unwonted temptations; who cannot stand before the tremendous physical and mental and moral strain of what we call civilization! What special need, then, that the mountaineer shall have just now the steadying, guiding influence of the Christian school and the enlightened Christian church!

I have stood at twilight in a wonderful valley in Tennessee, where iron and coal lie side by side in the mountains and are rolled down, by their own weight, straight to the blast-furnace below. I have watched the flare of the furnace fires against the deepening gloom of the mountainside; I have seen the molten iron run like fiery serpents down its path of sand, and heard the fierce hissing as the dross, shattered by streams of water, falls into the waste-pit; and it has all seemed to me a terrible parable. For there are men in these mountains as well as minerals, and industry digs them out, to separate them, and to transform those who are fit unto better things. But industry does not care for the poor, the weak, the handicapped. God does; and in his behalf the missionary must stand to supplement, sometimes to neutralize, the harshly beneficent work of the millionaire.

The Parable of the Blast-Furnace

II. THE EXPLOITATION OF THE MOUNTAINS BY LEISURE

The tender mercies of the millionaire at play, even when touched with much sentimental philanthropy, are no less cruel than those of industry. Mrs. Miles puts the case so justly, and with such fine feeling, that I quote at length:

The Passing "Spirit of the Mountains"

One day a hotel is built, a summer settlement begun, in some fastness of the mountains hitherto secluded from the outer world. The pure air, the mineral waters, are advertised abroad, and the summer people begin to come in. Good roads are built in place of the old creek beds and trails, and rubber-tired carriages whirl past the plodding oxen and mule teams. Handsome cottages are erected in contrast to the cabins, and sunbonnets turn aside in wonder at bright creations of roses and chiffon. The mountain people come in groups to look on, some from homes so deep in the woods that the children take fright at the approach of even a home-made "tar-grinder" wagon. They are easily bewildered, of course, and cannot at once respond to the need of a new standard of values. Perhaps instead of a hotel it is a factory or a mill of some kind that presents the thin edge of the wedge, but the results are as certain to follow.

When the cottages are occupied the trouble begins. The hotel may bring its own servants; but for the summer people there are washing and sewing to be done by the women, and work in the gardens and stables by the men of the place. Later, they are hired as house servants, and as caretakers during the winter season, when the houses must stand empty. All this is hardly to be avoided, perhaps, but a host of evils follow. Here is an easy way of making money, and the old pursuits are abandoned. Men neglect their farms and the fashioning of sturdy home-made implements and utensils. It is easier, far, to buy city tools with city money. Their teams are constantly in demand for hauling, moving households up in the spring and down in the fall. They have never worked so hard before, nor been so well paid. The strenuous life has laid hold of them. It seems for a

THE PASSING OF THE MOUNTAINEER

time that better days have dawned for the half starved and the ignorant among us.

Is it any wonder that false ambitions creep in? The lady of the hotel or cottage, when she packs her trunks to go home, leaves sundry trinkets out for the mountain girl who has served her — half-worn clothing such as the poor child has never seen before, trimmed hats, books and magazines, if she can read. The recipient plans for a similar donation next year. She does not willingly return to sunbonnet and homespun. Her old mother cares little for the new clothes, but sees at once how much easier it is to buy blankets than to spin and weave. So the loom and wheel are consigned to the barn loft, where they fall to pieces with dry-rot, and the woman forgets her coverlet patterns. The hand of the worker in wood and metal loses its cunning. The growing lads scarcely learn to shoe a horse; they are all too busy working for the city people.

The value of money, the false importance of riches, is evident to their minds before the need of education. They become avaricious, they who were wont to share their last chew of tobacco, and put the children to earning, by picking berries or what not, instead of sending them to school. For by this time the city people have helped to build a schoolhouse in the district. The old-time hospitality is crowded out of existence, and under the influence of women, who imagine that a man who does not know when to take off his hat cannot possibly be courteous, the fine old manners disappear. The old music is supplanted by cheap Sunday-school song-books, that contain shaped notes and directions so clear that the wayfaring man who has learned to sing on the do-re-mi-fa-sol basis, though he knows not one key from another, need not err therein. The homespuns, with their delightful dull colors of root and bark, are ousted by aniline-dyed calicoes which do not wear more than a season. The beauty of simple smoke-browned interiors is blotted out with newspapers pasted, coat upon coat, on the walls for additional warmth, since paper is easier come by than substantial chinking. Druggist barrel-house liquor takes the place of the clear, fiery product of the still, making the evil of drunkenness ten times worse. The old dances are given over to rowdies. A new standard of morals is set up amid the confusion. Even the old religion is passing, laughed away by empty-headed ones who never could understand a thing so sacred. This people who have no servant class are constantly made to feel themselves inferior to the idle newcomers, and so fall into servility. The old dignity has slipped from them before they are aware.[1]

I know a mountain community in which rich Charlestonians have their own church. They bring their pastor for the summer and hold services for the transient population. Then they lock the church and go away, leaving the natives to themselves.

Dubious Influence of the Tourist

The lonely missionary teacher, shut in with them by impassable winter roads, does not find the influence left by the careless flitters altogether sweet. The native lads, who have made easy money driving smart rigs full of tourists to admire the mountain scenery, prefer to loaf rather than to go to school until next summer. Their wholesome standards of life have been overthrown. They see only the lighter side of more privileged civilization, pick up its vices and seldom understand its Titanic industry and profounder meaning. Thus the mountaineer

[1] Miles, "The Spirit of the Mountains," pp. 190-194.

falls into the gap between the old and the new. The spirit of the mountains is broken before the spirit of the modern world captures him in its imperious but courageous grip.

The saddest thing about the millionaire's ministry to the mountains, whether of work or of play, is that it is so largely exploitation rather than permanent occupancy. Just now the nation is waking up to the bitter fact that much of its industrial progress has been a squandering of natural resources; and waste has been nowhere more rampant than in the South. I shall never forget the passionate appeal of one of the educational evangelists of Tennessee who argued that his state, however burdened with debt, must educate its mountain people in order to end its exploitation by alien capital; an exploitation which is not only sapping it of present profits but will be sure to leave its land stripped of original wealth. The mountains are full of decaying coal towns whose last state is infinitely worse than the first. John Fox's latest story vividly describes the collapse of land and mining schemes and their effect upon an Appalachian county seat.

Industry and Leisure both Exploit rather than Occupy

The story of the lumber industry as managed by American commercial wisdom is one of continuous economic atrocities. When the denuded mountainsides hurl down their torrents upon the lowlands, overwhelming the Carolinas, and inundating Augusta, the nation begins to hear and pity the lowlands. These have tongues, a press, prominent representatives in Congress, which even Speaker Cannon cannot utterly and forever ignore; hence agitation for an Appalachian forest reserve. But the first tragedy of the fallen forest is that of the mountains themselves, which are voiceless. The thin soil of their slopes and shoulders

Ravishing the Mountains of Beauty as well as Wealth

is swept away; stones bury the bottom farms, while sadder still, the people are robbed of their long heritage of the beauty of the hills — their one priceless possession. Or, with the tourist, comes the freebooter florist, whose pernicious activity is exterminating some of the most charming winter greenery of the Carolinas to deck Northern feast or fast. Must we bury our dead under branches filched from our Appalachian brother, leaving his body to lie amid crumbling stumps and his dust to be washed from his naked hillside?

With the passing whim of fashion, winter resorts come and go. The wreckage of a million dollar hotel near Cumberland Gap, bought for a song, now houses a mountain school. Two other schools to my knowledge have acquired buildings under similar conditions. The toilsome climb up Walden Ridge to Grand View Institute recently made every brick for a new dormitory cost double by the time it arrived. A railroad used to run up there, but was abandoned with the waning popularity of the region as a health center.

These ebbing waves of industry and leisure cause some of the chief embarrassments of missionary policy. Frequently what seemed a dozen years back a promising and strategic center of mountain life, turns out to be a decaying community, disillusioned, disheartened, hopeful neither for church nor school. Its more energetic people, the natural leaders, abandon it. The foreign blood and capital which tried to develop it are withdrawn. Sometimes they were genuine home-seekers trying to naturalize the fruit industry or even general agriculture in the milder climate of the mountains. Somehow they do not stay. Decaying homes and deserted schoolhouses are their tragical recessional.

A Tragical Recessional

THE PASSING OF THE MOUNTAINEER

Now all this raises the question of the residual strength of the hills to hold back permanently the fuller tides of civilization. The New York Central Railway following up the water level of the Hudson to the Mohawk gateway can travel several extra miles to Buffalo and still have immense permanent advantage over its nearest competitor, which must lift its trains over the comparatively slight Alleghany barrier. All the resources of the modern world cannot neutralize an additional thousand feet of elevation. How much less will they quickly obliterate the height and breadth of the Southern Appalachians! Thus Brigham writes:

The Residual Strength of the Hills

> A few tons of coal are now enough to overcome the Appalachian barrier, and it is from this point of view, apparently, that a recent writer treats the Appalachians lightly, as if they were no barrier. They do not now stop or turn aside the movements of men and commodities, but they still interpose a peculiar belt of climate, soil, field, and forest between the Atlantic and the Mississippi, and their influence in early days was enormous. Geographic influences are no less real because they blend with other types of control in the maturity of society.[1]

So much is clear: the old man of the mountains is doomed. Enough of civilization, especially of its evils, is sure to come to break his dreams and wreck his peace, while the mountain barrier, as a stubborn physical fact, remains to make the bringing of the better opportunities of life a slow and difficult task for the statesman and philanthropist.

[1] Brigham, "Geographic Influences in American History," p. 318.

III. THE UPLIFT OF THE MOUNTAINS BY EDUCATION

This is one of the two great national missionary problems geographically located in the South, toward the solving of which the organized Christian philanthropy of the North has reached out a brotherly hand. Shall these vast and impending changes make for human welfare and the nation's moral strength? Because of the crisis of the exploitation by industry and by leisure — because both of these disturbing forces are exploitations and consequently careless as to their human fruits — and because the mountains remain, even when exploited, a molding and restraining power, the work of the missionary is of central importance. May there be a transformation as well as an exploitation, from old into new men of the mountains — men keeping all pristine virtues yet assimilating them to the better spirit of the age?

Relative Magnitude of Southern Problems: Negro vs. Mountaineer

Relatively speaking, as a problem of an unassimilated human mass, this problem is many-fold smaller than the other one. There are at least ten, or probably twenty times as many un-Americanized negroes in the South as there are mountaineers. The negro's present deficiency, too, is deeper seated and his prospects more dubious than theirs. From the standpoint of the nation, also, the negro problem is the more dangerous and pressing. It confessedly contains social dynamite, while the forgotten highlander might rot amid his stumps without disturbing the preoccupation of the greater and busier world. Thus, just because it is less directly emphasized in popular agitation, or backed by self-interest, the regeneration

Black Mountain Academy, Evarts, Ky.

Elementary Grades, Black Mountain Academy

THE PASSING OF THE MOUNTAINEER

of the mountains makes a profound and unalloyed appeal to the Christian conscience.

The missionary agencies which seek to do this work follow policies and use methods generally similar to those illustrated in activities for the negro. As in his case, their work will be illustrated by the typical but uniquely unsectarian institutions of the American Missionary Association.

Its educational activities are frankly cooperative with and supplemental to the public school systems of the Appalachian states. The will to educate the mountaineer is everywhere present, as the will to educate the negro is not. In the former case, therefore, it is merely a question of the state's ability, and the awakening of the mountain districts to add local responsibility to the state's resources. Wise and heroically conducted campaigns to this end are being persistently carried on throughout the South, and preeminently in the mountain states, to which, through the General Educational Board and the Peabody Fund, Northern philanthropy has largely contributed. The building up of state school systems, on the one hand, has largely distracted interest and gifts from the more modest work of the missionary institutions; on the other, it has progressively relieved them of burden and will increasingly do so. The South is not yet able to educate its children without help; but as it becomes able it will develop white schools first. Thus for philanthropy the mountains are not merely a lesser problem than that of the negro, but a more rapidly diminishing one. Where mountain mission schools exist, cooperation with the state is close. At present all of the American Missionary Association's mountain institutions, save one, receive public

Cooperation of Missionary Agencies with the State

funds. These pay but a small proportion of the expenses of maintenance and contribute nothing to the support of higher grades of education; but they secure the prestige — and sometimes the educational handicap — of state supervision, and express the cooperative spirit. In the crusade for better public schools, missionary principals have been the educational leaders of their regions. Some have served as county superintendents of education. The preparation of teachers has been a chief element of all missionary endeavor. Pleasant Hill Academy, Tennessee, has sometimes put fifty public school-teachers into the field in a single year.

With this institution we may begin our review of typical mountain institutions of the American Missionary Association, ranging from elementary schools to colleges and theological seminaries.

Typical Missionary Institutions of Secondary Grade: Pleasant Hill Academy

Pleasant Hill Academy is a secondary school of the older type. Its field, Cumberland County, is notable upon the census maps for the poverty of population and of agricultural production. Its three hundred pupils come from a surrounding region, one of the most backward in the United States. Some sixty of these pupils are in the two years' normal course following the elementary school. There are a dozen teachers, including special instructors in music and girls' industries. While boys' industries are not at present systematically taught, the school has its own sawmill, and has on occasion burned its own brick, out of which it has built two three-story dormitories. This year a girls' industrial building was erected, chiefly by student labor. Pleasant Hill has the reputation of making a dollar go further than it does anywhere else.

THE PASSING OF THE MOUNTAINEER

Around the school has grown up a modest and wholesome community life. There are half-a-dozen stores and shops and a cluster of homes, much superior to those in the neighboring settlements. Dignified and intelligent religious services draw splendid audiences. The attendance at a mid-week prayer-meeting would be a surprise and a gratification in a metropolitan church. The school brings also a superior grade of lecturers and entertainers. Probably no mountain institution has so completely become naturalized in the heart of its region. There will probably some day be a high school at the county seat, fourteen miles distant, but the Academy is founded in the affections of the people. It has identified itself with their interests. Even though the region should develop adequate public schools it will be needed, because of its sentimental value. Dozens of New England academies are not educationally necessary, but antedating the public school systems, they have historic sanction. Pleasant Hill Academy has a similar guaranty of permanence.

Grand View Normal Institute, a school of about the same size, situated in an adjoining county, shows a moun-
<small>Grand View Institute</small> tain institution in process of change from the old missionary type into one adapting itself better to serve the expanding needs and economic problems of the mountains. Its four years' secondary course prepares for the University of Tennessee, but its particular ideal is to become an agricultural high school. A hundred-acre farm, including considerable tillable land, has recently been added to its domain, and a graduate of a Northern agricultural college has begun the task of applying the scientific principles of farming to mountain rural conditions. The raising of general crops will not be largely attempted, but gardening, horticulture, for-

estry, and stock-raising are all possible on the Cumberland Plateau. The science course in the high school has been reconstructed in correlation with practical farming operations. Laboratories and workrooms have been provided for instruction in domestic science and household management. A shop for the teaching of farm mechanics has been erected and awaits equipment. Grand View is about equally distant from six county seats, and the center of an area which in no human possibility will have adequate common school facilities for generations. Its permanence will depend upon a continuing need, but also essentially upon its adaptation to practical local interests.

Of graded elementary schools, with five or six teachers and from one to two hundred pupils, Joppa Institute, in Cullman County, Alabama, is an interesting illustration. The settlement itself consists of some thirty cabins, with two or three stores, a blacksmith shop, and two church-houses. By far the largest dwelling is our eight-room teachers' home. A little distance from it stands a well-built and commodious schoolhouse. To-day the sixth grade happens to be reading essays on pioneer life. The wise Bostonian, who makes the school-books, thinks it important that the children of the generation understand the life of their great-great-grandparents of Massachusetts Bay, which he describes in great detail — the clearing of the forest, the building of the log-cabin, the little patch of farm amidst the stumps, the hunt for venison and wild turkeys, and the solemn procession of Puritans to the meeting-house, each man with a gun in his hand. The children faithfully reproduce this valuable information as an exercise in English, while as a matter of fact every one of these experiences is a living reality for them, or

THE PASSING OF THE MOUNTAINEER

at least a memory of the present generation at Joppa. They know at first hand what it is to grub out a little farm in the forest; they are living to-day in log-cabins; the larder is still furnished with game; and their men too often "tote" guns to church. The school-bookmaker forgot that we have "contemporary ancestors."

In the narrow cabins of this little settlement were gathered some thirty pupils from other communities. There were no decent accommodations for them, no opportunity for studious quiet, and frequently an undesirable crowding of boys and girls in the same house. Sometimes whole families came to keep house for themselves in unfinished attics. Such conditions of life were no advance upon the homes from which they came, and the best the school could do for them scarcely overcame the handicap of their bad accomodations. It was felt that we must make a place where such students could have proper oversight and the influence of a well-ordered Christian home. There was a large store building which some too ambitious villager had begun and had been unable to finish. It stood exactly between the home and the school property. This was purchased, with some two acres of land, and transformed into a dining-hall and dormitory. One is almost ashamed to tell how little it has all cost. The lady teachers and student girls, under the charge of a competent matron, occupy this building. The old teachers' home has become a dormitory for boys under the charge of the principal and his wife. That we dared to attempt to make this great addition to our equipment was due to the fact that the principal, a veteran of mission service in Japan, was an expert carpenter and builder as well as preacher and teacher. The community cooperated most cordially, contributing the hauling of all material and much of the work. A fund for furnishing the new building was solicited by the teachers. A roomy but rickety barn went with the place, and this has been rebuilt so as to include a commodious shop for manual training. There is sufficient land for considerable work in agriculture, and the institution must have a horse, cows, pigs, and poultry. With these it might not merely educate its pupils, but also lead the community in rural efficiency.

Thus runs the simple story. The warrant for such a school's existence is the extreme present need of its neighborhood and constituency. It is admirably adapting itself at small expense to the day's task. Teachers from the hills are already demanding an advanced course to help them meet the rising educational standards of the state. As to the future, we shall see when the time comes; meanwhile, and for its own place, its service is indispensable.

The little mill village of Lynn, North Carolina, in the upper Pacolet Valley, shows the missionary school standing by the mountaineer in his hour of industrial and social transition. Gathered here in rows of company houses, he has put off many of the external peculiarities of his isolated cabin life. He has changed his clothes, but not his manner of speech, nor his inner habit of thought. The school is helping him to modify both. Winter residents from the North, who befriended many such enterprises, and the Lynn mill owner, have, in time past, cooperated in the school's support. There are two teachers and some seventy pupils. Last year they had hard times in the cotton industry, and the mill ran with a depleted labor force, consequently the school was full. In normal times it is a great temptation to the parents to send their children to work instead, and the philanthropy of the employer, when he is shorthanded, is not altogether proof against his covetousness of the child as a worker.

Lynn, a School in a Mill Village

THE PASSING OF THE MOUNTAINEER

The schoolhouse is the community's sole public building. Here in turn preachers from the neighboring town conduct services. The teachers assist the Sunday-school, devise entertainments, and make their mission home a center of social life for the young people. They go into the homes of the village with counsel and good cheer. With an additional worker the enterprise might be converted into a full-fledged social settlement. As it is, whatever Lynn has of intellectual and spiritual inspiration must radiate from two devoted women; otherwise it is drowned in the clatter of the spindles.

Ten miles or so up the mountain at Saluda is a girls' boarding-school, a favorite type of missionary institution. The mistress of the mountain home holds so critical a place in the redemption of her people that she deserves special training.

The Girls' Seminary, Saluda

She needs to be taught equally how to cook and how to hope; how to tend a household and also how to nourish ideals before she comes to have a home of her own. She will almost surely teach in the log schoolhouse of her settlement. There come also planters' daughters from the lowlands over the South Carolina border, from homes less poor but equally crude and devoid of the graces of life. Added to these are the children of a few winter residents and the village boys as day pupils. All told, they make a company of some one hundred and twenty-five.

School and home occupy, in common, an ancient and decrepit building set up in a gully in a day when the proximity of a spring was the chief consideration. Its stairways and halls are so illogical and labyrinthine that visitors sometimes threaten to unwind a skein of yarn to help them find their way out again. Yet here, in the companionship of half a dozen true and gentle women from the North, the mountain schoolgirl learns lessons of character and taste. Instinctively she catches new ways of dressing her hair and gathering her skirts. Her slackness is partly drilled out of her, and partly crowded out, by new desires and incentives to personal adornment. Apathy gives way to interest. I recall a rare day when a group of such girls had an outing down in a valley where a gentle-souled man had placed a pipe-organ in a gothic chapel. The tempered light streamed through cathedral glass, and shadows played in the recesses of the timbered ceiling, while he poured his own tenderness and devotion through the organ tones. The girls' eyes were big with wonder. They said little, but the memory will never die. New depths and dimensions of experience were added to the old enchantments of mountain spring and the glow of the full-blown rhododendron. Thus simple opportunity expands the mountain maid's heart. The dilapidated mission-school building is no longer an advance upon her standards of thought. She deserves a better one, and must have it — a worthy girl's home, safe, sanitary, and beautiful. The project has been begun. The village has given a hilltop overlooking the old gully and promises a thousand dollars — no small sum considering its resources — while the release of certain funds through the progress of the mountains, elsewhere, will permit the Missionary Association to erect a new dormitory at Saluda.

Outside of the actual mountains, as its name suggests — though in sight of them — is Piedmont College, at Demorest, in northern Georgia. It includes elementary, secondary, and college courses. As in the case of the higher institutions for negroes, only a small fraction of its students are of collegiate grade.

Higher Institutions: Piedmont College

The village of Demorest was founded in the eighties, by a company of Northern health and home seekers, who sought to give their children school privileges which Georgia was not furnishing, by the establishment of a local institute. With the years the original colony was broken up and dispersed, while the community grew by the coming of recruits from the neighboring Appalachian counties. Thus the opportunity of educational ministry to the native population increased at the same time that the hotels, boarding-houses, and other monuments of the colony's adventurous youth were on the market for a song. The situation was seized upon by representatives of the small but able and aggressive Congregational element in Georgia, centering in Atlanta, as an opportunity for the establishment of an institution which should both express their denominational aspirations and serve the roughest and neediest section of the state. In its missionary aspect it appealed also to the American Missionary Association, which finally acquired the property; it took over the Institute on a long-time lease, and has since been its chief source of support. The property consists of four large and several smaller buildings, commodious enough, but scattered, particularly on the several hilltops of the village, and ill adapted to school purposes. A board of trustees consisting of local citizens and representatives of the Association and of the Georgia Congregational churches manages the institution, subject to the approval of its financial budget by the Association.

The situation is not without its problems. Though not superior in equipment nor in results to the more modest schools, the elementary and secondary courses of Piedmont College — which numerically are over nineteen-twentieths of it — are conducted at unusual expense. This is because they are included in a collegiate scheme of administration and

Problems of the Higher Institutions

remuneration. The interesting and inspiring plan of uniting North and South, highland and lowland, in community and school is also expensive. A student minority, coming from the cotton belt, and even from the cities, is not satisfied with a standard of living which seems ample to mountain boys and girls. The lingering Northern tradition in Demorest is favorable to culture, but costs money. To attract and hold students of collegiate grade, especially in a state well supplied with higher institutions as Georgia is, the academic fashions of wealthier schools have to be imitated. This makes their financial support difficult, and their dependence on scholarship aid correspondingly great. Is it justifiable to take of scant missionary funds to do at Piedmont what (except for the college department) is done elsewhere at much less expense?

There is only one justification, namely, that Piedmont shall train leaders, that it shall make standards of the higher life for picked men of the mountains, as they return to share the transformation of their native sects, or follow opportunity to the lowlands and the city. It is a young institution, as yet an experiment, but a brave and hopeful experiment, which, under gallant and tireless leaders, is steadily endeavoring to make itself a vital and indispensable part in the redemption of the twenty-six Appalachian counties of North Georgia and of their needy and abounding human wealth.

Their Justification in the Training of Leaders

The case of this institution suggests two principles of missionary policy, which every supporter of such endeavor in behalf of our unassimilated peoples should understand.

The Inevitable Cost of Such Training

First, the inevitable cost of training for leadership.

PROFESSORS AND STUDENTS, ATLANTA THEOLOGICAL SEMINARY

GIRLS' DORMITORY, PIEDMONT COLLEGE

THE PASSING OF THE MOUNTAINEER

Provision for the higher education of any people must necessarily approximate that of the standard institutions of the nation. Shorn of all extravagances and reduced to the lowest terms of support sufficient for efficiency, colleges must have a collegiate grade of instruction and equipment. Their product must compete on behalf of their people with our best. If they are really to furnish competent leaders they must have adequate fitting. Missionary agencies should be very slow to undertake the responsibility of colleges, and very insistent that, after due testing, they be either properly supported or abandoned as higher institutions.

Second, the prior claim of the principle of diffusion of opportunity. This is the heart of missionary obligation. It must minister widely and in places of special need. This principle is fundamental from the standpoint of assimilating the under-Americanized; it is also inevitable in view of the relation of a missionary board to its constituency. The annual support of such a board comes chiefly from armies of relatively small givers, many of whom are by no means able to send their children to college, from feeble churches, from children and young people. They are told of the needy masses of alien blood and narrow opportunity. However important the education of leaders from the standpoint of the strategy of group development, the larger number of givers intend that their gifts shall minister to these people on the humble levels of their need. This fact sets a strict limit to the proportion of its resources which a missionary organization may justly spend on the higher or otherwise more expensive forms of education.

The Prior Claim of the Diffusion of Opportunity

CHRISTIAN RECONSTRUCTION IN THE SOUTH

The American Missionary Association has always held this principle sacred. As indicated in an earlier chapter, it has graduated into independence some of the largest of negro institutions previously under its control. Berea College, incomparably the most influential single mountain institution, was for many years fostered by the Association, which still holds certain trust funds in its behalf. Here are gathered about half as many students as in all the Association's mountain schools, but they are educated at an annual cost many fold greater. In technical trade-education Berea can do for the young mountaineer — as Tuskegee and Hampton can do for the young negro — what no school of the Association can do. Its work is abundantly worth all it costs, but it would not be a legitimate expenditure of funds for the Association to support at any one place in the mountains, a school at Berea's scale of expense. For a missionary board the diffusion of opportunity is the better part. The continuance of this principle necessitates the early graduation of another group of the Association's schools, both white and colored, into independent support. They are now absorbing more than a just proportion of resources. Their adequate development is impossible out of the current gifts of the existing constituency. This the Association has recognized by determining at its last annual meeting to make the centennial of Lincoln's birth the occasion of a campaign for the endowment of five of the most advanced schools. In the case of Piedmont College, both Mr. Carnegie and Dr. Pearsons have anticipated this plan with conditional pledges, as has the Association itself by a special endowment grant.

Graduating Missionary Colleges into Independence

Training for leadership in one line, namely, the minis-

THE PASSING OF THE MOUNTAINEER

try, is the accepted task of the Christian masses. Neither the state nor private philanthropy assumes this burden.

Training Ministers: Atlanta Theological Seminary

The churches expect, and more readily respond to appeals in behalf of schools for religious professional education. None has ever had so good a case as Atlanta Theological Seminary. The great city whose name it bears was created by the convergence of railroads at the southern extremity of the Appalachians. All the highways which touch the mountains meet here before passing on to every quarter of the South. The South, highland, and lowland combined, has but five independent Protestant schools for ministerial training, the most adequate of which are all located at the extreme northern boundary. Moreover the schism of social classes has left the churches of the humbler people virtually without an educated ministry. Undoubtedly, the relative provision for the training of negroes as ministers is greater than that for whites, whose need is not less. There are also some two hundred little, scattered, and chiefly rural churches bearing the Congregational name, whose ministers must be educated in the South, if at all. They are come-outers from unprogressive Southern sects, and for social prestige and financial ability by no means constitute a denominational asset. To furnish these with effective spiritual leadership is a task offering little sectarian, but great patriotic and Christian satisfaction. It touches the belated white man of the Southern lowlands, who shares the crisis of the sifting of the South as well as the mountaineer. Its acceptance at the beginning only complicates the race situation by introducing the problem of the ecclesiastical relations of white and negro churches. Before it is completed it will surely contribute to the Christian solution of that problem at the point where the clash of races is now most violent.

Externally, scarcely any school is less impressive than the Seminary. There is merely a none-too-modern brick dwelling-house, surrounded by the ruins of once pretentious grounds, on a wind-swept hill overlooking Atlanta. The students, many of them ordained men with families, constitute an interesting and earnest group. A virile and aggressive president carries as a personal burden the annual solicitation of nearly half the expenses of the institution, and pleads in faith for a modest set of buildings which shall decently house the school.[1] These are necessary to perpetuate present achievement and to provide for a spiritually magnificent future. A little group of professors, whose names have been honorable for eloquence, teaching power and missionary service, are giving their declining years to this splendid, underpaid ministry. The active pastors of Atlanta share their time gratuitously with the institution. It has as many students as three Northern Congregational seminaries. The earnestness and practical atmosphere of its classroom is in happy contrast with the dry-as-dust spirit and scholastic coldness of too many institutions, similar in name but not in practise. In a hundred years we shall garnish the sepulchres of these prophets; we are starving them now. Yet they are meeting a crisis where the mountain paths converge and where the feet of new pilgrims are passing into the broader ways and sterner conflicts of a new South, and of the nation of which it is a part.

Guiding the Pilgrims in their Crisis

In a region undergoing such radical transition as are

[1] Since the writing of the text, funds have been secured for a school building and a president's home.

THE PASSING OF THE MOUNTAINEER

the mountains, corresponding radical readjustments of missionary agencies are frequently necessary. Thus at Williamsburg, Kentucky, was located one of the largest and oldest of missionary schools, Highland College. The Northern preacher long preceded the railroad and reached the settlement before it ever had a church building of its own. Once a frame had been raised, and pulled down again on a drunken wager of ox-team against ox-team. For a quarter of a century a school was supported, which educated some of the brainiest of mountain politicians, which served as a center for educational and evangelistic activity, and set the standards of the higher life for the entire region. Meanwhile the race issue had arisen. Berea had maintained for years the coeducation of negroes and whites, and the Association's fidelity at Williamsburg to the same policy was the occasion of the establishment of a sectarian school. The deeper cause was the aroused spirit of progress in the mountaineers themselves. After the erection of the mission church in a neighboring settlement, they took hoes and scraped the primeval filth from the floor of the native meeting-house. At Williamsburg, emulation took the form of educational rivalry. With new ambitions came ability to satisfy them. The mountains at length produced the native millionaire.

Radical Transitions and Radical Readjustments

Through shrewd dealing in coal lands he made his fortune. He was willing to buy out the mission school at a price covering the entire property investment of twenty-five years. His sect represented two-thirds of the tributary population. Their school had caught the contagion not only of culture, but somewhat of liberality. Highland College was sold. It had

The Coming of the Native Millionaire: The Passing of the Old Men of the Mountains

[365]

done its essential work and the investment was more needed elsewhere. The community had not reached the standard of the more favored regions either in wealth or culture, but it was on the way. Its distinctive traits of a quarter of a century ago no longer dominated it, and remained only as the badge of the submerged classes. As a social group its people had emerged and developed the institutions necessary to conserve their gains. The cooperation of missionary and millionaire had hastened the passing of the mountaineer. The future, material and spiritual, was safe in the hands of their joint product, the normally equipped American. Thus, locality by locality, the mountains cease to present a national problem, needing the ministries of special nationalizing agencies. What was merely temporary backwardness in their peculiar life is left behind; the rest, bad and good, merges with the common life of the nation.

"I pass but cannot die."

So somehow within the deed and heart of America will abide the contribution of the Southern highlander.

XII. DOES THE PURPOSE OF GOD THWART THE SPIRIT OF CHRIST?

I. THE MORAL SIFTING OF THE NATION ON THE RACE ISSUE

CENTURY after century has marched by since that great movement began which has monopolized nine-tenths of recorded history and which we call the progress of Western civilization; but never has Aryan supremacy been challenged until within this decade. At-
<small>New Ardor and Stubbornness of Race-Feeling</small>
tila's Huns could not permanently threaten the racial balance of power; an awakened Orient does. Our breed of men has met this challenge with an ardor and stubbornness of race feeling new to Christendom. This feeling creates a crisis for Christianity itself.

Once the heathen was a perishing soul, hard to get at — and we loved him. Later he became a consuming body, part of a world-market, worshiping idols made in Connecticut — and we tolerated him. Finally he became a participating fellow in common civilization, a neighbor — and we hated him. Recently he has taken an active hand in affairs — and we propose to put him out. Everywhere it is the same — in Australia, South Africa, Canada, the United States; all the seats of Anglo-Saxon Empire raise the cry, Exclusion! Deportation! Race prejudice, a natural self-protective instinct, has roused and shaken itself. This compels heart searching in all our traditional Christian activities, and puts the missionary impulse itself on trial.

Let us clearly understand why. Race-feeling to-day rises in the face of a tremendous fact, a new world-unity.

It is Forced to Extremes by Revulsion from the Social Applications of Christianity

World-politics, world-science, world-commerce and industry have made this earth an open-doored commonwealth of mankind. It also confronts a new religious ideal. Within this new world men have seen the social vision of the gospel which compels them to look beyond individual salvation to the actual and active contacts of redeemed men in the kingdom of God. The impact of these two facts immediately forces race-feeling of a naïve, instinctive character and compels it to forge weapons. Slave-holder theology believed in heaven for human chattels; mercantile philanthropy thanked God for souls new-born in India; the old missionary evangelism converted a heathen and left the institutions of Turkey or China to stand the moral shock and take the social consequences; but convert a heathen at home, and American institutions have to stand the moral shock and take the social consequences. What these consequences are, race-feeling clearly discloses. One cannot evangelize a man and then shut the door of human fellowship in his face. Within twenty-five years, I venture, no American with a shred of honesty will dare engage in foreign missions unless race-feeling in America is conquered. These comparatively insignificant race-contacts will inevitably follow the spirit and fashion of the massive, permanent, and significant contacts within the national life.

The Pickets will Cease to Fraternize when the Armies Begin to Fight

Christianity must face the social consequences of asking men into the family of God. The very missionary impulse is at stake in the struggle with ascendant race-feeling; for missions in the modern world must mean the participation of men

THE PURPOSE OF GOD

in common civilization. Whether we shall evangelize at all is to be determined *here* — under the stars and stripes.

A momentous phase of the present race issue in the United States is the growing consciousness that it is con-

<small>Critical Significance of American Solutions of Race-Issue for all Mankind</small> tinuous with the world-struggle of classes and races and that its outcome is profoundly significant for all mankind. Race adjustment is a universal problem of civilization. The echoes of this fact already are heard in our controversial literature. Our negro press took on a tone of triumph at the victory of Japan over Russia as that of a colored over a white race. The later apologies for the white South's race-policy deliberately argues from Anglo-Saxon practise at the antipodes. Mr. Ray Stannard Baker shows [1] that in the large the negro's unrest is of a piece with the under-man's struggle all over the world. America is naturally the central theater of this struggle; for here we have theoretically taken the most ideal ground upon race relations. The world is concerned in our endeavor to make good our theories. Succeeding or failing, we are molding the destinies of mankind.

II. MORAL STRUGGLE COMPLICATED BY INTELLECTUAL DIFFICULTIES

<small>Assumed Authority of Science: Alleged Verdict Concerning Races</small> The moral struggle in which we are thus involved is peculiarly complicated to-day by intellectual difficulties. The most critical of them is a peculiar authority which race-feeling gets from the belief that it is justified by science. Yesterday Scripture was appealed to in its favor; to-day, Sociology. For the myth of divine origin

---

[1] "Following the Color-Line," p. 269.

of favored stocks we have substituted the doctrine of chosen people by natural selection. The past, it is taught, revealed the sifting of human races; the present sees the crowning of the fit to rule; the future must witness the elimination of the unfit who else will inevitably beguile and entangle the chosen races to their doom. As a counsel of practical duty this doctrine takes two forms: first, it is a doctrine of the active suppression of the unfit — applied Darwinism, the gospel of racial aggression, which is the name of a better humanity, would crowd the nature peoples from the earth; second, it is a doctrine of the passive suppression of the unfit — race segregation, which is to be vigorously enforced by social policy until nature eliminates the unfit by her slow, inexorable processes.[1]

In its application to races this doctrine of the survival of the fittest gets the unfair backing of many instinctive and carefully cherished prejudices. It can only be judged fairly in its broadest and most general application *not to races but within races*. Logically it ought to demand the elimination of our parents when they are old, of our children while they are weak, and of ourselves when we are sick. It saves, at best, not all Aryans, or Anglo-Saxons, but only long-headed blondes. President Roosevelt ought to have been slaughtered, and Sir Walter Scott before him, because of their puny youth. Actually the issue is often theoretically raised in most serious and authoritative scientific discussions of heredity as related to the pauper, the consumptive, or the alcoholic. In a savage society these would soon succumb. What is the effect on the future health and strength of the race of their preserva-

Stated in its Widest Bearings

[1] Finot, Race Prejudice, Pt. I, ch. i, "The Gospel of Inequality and its Prophets," §§ 5, 6.

tion by the humane ministries of modern society — charity, the hospital, moral reform? By example and by heredity will they not perpetuate their weaknesses to the deterioration of the race? Is it not better that present victims be sacrificed than that the unborn should suffer?

Logically this is a serious dilemma; practically it involves profound problems. It can only be met by an adequate scientific answer, which later we shall attempt to suggest. Yet when it touches those near-at-hand classes who are protected by the humane sentiment, the average man dismisses it with the crass comment of his morning paper, "a scientist talks nonsense."[1] We take this doctrine complacently, however, when applied to the man of other races than ours. Half of us are quite willing to give him a push over the precipice (to use Nietzsche's kindly metaphor); most of the other half are easily resigned to leaving him outside the pale of civilized associations till he vanishes before our expanding empire.

There is still a further step; the missionary impulse is formally arraigned by the dogma of race inferiority on the authority of science. Pro-Aryan champions take a vein of high solemnity.

The Missionary Impulse Formally Arraigned

"You can't afford to be kind to the lower races; it is wicked." The spirit of Christ is definitely rebuked when it would exercise its nature toward the backward folk. Scientific qualms turn pious. We are warned "especially against the emotions of sympathy, of pity for the unfortunate race, the 'man of yesterday,' whom the unfeeling processes of nature demand in sacrifice upon the altar of the Evolution of

---

[1] See editorial in New York Times on Prof. Wm. Ridgeway's address before the Anthropological Section of the British Association, September 7, 1908.

Humanity." The issue is frankly put: "May not the strong Caucasian lend a helping hand to his weaker African brother, lift him up, and the two walk along hand in hand through the centuries? This is a very idyllic picture — but a moment's reflection must show how inadequate and unreal this dew of Hermon."[1] "All flesh is not the same flesh; star differeth from star in glory"; therefore concerning the races we are solemnly adjured, "What God hath put asunder, let not man join together."

In like vein writes a Southern reviewer of "The Negro in the South" (by Dr. W. E. B. Du Bois and Booker T. Washington). He finds the keynote to Dr. Du Bois' contribution in the following quotation: "Who can doubt that if Christ came to Georgia to-day one of His first deeds would be to sit down and take supper with black men, and who can doubt the outcome if He did?" The reviewer's comment is: "Upon the short-sightedly sentimental ideal or Christian basis it may be admitted that Professor Bu Bois has the best of the argument. But," he goes on to remind us, "the laws of nature and not the imperfect and changing interpretations of the principles of any ethical system, Christian or other, determine the fates of men and of races in bulk." He concludes: "As the nation could not exist permanently half slave and half free, so it cannot exist permanently seven-eighths white and one-eighth black. White or black must perish in the end. Which is the most likely to perish?"[2] The negro, it appears. His elimination is declared to be "an inevitable, far-off divine event," against which it is both foolish and wicked to strive.

The axe is thus laid at the root of the tree of Christian

[1] Smith, "The Color-Line," pp. x, 188.
[2] "H. I. B." in New York Times.

missions and its edge is this: Does the purpose of God thwart the spirit of Christ? May we evangelize and educate, or does God forbid? When Jesus says, "Make learners of all nations," does God say, "No, some haven't brains enough"? When the voice sounds, "Feed my sheep," must we reply, "Yea, Lord, thou knowest that we love thee, but what you take for sheep are only goats"?

The Axe at the Root of the Tree

This is no academic question. So subtle are the infections of race-feeling that thousands of men of Christian instinct (whether they have articulated the fear or not) are not sure whether, after all, God himself is not against missionary endeavor for the most backward races; whether the full Christian hope, especially for the negro, is not mistaken; whether the participation of his race with ours, in the Christian civilization of America, is not impossible, because of natural racial inequality which God intended.

III. EXAMINATION OF THE ALLEGED VERDICT OF SCIENCE

The remedy for this condition is chiefly moral. As a challenge to the Christian spirit it must primarily be met by the Christian spirit. Concerning instinctive race antipathy we have nothing to say; the passion of brotherhood must conquer it. But in so far as the difficulty is intellectual, it admits of intellectual treatment. The alleged findings of science may be met on their own ground. These Philistines also are men, and as such we may fight them.

Anthropology

Race antipathy instinctively seizes upon distasteful physical peculiarities in other human varieties as evidences of their inferiority. Color is the most outstanding example. To say authoritatively what significance color may have, if any, is the business of anthropology; and to this science we first appeal.

First, then, the most violent pro-Ayran anthropology is infinitely milder than the popular prejudice it is alleged to justify. That prejudice sees the lowest white man on the throne and the highest colored man licking the dust under his footstool. A supposed justification of it is found in the conception that there are feral races, physically intermediate between true man and brute. This view has not the slightest scientific standing. The contrary facts are that physically each race approaches the brute at some points, and departs at other points, but no race is feral at all points, or at so many more than others that it is thus distinguished. If in the exchange of interracial amenities, for example, one is moved to exclaim, "You great black brute!" the retort courteous might be, "You great hairy brute!" If one says, "Your long arms remind me of an ape," the scientific reply would be, "Your short legs remind me of the same beast." In brief, the white race has simian characteristics which the black race lacks, and *vice versa*. But the utmost that any anthropology claims is *a slight average superiority* in the white race. In height, bulk, strength, brain weight, skull capacity, development of forebrain, fecundity, longevity, or any other proposed test, that is all. Through most of their ranges of mental capacity the races are overlapping; most of the individuals of a given race have individuals to match them in any other. This means, to take the nearest case, that if one should line up all the American whites and grade them on the scale of 100, he would probably find few blacks to match those above 90, more to match those from 80 to 90, more

THE PURPOSE OF GOD

still as he went down the scale, the middle ranges being proportionately equal. No negro can possibly be lower than some white men. The bottom of hell is level. No one can say dogmatically that there are not ten million American whites who could be married to the ten million American negroes without biological injury to posterity. Of course the social injury would be immeasurable.

But overlapping races can participate in a common civilization.

Again some one will say — call his name Charles Francis Adams — " If the backward people have high natural capacity why don't they show it? Measure the unutterable distance between London and Khartoum! If negroes have brains why don't they use them?" The answer is, They do. The backward peoples positively manifest a high order of mental capacity.

<small>High Capacity of Backward Peoples</small>

We are not brainier than our fathers; no one argues that we are a biological advance on the Teutonic barbarians. They showed genius in the German forest as the savage in the African jungle. How? By not pronely accepting the world as they found it; by actively attacking and transforming their environments. As evidences of sheer ability to conquer by intelligence, no subsequent steps in civilization can remotely compare with the first. Edison is a poor second to Prometheus and Luther Burbank to the squaw who tamed the first dog.

Still further, their method of mental procedure is exactly that which we glorify by the high sounding titles of abstract reasoning and scientific method. Modern logic is teaching us that every fruitful idea is simply a plan of action, the validity of which we discover by trying it. We have absolutely

<small>Superior Intellectual Processes</small>

[375]

no other resource, no esoteric Aryan guaranty of truth. Did the Hawaiians plant Captain Cook's iron nails thinking that they would grow? Absurd? Then yesterday's physical science was equally absurd in its static conception of matter. That iron would grow, and that matter was made up of atoms, were both perfectly worthy hypotheses, but neither worked. Consequently the savant ceased to treat matter atomically; the savage ceased to plant nails. Each used the same method, one professionally, the other popularly. One had more accumulated knowledge, but he was not wiser than the other; particularly he did not show some exalted mental faculty which the other lacked.

Moreover, the most significant wisdom of all is that which counsels concerning human life. This is the core of all philosophies. The Aryan masses do not know Plato, but they have a popular philosophy infinitely more revealing of the race mind. But so has the West African. "Full-belly child says to hungry-belly child, 'Keep good cheer.'" We say, "It's easy to bear others' misfortunes." Is our version better? "I'm not so angry at the man who killed me as at the man who hurled me on the ground afterward." Is "adding insult to injury" apter? "Quick marrying a woman means quick unmarrying a woman." What more can one ask as a passport to our Christian civilization? In brief, the practical philosophy of life is for savage and civilized essentially similar.

Practical Philosophy

Or turn to the supreme moral quality, self-control. Are the nature-peoples popularly characterized as impulsive, subject to uncontrollable instinct and chance passions? Yet no life is so bound as theirs with ceremonialism, and ceremonialism means the subor-

Capacity for Self-Control

dination of impulses. The law of *tabu* hedges conduct at every turn. It says " No " to the most imperious impulses and is obeyed. Would the American starve rather than eat the sacred seal sporting before his hut? The Eskimo will. Would he take the holy serpent's fang in his breast rather than kill it? The West African will. Are our cities safe from civic looters because an unseen power guards them? The Hottentots' possessions are in the jungle. The natural man is probably challenged and restrained by law at more points — not the same points, to be sure — under heathenism than under Christianity. Moral control is not a whit less real, inclusive, or effectual.

In significant achievement, then, as well as in natural capacity, the races are overlapping. All of this does not prove equality. We are not talking about equality, but about the inclusion of the backward races in a common civilization. Can the negro be fitted for American citizenship? So far as anthropology testifies of his natural capacity, Yes. No race can be saved wholesale; nor need any race be lost wholesale. All races, biologically speaking, are fit to survive and participate in and contribute to human society.

<small>No Race Unfit for Civilization</small>

But the argument must be pushed still further; for however favorable the verdict of anthropology concerning the backward races, and however conclusive against doctrines of their necessary elimination, either by the active or by the passive method, it is not immediately applicable to social perplexities. We asked whether the races could participate in a common civilization and were assured that all were capable and fit to survive. That is not an answer to our question. For such an answer we must go to Sociology — the sci-

<small>Sociology</small>

ence of human association. Specifically, our question is this: Granting corresponding natural capacities and general mental endowments, may not the *difference in detail* in the mental tendencies of the races be so fixed as to make their inclusion in common interest and activities forever impossible? We know of brilliant individuals who could by no means live together. May not this be the case also of capable races? We answer, They may learn to live together. There are no specific differences of race mind which are beyond the control of education.

The organic basis of race traits can only be interpreted in terms of instinct. There are inborn tendencies which make the white act in a different manner from that in which the black would act in the presence of the same stimulus. But what of it? Similar and not smaller tendencies exist to make one white man act differently from another. Besides, there is nothing fixed or invincible about these differences. Psychology knows nothing of relentless instincts. Every one has lost dozens of them. Thus it is no excuse for race antipathy to call it "instinctive." Unchastity is equally instinctive. No specific race-trait is half so deep-seated as the common and elemental impulses which the moral life undertakes to control. Of those which intrude into the moral realm only two — the instincts of self-preservation and of the propagation of the kind — are especially unyielding. All the rest may be molded, suppressed, or recharged. Most of them, unless fixed and reenforced by habit, die of themselves. And among the most fleeting of them, the feeblest and latest born, are the instinctive race-differences.

Mental Traits of Race not beyond Education

The proof of such actual modification and the assimilation of one mental type to another is everywhere at hand. I will risk an illustration from our negro Congregational brethren. I sometimes go to their church conferences and find a gravity of manner, a sobriety of expression, a restraint of religious utterances which I think overdoes the matter. They have, in short, the general denominational lack of religious spontaneity.

Now, does any one believe that this result is due to a superhuman self-control whereby each colored brother painfully suppresses his inner tendency to explosive Hallelujahs? This is to attribute to him a grip on himself which we have not. Is it not rather clear that the tendency itself has suffered change; that liveliness of emotion, a proverbial negro trait, has been radically modified? In this particular our brother has ceased to be a negro and has become a mere Congregationalist. It has been a change for the worse, too. Many negro traits *may be, but ought not to be*, obliterated by education, being of positive and sometimes of unique value to the world.

But still the objector has a parting shot. "If race traits have no deeper organic roots than you say, why are they actually so persistent, so stubborn?" Again the answer is easy though the application is hard. Race characters persist because individuals coming into life, one by one, with perfectly plastic racial instincts, have these instincts fixed, one by one, in a similarity of habit, under the action of a common mental and social environment. The negro infant develops a negro mind because he grows up within a race tradition. He has a negro mother, a negro home, a negro community, a negro place in society. These give certainty and permanency to the faint organic racial tendencies which were otherwise lost. The technical name for this process is "social heredity," the

<small>Actual Perpetuation by Social Heredity</small>

newly recognized significance of which is effectively stated by Prof. Simon N. Patten:

> The striking aspect of the recent development of thought is the changing concept concerning the part heredity plays in life. Men have been trained from the earliest times to attach great importance to the influence of blood descent upon racial and individual character. Some families and peoples are said to be inherently superior to others, because they have possessed, generation after generation, well-marked qualities which others did not have. The differences between them were readily explained by heredity, so readily, in fact, that more influence was soon given to ancestry than to the environment into which a man was born. This unequal division of power seems to be destroyed by recent discoveries in biology, which are establishing a new equilibrium between natural or inherited qualities and those acquired after birth. Many qualities are inherited, but the number is smaller than it was thought to be, and many of them may be readily suppressed by the action of the environment in which men live, so that they do not show themselves for long periods in a particular family or a given race. This curtailment of the force of physical heredity gives more power to the acquired qualities handed on from generation to generation as a social tradition. A physical inheritance, simpler than we thought, is ours at birth; but there is a larger and increasingly important social heredity which must be constantly renewed through the conscious efforts of parents and teachers.[1]

The conflict of the educator therefore is not with physical heredity, but with that part of the social heredity

[1] "New Basis of Civilization," pp. 204, 205.

of his pupils which he cannot control. A classic example is the acknowledged inability of the schools to teach the masses the mother-tongue. The trouble is not that babes are born predestined to erratic spelling and grammar, but that homes and streets are also educators, and have the first and longest chance at the child. Now, no remoter guiding or reforming agency can interpose early or often enough between the mother and her child, the intimate group and its members, the isolated race and its people. Consequently family, group, and race traits are perpetuated from generation to generation, much as if physical heredity were the controlling factor. But for all that it is not the controlling factor. Social heredity is; and against it the teacher and reformer may do something immediately and in the long run, much.

Control through, and of, Social Heredity

One thing of vast import that he may immediately do is to modify the beliefs of men. On the whole this is more significant even than any ability to change outward conditions. A belief, in a peculiarly intimate sense, expresses a man. Change it and the man is changed — as in the case of the mulatto. His case is of pathetic and thrilling human interest. On the misunderstanding that it was chiefly to be explained by the potency of white blood it has been used to rob the pure negro of most of his racial achievements.

The Rôle of Changed Beliefs in Social Heredity

The true explanation is essentially psychological.[1] Undoubtedly the progress of the American negro has been

---

[1] Contrast with this the biological explanations of Stone, Studies in the American Race Problem, ch. ix, "The Mulatto Factor." In general harmony with the position of this book, see Ross, "Foundations of Sociology," pp. 320, 321.

disproportionately the progress of a mulatto group; its leadership disproportionately mulatto leadership. Because the mulatto is biologically superior? No; because he believes in the superiority of his trickle of white heredity. Repeatedly I've heard from men of low mentality, "You can't scare me; I've white blood in me." Result: they are not scared. Mere belief? Well, there is nothing mightier in the universe. "By faith the walls of Jericho fell down." The latest word of philosophy is that the nature of a thing is what it does. "That is different which makes a difference." Mentally the mulatto is not a negro, not because he is the product of mixed blood, but because he is the product of a mixed and modified race tradition. Any social group which experiences common modifications of an old race tradition is a new type, as worthy of scientific recognition as an "original" race. To think otherwise is a pure superstition of classification. "If any man is in Christ there is a new creation." This is a rigidly scientific statement. Social psychology teaches that men are transformed in essential personality by the renewing of their minds. There is no biological fate sundering the races, no inexorable processes of nature thwarting the new faith in one's self and one's brethren inspired by the spirit of Christ.

<small>Control through Social Heredity</small>

In so far as hard and cramping tradition is not challenged and broken through by new and energizing beliefs, social heredity works out human destiny as relentlessly as if it were true physical heredity, and consequently beyond human control. Its effective results come to much the same thing. According to its dictates men are selected for high or low estate. Custom, law, institutions, possessions,

<small>Selection according to Social Heredity</small>

THE PURPOSE OF GOD

and social pressure conspire to bring some into life, heirs of self-confidence and traditional prestige, controlling the accumulated wealth and the manifold machinery of civilization. Others, by arbitrary discrimination of birth, lack all these advantages and go in the mass as though naturally predestined to a lower place. As between races, belief and wealth exalt the white as the socially elect, and abase the black; within the white race, they exalt the rich and abase the poor. There is not a vestige of scientific proof that these contrasts in any wise register the distribution of natural capacity by physical heredity. Its distribution is indeed unequal *but it does not at all follow racial or class lines.*

Vast and unmeasured numbers of the disinherited are simply normal human beings whose average capacities are socially suppressed; partly through under-nourishment and other environmental handicaps which lower their physical tone, and partly through paralyzing beliefs in natural inferiority which forbid them to hope for themselves and prevent society from doing its best in their behalf. The rich and the successful as a class have not more strength and capacity than the average run of natural men, nor the poor less; but social environments in the latter case do not allow the effective expression of nature's gifts, nor even their self-discovery. An alien and pauper race included in a highly self-appreciative and arrogant civilization becomes, in the nature of the case, a suppressed class. It shows the typical traits of poverty-men which, in its case, especially, are mistakenly charged to physical heredity.

<small>Suppressed Classes</small>

Such a social situation hardens into a caste system whenever ultimate sanctions are supplied to fix the results of arbitrary social sifting. Whenever the philosophy and religion of a dominant group unite to justify its present advantage, and especially whenever a disinherited group comes to accept its place as in the nature of things, a deadlock is reached which is more hopeless than if it were indeed the result of physical heredity. For physical heredity admits of great, though limited, possibilities of modifying the individual after he is born; but the fatalism of the caste doctrine makes all endeavor hopeless. Such fatalism is the essential attitude of much American thought, particularly in the South. The Booker Washington program is declared to be no better than that of the negro radicals: it simply will prolong the agony a little; the negro problem has no solution. Such an attitude reveals the suppressive weight of social heredity at its worst. "Our wrestling is not against flesh and blood," but against diabolical ideas, against "spiritual wickedness in high places."

The Caste System

A consideration of the fatal power of the caste idea should finally and forever forbid any confidence in statistical comparisons of social or racial classes in their present status as having any bearing upon relative natural capacity. In the most advanced civilization eighty per cent of the population still belong to the "lower classes."

Its Results no Measure of Natural Capacity of Men

Prof. Lester Ward writes:

> Statistical investigations prove that notwithstanding their superior numbers, they furnish less than ten per cent of the agents of civilization, and that relatively to population they furnish less than one per cent. Their influence in the progress of the world is therefore practically nil, although their capacities are the same as those of the higher classes, to whom, notwithstanding their small numbers, nearly all prog-

THE PURPOSE OF GOD

ress is due. This is entirely the result of the social stratification caused by artificial inequalities. The abolition of social classes, could it be accomplished, would therefore increase the efficiency of mankind at least one hundredfold.[1]

This means that defective social selection, through false tradition and unequal environment, is robbing the race of most of its natural human wealth. However important, then, the improvement of the breed through eugenics, manifest duty and economy demand that society first cease to waste what it already has.

Modern sociology, furthermore, comes squarely forward with an answer to the demand that the human stock be improved by the elimination of the unfit.

Progress without Elimination through Social Control — In the first place, do our best, we cannot defeat the elimination of the least fit. Nature peremptorily dismisses them. That radically defective individuals should not be allowed to reproduce their kind, all agree. But the ordinary version of the doctrine of the survival of the fit attacks whole classes and races of probably average natural capacity. It proceeds upon the false assumption that those are unfit who could not survive the struggle for existence on the brute or savage plane; or, more moderately, under American pioneer conditions, or under such suppressive social institutions as, for example, the negro experiences in the South. But life is no longer under such conditions — at least necessarily. We have a new basis of civilization, "a kingdom of man," in which environment has been radically changed so that more and more of those who formerly were doomed to death are now adapted to sur-

[1] American Journal of Sociology, "Social Classes in the Light of Modern Sociological Theory," vol. xiii, p. 627.

vival. Fitness always means fitness under given conditions. Artificial modifications have become permanent and therefore natural. The stall-fed ox would be no equal competitor with *Ursus* of the ice age, nor could it endure exposure with the cattle of the Montana range; but it will never have to; domestication is its permanent lot. Weaker than its ancestors, it is better and fitter to survive under present conditions. Similarly — to borrow Professor Patten's illustration — it is useless to "toughen" a child by making him go barefooted in the winter. The ability so to do is no superiority in a race which for good and all has adopted shoes and stockings. The efficient strength of the civilized man is greater than that of the savage, though the former is not adapted to survival in the jungle. Resources are now funded and may continue to be so indefinitely. "None of us liveth to himself." Under a life more fully socialized, the human units are not only individually sounder and more potent relative to their environment, but, also, in combination, even weakness is made strength. Thus for a long, long time, and with no limit which we can see, civilization may maintain its standard and still admit to privilege an immeasurable number of the now disinherited classes.

Such a society will not merely have physical and moral health; it will possess also the inner forces of progress. Suppressed genius will be unloosed for its enrichment; and, through organization, the present supply of genius will be made instantly serviceable to the world at large.

When culture becomes cosmopolitan, as it is to-day, the success of a race turns much more on the efficiency of its average units than on the inventions and discoveries of its geniuses. The heaven-sent man who invents the locomotive, or the dynamo, or the germ theory, confers thereby no exclusive advantage on his people, or his race. So perfect is intellectual commerce, so complete is the organization of science, that almost at once the whole civilized world knows and profits by his achievements. Nowadays the pioneering genius belongs to mankind.[1]

Thus any man, group, or race which shall prove capable of serving the present age may be preserved without fear of his influence upon the future.

Scientific Optimism concerning Backward Races

Of revolutionary significance for problems of race is sociology's extension to despised backward peoples of the principles of judgment which she applies to the disinherited classes in white civilization. Thus Ross says:

> Social psychology ignores uniformities arising directly or indirectly out of race endowment — negro volubility, gipsy nomadism, Malay vindictiveness, Singhalese treachery, Magyar passion for music, Slavic mysticism, Teutonic venturesomeness, American restlessness. How far such common characters are really racial in origin and how far merely social, is a matter yet to be settled. Probably they are much less congenital than we love to imagine. "Race" is the cheap explanation tyros offer for any collective trait that they are too stupid or too lazy to trace to its origin in the physical environment, the social environment, or historical conditions.[2]

In some quarters the whole science of sociology is now written without resort to the word or idea of race. So-called "races" are regarded as merely human groups with

[1] Ross, "Foundations of Sociology," pp. 374, 375.
[2] American Journal of Sociology, "Social Psychology," ch. i, vol. 13, p. 578.

special histories, temporary environmental marks, and signs of common social lot. Their heredity does not especially need improvement; it is already as good as the human average to which nature ever pulls back her more precocious children. Their special characteristics are easily modifiable. The gains of genius from any human quarter are easily transmissible to them. The uncontrollable powers of nature are as apt to fight for as against them, spontaneous variation being quite capable of bringing good out of Nazareth. What they need is to have adverse social pressure taken off, and to have the forces of social control exercised in their behalf. This is no interference with nature but the expression of the true nature of the human world as revealed by social control following Christian ideals.

IV. THE PURPOSE OF GOD AND THE RACE QUESTION

If God is the ruler of the universe it is proper to expect to find some indication of his purpose in the natural tendencies of things. The argument of this book has been that these tendencies are not unfavorable to the backward peoples, and do not forbid the effort to assimilate them to American civilization under the ideals of democracy and of Christian brotherhood. When the social distortions of their natures are removed, all stocks and varieties of men express full human capacity and show promise that ultimately the downmost may be raised to participation in the life of the highest. To this effect we read the reasonable verdict of science.

Futility of Scientific Verdicts to convince concerning Human Issues

We do not expect this reading of the verdict, however,

Rev. Joseph Smith, Chattanooga, Tenn.

Prof. William Pickens, Talladega College

TYPICAL MAKERS OF EVIDENCE ON THE RACE PROBLEM

to convince those who on instinctive and dogmatic grounds deny the possibility of a democracy across the color-line. Not one human conviction in ten thousand is actually arrived at on scientific grounds. It was confessed at the outset that the argument could expect only to clear away certain intellectual difficulties for those who want to believe the best for all men. It will not move the South — the South where thousands of earnest Christians passionately hold that the inexorable laws of the universe doom the negro to hopeless inferiority; that its irreversible processes condemn him to extinction; and that the attempt to raise him ("above his natural station") is contending against the purpose of God. They cling, therefore, with desperation to the policy of social separation, fearing that any relaxation of it will mean intermarriage and the deterioration of the white race. Suppose that, scientifically, they were right and we wrong? What would we do about it?

Having honestly attempted to put myself in the attitude of a Christian Southerner, I believe that there are two considerations that go deeper than anything by which he thinks to justify the racial policy of his section, or of any other like-minded Anglo-Saxon group. First, the dignity and finality of personal solutions of human problems. Whenever a negro has achieved character and self-respect; whenever he has reared a home, brought up children, acquired a modest competency, done useful work, counted on the side of social order, kept courage in his own soul and brought cheer to his fellows, honored God in his heart and in the deeds of his earthly pilgrimage, then the fashion and force of such a life has raised it above race barriers. And whenever a white man,

Two more Fundamental Considerations: 1. The Dignity and Finality of Personal Solutions

the master of like achievements (and none can do more than these) has looked upon his negro brother without scorn, reverencing in him the same struggle and victory that he knows in himself, appreciating, yes and loving, the simple, effective goodness of him and the glory of his aspiration, then the galling, maiming, fatal aspect of the race issue is obliterated. Whenever these two men, disregarding classifications and traditions in the presence of vital experience, see eye to eye, so far as men may, understanding each other in part, and for the rest bowing before the mystery of the unique selfhood of each soul, the race problem is altogether solved. Any one may solve it who will — a case at a time. It is solved between the Texas judge and his " Ned, nigger and gentleman." Wisely said Chancellor Barrows of the University of Georgia at the inauguration of a Northern white president over a negro university, " Forget race: think only of the individual." Whoever does this in one case, giving the individual simply and completely a standing of individual worth, is beyond challenge. The case does not conflict with racial verdicts of science, for or against; it is simply outside of them.

Now, such saving personal adjustments are everywhere admitted. They are infinitely more common South than North, and are the moral leaven of the race situation. Nothing could do the Northern philanthropist more good than to learn the cordial, affectionate, thoroughgoing Southern appreciation of the individual negro and the genuine equity of some of its relations with him. But, theoretically speaking, such adjustments are disregarded as exceptions.

But what is an exception? In answering we will doubtless be accused of lugging in a whole philosophy by the

THE PURPOSE OF GOD

Exceptions are the Foundation-Stones of the Universe

ears. Not so; for in any attempt at a thorough-going answer a whole philosophy plunges in, inevitably, of its own accord. As we understand the nature of the universe, whenever any "two of you shall agree on earth as touching anything"— whenever personalities, respecting and inviting each other to express whatever there is in them, come to an untrammeled, vital adjustment, there is created a new center of being and energy. Such a contract is a bit of the real thing — Reality itself — and whatever else exists is only more of the same sort. All that appears as "star" or "sun," all that operates as the "tendency of nature," or lords it as "law," is at bottom some adjustment of personalities. Here is a process which cuts under any other. Was there a law of nature to the contrary a moment ago? It is now abrogated by the original and underived sovereignty of the two who agree. Vast and venturesome language, this? At least it is time we were learning it. Too long have we been kept by conceptual scarecrows from the dearest of human possessions — the possibility of universal brotherhood. "Race," a mere word; a classificatory device intended as a labor-saving instrument of human thought; a generic term, used of masses but true of no single individual, has fooled us into unmanly slavery. Philosophically speaking, race does not exist but only individuals.

> "For there is neither East nor West —
> Border nor breed nor birth;
> When two strong men meet face to face,
> Though they come from the ends of the earth."

This is not poetical "bluff"; it is the direct and logical outcome of a philosophy which believes that personalities are the ultimate stuff of the universe, and that in their mutual interactions the world is a-making.

There is another side to this doctrine. Whoever forces an adjustment with another personality which denies the full nature and right of both; whoever overbears the essential dignity of his brother's aspiration, and has contempt for its unique sanctity, he also creates a fragment of Reality, but creates it wrong. There is no blacker sin than contempt. " Whosoever shall say to his brother, Thou fool, shall be in danger of the hell of fire." That race antipathy is deeply entrenched in the universe we have no mind to deny; we only deny that it is entrenched behind unyielding laws of nature. Its actual citadel is the unbrotherly spirit, the stubborn and baffling fact of which we dramatize as the Problem of Evil.

This introduces the second consideration, which I venture to think goes deeper than any of the philosophical foundations of the South's race policy, namely, that the existence of evil in the universe presents a moral dilemma of which the final solution is not an explanation but a choice. Some of us believe that the order of nature is for us and for human hope; but if not we would go on doing just as we are doing.

2. The Final Solution not an Explanation but a Choice

We do not for a moment admit that the trend of natural processes has to be identified with the purpose of God. We do not find complete moral unity in the universe as it stands. It seems to us there is some real evil in it. Admitting that, we do not feel under obligation to worship anything which looks like evil. In a universe in which one slaps a mosquito, he reserves the right to take issue with the law of gravitation, if need be. A big mosquito is not God; a big evil is not holy. The bigger, the worse! If cruelty has entrenched itself in the processes of nature, so much the worse for them. We will follow the impulse of brotherhood against evolution as quickly as with it. Who says we must knuckle down to the physical universe? We simply do not know yet how far it will prove plastic to moral effort; therefore we will make the hypothesis of faith, "He has put all things under his feet." That this is faith, not demonstration, we cheerfully confess. "We see not yet all things subjected to him, but we see Jesus," and choose to take his part whoever or whatever is against him.

Is there other ground of hope for anybody? Is Anglo-Saxon salvation based on the shape of the skull? Was science crucified for you or were you baptized into the name of anthropology? As a mortal man, is the white less transient and futile than the black? Has he any special revelation, a peculiar demonstrable clue to the mystery of life? When the author of "The Color-Line" dismisses negro optimism with the assertion "that the hopefulness of the majority is quite artificial, based on some religious faith or moral trust, and that the really weighty answers are given by the hopeless minority," [1] does he really mean to say that his own exceeding confidence in the earthly future of the white races is not also artificial in the sense that it is based on "some religious faith or moral trust"? If not, on what, pray, is it based? I at least know nothing beyond the apostle's plea:

Salvation for All if for Any

> Who shall change our vile body, that it may be fashioned like unto his glorious body, according to the working whereby he is able even to subdue all things unto himself.

[1] Smith, "The Color-Line," p. 177.

If this avails for any, it may for all; it cannot be bounded by the color of the skin.

If, then, the most unfriendly anthropology should triumph over the lower races; if they were scientifically branded unfit; if it were certain that their participation in our civilization meant a lowered physical stamina, a decreasing mental capacity, an increasing moral tragedy for all, we would still carry out the program of the gospel at any cost. We may be beside ourselves, but "the love of Christ constraineth us; because we thus judge, that one died for all, therefore all died; and he died for all, that they that live should no longer live unto themselves, but unto him who for their sakes died and rose again. Wherefore we henceforth know no man after the flesh."

<small>Facing the Alternative</small>

I have held in my hand the diary of Snelling. With a dozen Micronesians, including women and children, he was lost while making an evangelistic tour of scattered islands, and drifted in an open boat for fifty-one days. With vivid simplicity the daily entries tell how they starved to death and kept the faith. As the end approaches, the few survivors are practically crazy, and lie in a delirium of worship, praising God and gasping life away. I do not count that an inglorious end. I would be willing to have humanity finish earth like that!

Humanity is out on the uncharted bosom of the universe in as frail a boat, a huddle of black, white, red, and yellow. They do not know that any of them will get to land. Science least of all guarantees it. We live by faith.

The white man might throw the colored man overboard — though since the Japanese-Russian war it's a question who'd go over first; but craft might prevail against numbers; the white man might take all the food for himself; it might sustain life until land appears; he might reach his desired haven. Suppose he could.

In a recent magazine story, Bully McLean, the "bucko-mate," finds a similar problem confronting him:

> The captain raised his voice and called to the mate to come aft.
>
> "All right, Captain, I'm coming," bawled the mate. "Shake her up, now, you lubbers; and don't you stop work, or I'll be the death of you. Walk her round, bullies! I'll be back in a brace of shakes."
>
> As he waited, the captain wondered how the mate would take the proposal to abandon the ship and leave the blacks to drown. Bully McLean hated all negroes, he knew — hated them whole-heartedly and impartially, because a gang of them had once tried to murder him in Baltimore. Indeed, he had shipped in the *Brynhilda* only to get a chance, as he expressed it, "to bullyrag a crowd of bloody blacks and raise Cain and kill Injuns generally." But then, these bucko-mates were not without a code of honor of their own, and one could not always forecast their conduct under given circumstances.
>
> "What do you want, Captain? I can't leave those black rascals long."
>
> The captain, suddenly confronted by the towering form of the first officer, asked nervously how much water there was in the hold.
>
> "About six feet, but not gaining as fast as it was."
>
> "She'll go down pretty soon now," said the old man; "and I guess — I think we'd better abandon her at once."
>
> "Well, I'll get the other boats over, then; but I think we could keep her afloat till daylight."

"The other boats are smashed up," the captain said hurriedly, hoarsely. "No use to launch them."

"Well, that's bad," commented the mate quietly. "The quarter-boat won't carry all hands."

"No. It'll hold the white crowd, but not the niggers. We'll have to leave them."

"What? You mean the afterguard are to save themselves and leave the crew to drown?"

"There's nothing else to do, Mate. All hands can't go in the boat, and white men take precedence over black."

"Well, Captain," said the mate coolly, "you can do what you please, but I stand by the crew. What a captain's duty under the circumstances may be is not for me to say; but a mate's first duty is to his ship, and his second to his crew, white or black. If I saved my life by leaving my crew to drown, I'd never be able to — to hold up my head again among honest men."

The captain emitted an energetic grunt, then muttered bitterly: "Oh, yes; a captain should go down with his ship — that is all very fine, very heroic. But when a man has a wife and children dependent on him he's got to think of the bread-and-butter aspect of things."

"Maybe so — maybe so; it's all in the point of view, I dare say." [1]

"It's all in the point of view"; the Judgment Day is no more. There is a point of view which thinks it sees that there is one moral law for the individual and another for the race; that the latter must save itself at all costs.[2] Authority cannot settle that issue; it is a matter of moral taste, of an inner sense of the fitness of things.

[1] McClure's Magazine, vol. xxx, p. 694.
[2] See Smith, "The Color-Line," p. 190.

We can merely testify to our point of view. Whatever the duty of captains it seems to an every-day mate not worth while to live at the expense of his crew — white or black.

See the other alternative! In the splendor of morning the super-man stands in blonde glory on a fairer shore than ever man trod. He builds his new life as far above ours as ours above the brutes. Intellect is ennobled, beauty perfected, gentleness enthroned. Women are more glorious than any dream, and all men walk in kingly freedom. They look into each other's faces, white and glowing, and are happy — until they go out to meet the silent and unwearied contempt of the stars, to hear all the sounding voices of the seas cry, " Where is thy brother? " The finest breed of human animals may inhabit a moral hell. Better be lost on the pitiless waters, starving with a huddle of colored folks, delirious but not despicable, agonizing but not ashamed. For not idly is it written, " It is better for thee to enter into life maimed, than having two hands to go into hell." And what shall it profit the Anglo-Saxon if he gain the whole world and lose his own soul?

[marginal note: Man and Super-man]

INDEX

INDEX[1]

Abbott, Lyman, quoted, 270
ACADEMIC AND INDUSTRIAL SCHOOL, Kowaliga, Ala., 136
Adams, Samuel Hopkins, quoted, 178
Africa and African traits, 117, 141, 197, 234, 248
Agriculture in South, 52, 107, 133, 146, 190, 233, 247 ff.
Alabama, 47, 66, 69, 73, 122, 136, 137, 140, 147, 150, 219, 263, 304,
Alaska, 23
Alderman, President E. A., 50, 55, 56, 111, 113, 121, 174, 185
Aliens, congestion of, in cities, 26
ALLEN NORMAL SCHOOL, Thomasville, Ga., 87, 95, 215, 239
Alston, Leonard, quoted, 117
Amalgamation of races, 31, 32. *Vide* Miscegenation
American Indians, 20, 23, 29, 45, 62, 300, 314, 320
AMERICAN MISSIONARY ASSOCIATION, vii, 34, 36, 40, 62, 73, 87, 90, 132, 135, 158, 161, 209 ff., 268, 289, 291, 351, 352 ff.
American Negro Academy, Publications of, 267
Anglo-Saxon, 112
Appalachian Mountains, 80, 304 ff., 308 ff., 312
Arkansas, 46, 53, 236
Armstrong, Samuel Chapman, 265, 268 ff.
Asheville, 80, 304

Athletics for negro, 255
ATLANTA THEOLOGICAL SEMINARY, Atlanta, Ga., 363
Atlanta University, 210, 214, 241, 243, 247, 252
Atlanta University Publications, quoted, 150, 151, 153, 155, 156, 158, 275
AVERY NORMAL INSTITUTE, Charleston, S. C., 228, 256

Baker, Ray Stannard, quoted, 42, 85, 105, 221, 369
BALLARD NORMAL SCHOOL, Macon, Ga., 224, 228
Banks and savings institutions, 142, 147
Baptists, 148, 150, 151, 152, 154, 155, 159, 209, 259
Barrows, Chancellor, 390
BEACH INSTITUTE, Savannah, Ga., 175, 225, 227, 228
BEACHTON SCHOOL, Beachton, Ga., 214
Berea College, 210, 212, 316, 320, 362, 365
"Black Belt," 72, 81, 86, 136, 210, 218, 219
BLACK MOUNTAIN ACADEMY, Evarts, Ky., 313, 328
Border States, 100
Bowman, Rev. Charles E., quoted, 60
Bratten, Bishop, quoted, 115
BREWER NORMAL SCHOOL, Greenwood, S. C., 236

---

[1] For the convenience of those wishing to make a detailed study of the American Missionary Association, titles relating directly to its work are capitalized.

INDEX

BRICK SCHOOL, Enfield, N. C., 38, 132, 251, 257, 262, 291
Brigham, Albert P., quoted, 19, 54, 307
"Brown Fellowship," 75
Brown, William G., 78
Brunner, Dr. W. F., quoted, 175
Bryce, James, 71, quoted, 112, 113
Building and Loan Associations, 143, 162

Calhoun, John C., 267
Calhoun School, 137
Canada, negro refugees in, 62
Carmack, Senator, x
Carnegie Building, 38, 242, 362
Carver, Professor George N., 42
Census Bulletin, quoted, 171, 305
Charleston, S. C., 74, 104, 177
Charleston News and Courier, quoted, 54
Chattanooga Tradesman, 190
Child labor, 186, 337, 356
Christianity and race problems, 367 ff.
Church as Americanizing agency, 58
Cities, problems of negroes in, 163, 254
"Color line," 101, 105, 116 ff.
Columbia State, quoted, 103, 189
Commissioner of Education, reports referred to, 47, 49, 51, 52, 100, 210
Commons, Professor John R., quoted, 21, 24, 31, 32, 81, 122, 188, 191
Competition between races, 106, 120, 183, 185
Conference of Education in the South, 64, 157
Congregationalists, 90, 152, 156, 159, 160, 161, 163, 164, 227, 232, 359, 363, 379
Consultative Committee on Higher Elementary Education, 280, 282

Cooperation, economic, 121, 143; in education, 63
Cotton, 71, 73, 79, 136, 146, 336
COTTON VALLEY SCHOOL, Fort Davis, Ala., 220
Criminals, negro, 37, 75, 82, 135, 164, 198, 202
Crummell, Alexander, quoted, 267

Davis, Jefferson, 66, 102
Death-rate, 75, 82, 168, 206, 226
Democracy, 28, 30, 32, 34, 64, 125, 295 ff., 382 ff.
Denominational boards, 61
Department of Agriculture, 71; Year Book of, quoted, 52, 53
Destiny of negro, 206, 338 ff.
Deveaux, Colonel, 226
Dewey, Professor John, quoted, 266
Distribution of population, 72, 132
District of Columbia, 140
Dixon, Thomas, 103
Domestic science, education in, 249, 352 ff.
DORCHESTER ACADEMY, McIntosh, Ga., 232, 235
Dowd, Jerome, quoted, 184
DuBois, Professor W. E. B., 115, 135, 164, 165, 252, 372
Dunbar, Paul L., the poet, 164

Education, in Northern States, 47, 51; in Southern States, 47, 51, 55, 57, 58; principles of, in a democracy, 34, 57, 64, 278 ff., 295 ff.; of negro (see Negro education); as served by negro educational experiments, 265, 281
"Educational Revival," 57
EMERSON INSTITUTE, Mobile, Ala., 140
Entertainment for the negro, 255
Episcopal Church, 59, 95, 104, 152, 154, 156, 209, 227

INDEX

Ewing, Rev. Quincy, quoted, ix
Extension work, 257

Faduma, Rev. O., 158
"Farmers' Day," 262
Farmville, Va., 150
FESSENDEN ACADEMY, Fessenden, Fla., 37, 236
Fifteenth Amendment, 123
FISK UNIVERSITY, Nashville, Tenn., 100, 132, 163, 215, 241, 242, 243, 246, 247, 252, 291
Fleming, Walter, quoted, 73, 124
Florida, 37
Forests, 54, 72
Fox, John, 316, 325, 326, 328, 347
Freedman's Bureau, 63, 268
Friends, Society of, 209
Frissell, Principal, 289
Frontier, social effects of, 25

Galloway, Bishop, quoted, 115
General Education Board, 65, 351
Geographic divisions in South, 66, 69, 70, 304 ff.
Georgia, 60, 73, 86 ff., 100, 122, 123, 124, 134, 146, 152, 163, 172, 174, 175, 185, 209, 224, 226, 232, 235, 292, 304, 310
Georgia Medical Association, 89
German elements, 68
Giddings, Professor Franklin, quoted, 182
GIRLS' INDUSTRIAL SCHOOL, Moorhead, Miss., 264
Gloucester Co., Va., 135
GLOUCESTER HIGH AND INDUSTRIAL SCHOOL, Cappahosic, Va., 135, 143, 236
GRAND VIEW NORMAL INSTITUTE, Grand View, Tenn., 348, 353
Group-economy, 84, 93, 96, 142, 146, 165

Hall, President G. Stanley, quoted, 297
Hampton Institute, 135, 210, 232, 251, 265, 268, 270, 274, 288, 289, 290, 291, 294
Hargis, Judge, 66, 326
Harlan Co., Ky., 311
Hart, Professor A. B., 28, 74
Hawaii, 22
Health of negro, 118, 168, 171 ff., 256 ff.
Highland College, Williamsburg, Ky., 365
Hill, O. J., 190
Hillsboro School, Hillsboro, N. C., 218
Hoffman, Frederick H., quoted, 185, 189
Holloway, Rev. William H., xii, 86, 96
HOWARD UNIVERSITY, Washington, D. C., 161, 210, 240, 241, 249
Hutchinson, Dr. Woods, quoted, 254
Hyde, President W. D., 273

Idaho, 132
Illiteracy of negro, 46, 55; of Southern whites, 46, 305, 310
Imitation, psychology of, 129
Immigration to United States, 20, 26, 121, 145
Immigration Congress, 107, 190
Inborden, Principal T. S., 257 ff.
Indian Territory, 46
Industrial Education, history of, 268 ff.; theoretical considerations, 269 ff.; European experience with, 279, 281 ff.
Inefficiency, psychology of, 292
Insurance, negro and, 94, 142, 147
Iowa, 48, 50, 132
Italians, 105, 190, 191, 192

[403]

INDEX

Jamaica, 62
Jeanes Board, 120
Jefferson, Thomas, 23, 63
Jews, 26, 29, 105
Jonesboro (Tenn.) School, 132

Kelsey, Professor Carl, xii, quoted, 36, 72, 81
Kentucky, 47, 55, 69, 100, 304, 310, 326, 339, 341
Kowaliga enterprise, *vide* Academic and Industrial School, Kowaliga, Ala.

Labor problem and race conflict, 77, 92, 106, 121, 145
Land, how negroes acquire, 136, 258 ff.
Lee, R. E., 66
LE MOYNE INSTITUTE, Memphis, Tenn., 228, 255, 256, 257
Library, Public, 257
Lincoln, Abraham, 66, 117, 331, 362
LINCOLN ACADEMY, King's Mountain, N. C., 236
LINCOLN NORMAL SCHOOL, Marion, Ala., 236, 263
Louisiana, 46, 53, 108, 161, 236
Lumber industry, 347
LYNN SCHOOL, Lynn, N. C., 356

Maryland, 304
Massachusetts, 47, 49, 278
Massachusetts Commission on Industrial Education, quoted, 279, 281, 284, 285, 286
Mathers, Sir William, quoted, 284
Mayo, Dr. A. D., quoted, 209
Mayor's Report, Savannah, Ga., quoted, 179, 209
Memphis, Tenn., 255, 257
Methodist Episcopal Church, negro, 148, 150, 154, 155, 159, 209; Southern, 59, 60; Northern, 156

Miles, Mrs., quoted, 322, 328, 343
Miller, Professor Kelly, quoted, 159, 275, 294
Millsaps, Major R. W., 41
Miscegenation, 104, 238
Missions and missionaries, competency of testimony, 35, 43; to various regions of United States, 45; in South, 59, 61; in negro education, 209 ff.; to Appalachian Highlanders, 350 ff.; various activities of, 36, 63, 209 ff.
Mississippi, 41, 54, 55, 71, 72, 100, 105, 132, 191, 209, 236, 264, 275, 278
Missouri, 20, 46
Mobility of negro, 81, 120, 132, 194
Montana, 132
Movements of population, 79, 81
Mulatto, 74, 85, 244, 381
Murphy, Rev. Edgar Gardner, quoted, 40, 126, 207

National Educational Association Report, quoted, 48
National Playground Association, 254
"Negro a Beast," pamphlet, 114
Negro, alleged shortcomings of, 166 ff.; physical, 171 ff.; economic, 183 ff.; moral, 114, 198 ff.; explanation as racial traits, 205 ff.
Negro, American; numbers, 23, 46, 55, 62, 132, 166; occupations of, 38, 82, 91, 133, 183, 226; farmer, 42, 134,*185, 193; tenant, 89, 220, 258 ff.; domestic servant, 40, 238, 239; artisan, 38, 40, 82, 97; professions, 83, 90, 93, 97, 226, 247 ff., 274; ministers, 90, 248, 362; business, 37, 38, 40, 42, 74, 89, 91, 98, 107, 190, 191, 202, 226; federal service, 90, 140; material progress of, 74,

[404]

INDEX

87, 88, 204, 219, 226; ownership of property, 88, 134 ff., 162, 219, 232, 233; landlords, 234; wealth, 76, 139, 219; institutions, 60, 95, 140 ff., 209 ff., 234, 257; home and family, 85, 88, 141, 186, 201; marriage, 85, 88, 141; economic institutions, 94, 142 ff.; publications, 151, 267; churches and religion, 148, 152 ff.; schools sustained by, 60, 100, 209 ff.; philanthropies, 95, 119, 164; social classes, 75, 84, 120; race leaders, 85, 119, 164, 265 ff., 360; public opinion toward, viii, 101, 102, 104, 110, 113, 200 ff.; handicaps, 116, 118, 169–170, 186, 187, 200 ff.; esthetic expression, 38, 83, 164, 245

Negro education, 47, 56, 209 ff.; ungraded, 213; elementary, 57, 216 ff., 281, 288; secondary, 100, 223 ff., 237 ff., 282, 288; collegiate, 90, 240 ff.; professional, 90, 248 ff.; industrial and agricultural, 215, 223, 230, 250 ff., 271 ff.; controversy over, 57, 211, 271 ff.; diffusion and concentration of schools, 210 ff., 240, 361, 362; discipline, 244; equipment, 242; constituency, 243

"Negro, new," 85

Negro women, numerical excess of, 200; moral peril of, 117, 200, 222, 237; as breadwinners, 83, 89, 179, 186; education of, 237 ff., 249 ff.; organized activities of, 95, 142, 164; as home-makers, *vide* Negro, American, home and family

New Mexico, 46

NORMAL AND INDUSTRIAL COLLEGIATE INSTITUTE, Joppa, Ala., 354

North Carolina, 46, 68, 69, 73, 100, 132, 137, 158, 160, 218, 275, 304, 310, 338

Northern people, attitude of, toward negro, 117, 166; toward the South, vii

Northern States, wealth, 50; education (see Education in); comparative progress, 47–51

Norwood, Judge, 197

Nurses, training, 250

Ogden parties, vii
Ohio, 66
Oklahoma, 101, 132
Orientals in America, 24, 29, 45, 105, 367
Oyster industry, 135

Page, Thomas Nelson, 125
Parks and playgrounds, 254
Patten, Professor Simon R., quoted, 142, 145, 196, 380, 386
Payne, Bishop Daniel, 149
PEABODY ACADEMY, Troy, N. C., 158
Peabody Fund, 351
Peabody, George F., 64, 243
Pearsons, Dr., 362
Pennsylvania, 67
Peonage in South, 188
Physiography, 68, 69, 71, 73
PIEDMONT COLLEGE, Demorest, Ga., 358, 362
Piedmont region, 56, 67, 72, 81, 218, 312
Pilgrim Fathers, 17
Plato, quoted, 120
PLEASANT HILL ACADEMY, Pleasant Hill, Tenn., 352
Politics, negro and, 122, 124
"Poor white," 75, 77, 102
Porto Rico, 22
Pou, Hon. James E., quoted, 137

INDEX

Presbyterian Church, Southern, 59, 154, 159, 209
Price, Principal, 143
Proctor, Rev. H. H., 163
"Prophet of the Great Smoky Mountains, The," 76
Psychology and race, 128, 196
Public schools for negroes, 224, 227

Quakers, 68

Race and race problems, ix, 28, 99, 116, 206, 367 ff.
Race consciousness, 93, 101
Races in America, 68
Reading-rooms, 257
Refugees, negro, 62, 216
Reversion of race, 234
Rockingham (N. C.) Church, 160
Roosevelt, O., President, 110, 254, 370
Rose, Professor Wycliffe, quoted, 49
Ross, Professor E. A., quoted, 76, 118, 128, 170, 171, 181, 185, 387
Rural conditions and problems, 49, 230 ff.
Russell, Assistant Attorney-General, quoted, 188

SALUDA SEMINARY, Saluda, N. C., 357
Savannah, Ga., 174, 197, 198, 202, 225, 226
Scotch-Irish, 67, 68
Secret societies, 142
Segregation, 84, 87, 96, 119
Selection, biological, 373 ff.; social, 78, 84, 377 ff.
Sex and race, 109
Shaler, Professor N. S., quoted, 184
Slavery, 23, 33, 34, 69, 74
Smith, Governor Hoke, 122, 287, 288

Smith, Professor W. B., quoted, 128, 173, 393, 396
Social classes, 278
"Social equality," 110
Sociology and race doctrines, 75, 114, 128, 141, 205 ff.
Soil survey, 71, 74
South Atlantic Quarterly, viii, xi
South Carolina, 55, 103, 189, 304, 310
Southern churches, characteristics, 58; work for negroes, 59
Southern Educational Association, quoted, 295, 297, 310
Southern Immigration Congress, 107
Southern Mountaineers, 56–70, 304 ff.; history of, 19, 69, 130, 318; social types and diversities, 80, 306 ff., 317–334; in politics, 69, 320; in industry, 335 ff.; effect of recent movements upon, 79, 332; missionary work for, 62, 63, 343, 350 ff.; esthetic expression, 325
Southern States, geographical variety, 66, 70; natural resources, 50; composition of population, 75; political and social traits and tendencies, 77, 100; educational problems of, 46, 224; race problem in, 99 ff., 119 ff.; racial creed of, 114 ff., 226, 238, 263, 270, 287
Southern Workman, quoted, 135
Speer, Judge Emory, 185
Standard of living, 194
State as Americanizing agency, 57, 251, 296
"State of Franklin," 76
Statistics, of negroes in United States, 132 ff.; of Southern education; of comparative sectional progress; limitations of, 76
Stewart, Professor J. S., quoted, 293

[406]

INDEX

Stone, Alfred Holt, quoted, 33, 41, 171, 172, 185, 191, 194
STRAIGHT UNIVERSITY, New Orleans, La., 228, 256
Student life, of negro, 238, 240 ff.
Supreme Court of South Carolina on labor contracts, 189

TALLADEGA COLLEGE, Talladega, Ala., 213, 241, 242, 243, 246, 247, 248, 250, 252
Tanner, H. O., the painter, 164
Taylor, Coleridge, the composer, 164
Teachers, professional training of, 240 ff., 247 ff.
Temperance, 38, 258
Tennessee, 48, 50, 69, 73, 100, 151, 216, 257, 304, 310, 339, 341, 347
Texas, 100, 101, 114, 211
Thomas, Professor W. I., quoted, 298, 299
Thomas Co. (Ga.), churches of, 152
Thomasville (Ga.), negroes of, 86 ff.
Thompson, Holland, quoted, 68
Tillinghast, Joseph A., quoted, 36, 181
Tillman, Senator Benjamin, 102, 103
TILLOTSON COLLEGE, Austin, Texas, 228
TOUGALOO UNIVERSITY, Tougaloo, Miss., 139, 161, 241, 247, 251, 264
Trade unions, 144, 226, 289
TRINITY SCHOOL, Athens, Ala., 216

"True Reformers," 147
Turner, Frederick J., quoted, 67, 68, 70
Turpentine industry, 37
Tuskegee Institute, 42, 219, 232, 251, 268, 270, 272, 274, 287, 288, 289, 290, 291, 294

Vagrants, 37, 38
Vardaman, Governor, quoted, ix, 102
Vice, 180, 198 ff.
Virginia, 71, 81, 114, 135, 141, 143, 146, 147, 153, 209, 211, 304, 310
Vocational education, 247 ff., 270, 278, 280

Ward, Professor Lester, quoted, 384
Warner, Charles F., quoted, 284
Washington, Principal Booker T., quoted, 110, 120, 157, 164, 165, 167, 268 ff., 271, 286, 291, 372
West Virginia, 69, 304, 310
Whitt, Rev. M. W., 161
Wilberforce University, 151
Wiley, Principal, quoted, 39
Willcox, Professor Walter F., 171, 172, 173, 183
Williams, Senator John Sharp, 103
Wilson, President Samuel T., 307
Women in labor problem, 77; in education, 277; progress of, 277, 297, 301, 302
Woodworth, President F. G., 161
World's Work, quoted, 54, 55, 56, 147

DATE DUE

ill. 7909794 8/26/88			

GAYLORD   PRINTED IN U.S.A.